# MAIN

# INDIAN HISTORY

This book deals with the main currents of Indian history—political, religious and social—from the earliest times to the post-independence period. It is primarily intended for those who have neither the leisure nor perhaps the inclination to go through big volumes on the subject but who would still like to possess authentic knowledge of India's past, knowing that the present image of the country owes so much to its past greatness. This book will thus enable such readers to bring a well-informed mind to bear upon a proper solution of some important problems which face the country today, such as national integration, caste and communal issues which do not take into consideration many relevant facts of India's past history but have an important bearing on the formulation of policies for the future. Originally written by Dr. R.C. Majumdar and brought up to date by Dr. P.N. Chopra, this book, it is hoped, will make a substantial contribution to the understanding of many current problems in the light of past achievements and failures.

*An eminent historian of India and former Vice-Chancellor of Dacca University, the late Dr. R.C. Majumdar was Vice-President of the International Commission for publishing* A History of Mankind *sponsored by UNESCO. He was President of the All India History Congress, All India Oriental Conference and President of the Section on Indology of the International Congress of Orientalists. He was a visiting Professor to many universities in India and abroad. He had a number of highly acclaimed publications to his credit besides over hundred articles published in research journals.*

*Dr. P.N. Chopra, Chief Editor,* Towards Freedom Project, *Indian Council of Historical Research, and formerly Editor,* Indian Gazetteers, *is a well-known historian and scholar. He has to his credit a number of works besides three volumes of the* Gazetteers of India *which are regarded as the most authoritative works on India and its people. He has also published three volumes of* Who's Who of Indian Martyrs, History of South India *(3 vols.),* A Social, Cultural and Economic History of India *(3 vols.),* Quit India Movement of 1942.

Published by
Sterling Publishers Private Limited

# Main Currents
# of
# Indian History
### (Revised & Enlarged Edition)

R.C. Majumdar
P.N. Chopra

A Sterling Paperback

STERLING PAPERBACKS
An imprint of
Sterling Publishers (P) Ltd.
L-10, Green Park Extension, New Delhi-110016
Ph.: 6191784, 6191785, 6191023 Fax: 91-11-6190028
E-mail: sterlin.gpvb@axcess.net.in

*Main Currents of Indian History*
©1994, R.C. Majumdar and P.N. Chopra
ISBN 81 207 1654 x
First Edition 1984
Second Revised & Enlarged Edition 1994
Reprint 1996, 1998

*Published by* Sterling Publishers Pvt. Ltd., New Delhi-110016.
*Lasertypeset by* Rasleen Art Printers Pvt. Ltd., New Delhi.
*Printed at* Print India, New Delhi.
*Cover Printed at* Roopak Printers, Delhi.
*Cover design by* Adage Communications

# Preface to the Fourth Edition

It is indeed a matter of gratification that the third edition of the *Main Currents of Indian History* was sold out in a short time and its fourth edition is being brought out. In the revised edition the last part entitled 'India since Independence' has been completely rewritten and brought up-to-date (1992). The necessary additions and alterations have been made in the rest of the volume wherever necessary. It is hoped that this volume will be welcomed by all those who are interested in Indian History and Culture.

**P N Chopra**

# Contents

*Preface*                                              v

I. **Ancient Period**                                 1-73
   1. The Indus Valley Civilisation
   2. The Aryans
   3. Rise of Heterodox Religious Sects
   4. The Maurya Empire
   5. The Gupta Age
   6. The Struggle for Empire
   7. Sultan Mahmud—the Beginning
      of the Muslim Conquest
   8. The Last Days of Hindu
      Independence in Northern India
   9. The Deccan
   10. Southern Indian
   11. Retrospect and Review

II. **Medieval Period**                               77-125
   1. Muslim Invasion of India
   2. India under the Turks
   3. Pre-Mughal Muslim Rule : A Broad Survey
   4. The Mughal Empire
   5. The Fall of the Mughal Empire

III. **Modern Period**                                129-198
   1. The European Trading Companies in India
   2. Consolidation of British Power
   3. Reforms During the First Century
      of British Rule
   4. The Outbreak of 1857 War
   5. English Education

6. Social and Religous Reforms
7. Political Regeneration
8. The Era of Administrative Reforms
9. Mahatma Gandhi
10. The Last Decade of British Rule
11. Retrospect and Review

**IV.   India Since Independence**      201-232
*Bibliography*      233-235
*Index*      237-251

# I
# Ancient Period

# 1

# The Indus Valley Civilisation

History is a record of the achievements of men, organised in communities and living within a definite geographical region. It differs from legends inasmuch as it is based on some definite evidence and not merely drawn from imagination. The history of a country or a group of men living together, therefore, begins only when some evidence of their life and activities is available. As far as India is concerned, we know definitely that men lived in various parts of the country about five hundred thousand years ago, but the evidence of the life of the oldest inhabitants is very scanty. The only traces they have left behind are the stone tools they used and a number of pictures they drew on the walls of the caves in which they lived. They had no idea of cultivation and lived on the fruits of trees and the animals and fishes which they killed with their stone implements. They did not know the use of any metal, could not make any fire and did not build any houses. So they had to live in caves and had to eat fruits and raw meat.

The evolution of the culture of these people is, however, marked by the gradual improvement in the artistic finish of the stone implements, knowledge of how to make a fire and how to build a primitive type of house to dwell in. At a much later stage they gradually learnt the use of metals, first copper or bronze (an alloy of copper and tin),then gold and silver, and lastly the use of iron, the hardest metal. They also acquired the technique of making potteries and many sharp instruments of iron which established their supremacy over animals and made their livelihood secure by means of hunting. Still later, they learnt cultivation which enabled them to settle down in a particular locality without being compelled to move from place to place in search of food when the supply of fruits and animals was exhausted. No definite date may be assigned to the different stages of these developments, but we have evidence that they had passed through most of these stages before 3000 B.C. What we have said above is mostly true of all branches of mankind living in any part of the world, and what we may call the history of India proper also begins about 3000 B.C.

India, which has been known by this name or its equivalent since time immemorial, is marked off by a series of hill ranges from the rest of Asia. The great Himalaya mountains in the north including several parallel ranges with valleys between them cover an almost inaccessible region 1,500 miles long and 150 to 200 miles in breadth and stand as an insurmountable barrier. Running, respectively from the western and eastern ends of the Himalayas, two ranges of mountains run southwards to the sea which surrounds the remaining part of India. Thus India was almost unapproachable from the north except through a few passes in the hills on the north-west, specially the Hindu Kush, and those in the north-east. The rest of India was protected by the sea. The territory comprised within this area is about 2,500 miles from east to west and 2,000 miles from north to south, with an approximate area of 1,800,000 square miles. Its land and sea frontiers measure respectively about 6,000, and 5,000 miles. India is really a subcontinent rather than a country.

The interior of India is divided into three well-marked regions. The first is the vast North Indian plain, between the Himalayas and the Vindhya, extending from the Punjab to Assam. To the south is the Deccan plateau sloping down from the west to the east, bounded by two ranges, the western and the eastern ghats, which leave a narrow coastal plain both on the west and on the east. The Krishna river and its tributary, the Tungabhadra, separate the plateau from its southern extension up to the sea generally known as the South Indian peninsula.

There are many rivers, the most notable being the Ganges, the Yamuna and the Brahmaputra in the North Indian plain, the Narmada and the Tapti between this plain and the Deccan plateau and the Cauvery in South India in addition to the Krishna and the Tungabhadra and the innumerable branches and tributaries of these rivers.

It is likely that in addition to a number of people belonging to various races who may be called autochthonous, *i.e.*, inhabiting the land for a very long period—how long none can tell—new races of men came to India from time to time both from the east and the west, and it is not unlikely, also from across the sea. No definite information of these is available though it is almost certain that many of the present primitive peoples like the Santhals, Mundas, Garos, Khasis, and others are their descendants. The oldest of these newcomers of whom we know enough to enable us to form a general picture of their civilisation, if not history, lived in the Valley of the Sindhu or Indus river and must have come from the west some time in the third millennium B.C. Our knowledge about them is derived almost solely from the archaeological excavations carried out at Harappa, Mohenjodaro and other localities in the Punjab, beginning from the epoch-making discovery at Mohenjodaro of a big mound situated in the Larkana District of Sindh (now in Pakistan) in 1922-23. The following account is based on the excavations carried out in Mohenjodaro for many successive years, though supplemented here and there by similar excavations carried out at Harappa and other places in the neighbourhood at a later date. Excavations have revealed the existence of seven cities, each built upon the ruins of another destroyed by the inundation of the Sindhu river or some other cause.

The first thing that strikes one is the remarkable skill shown in town-planning. The principal streets duly oriented to the points of the compass, intersected at right angles and ran straight, dividing the city into a number of square or rectangular blocks, each of which was divided both lengthwise and crosswise by a number of lanes. There was an elaborate drainage system which opened into great culverts emptying into the river.

Along with small houses, there were also palatial buildings made of well-burnt bricks, sometimes two storeys high. Many of the houses had a well, a bathroom and covered drainage connected with that in the street. There was a great public bath measuring 180 ft. by 108 ft. with a bathing pool 39 ft. long, 23 ft. wide, and 8 ft. deep, which could be filled and emptied by means of a vaulted culvert. Among other public buildings may be mentioned a big granary 150 ft. by 75 ft. and a pillared hall 80 ft. square with long corridors and low benches, which probably served as an Assembly Hall. There are ruins of other buildings, the exact nature and purpose of which are not quite clear. It may be mentioned that there was even a large granary at Harappa, 169 ft. by 135 ft. and it had strong fortifications of which only slight traces have been found.

Wheat and barley were regularly cultivated and probably rice was also grown. In addition to these, date-palm and other fruits, vegetable, milk, fish and flesh of various animals—beef, mutton, pork and poultry—formed the principal items of food.

Both men and women used two pieces of cloth, covering respectively, the lower and upper parts of the body, and various ornaments made of gold, silver, copper and other metals with beads of semi-precious stones such as carnelian, lapis-lazuli, turquoise, amethyst, etc. and marked by various designs giving evidence of high technical skill. The ladies wore a fan-shaped head-dress and used cosmetics, lipsticks, bronze oval mirrors, ivory combs and even small dressing tables.

Great progress had been made in pottery, spinning, weaving, dyeing and shipbuilding, and trade was carried on not only with other parts of India but also with many centres of ancient civilisation in Western Asia. Figures of men and animals show a high degree of skill, and two small statues found at Harappa rank as very high class art indeed. The most remarkable finds at Mohenjodaro are more than two thousand seals made of ivory, faience, and steatite. Some of these are engraved with figures and designs, undoubtedly a sort of pictorial writing, like the hieroglyphs of Egypt. But unfortunately, no one has yet been able to decipher it so that we are for the present, left with archaeological evidence alone to tell the tale of the lives of people who built this wonderful culture and civilisation. That it was of a very developed character with centuries of effort behind it is indicated by what has been stated above and also by what we know of their furniture and utensils from the actual remains and what we may reasonably infer from their religious images and icons found. Special mention must be made about furniture and utensils, of beautifully painted pottery of diverse types and designs, needles, awls, knives, axes, saws, sickles (made of bronze or copper as well as ivory), chairs and bedsteads made of wood, stools of wicker-work, mats of reeds, marbles, balls, dice, measures of weight and length, and bullock carts. Of special interest are toy clay carts as these are the earliest specimens of wheeled vehicles so far discovered in the world. The discovery of wheels may be regarded as one of the greatest inventions in the development of human civilisation, comparable to that of electricity or steam engine in the modern age. Equally remarkable were the toothed saws which were unknown to the ancient world. Mention may also be made of the weapons of war such as axe, spear, bow, arrow, dagger, mace, sling and sword made generally of copper or bronze as well as shield and scale of armour.

So far as may be inferred from actual images, without the help of any literary texts, we may say that the worship of female energy in the shape of the Mother Goddess, which was a popular cult in most ancient civilisations of Western Asia, was also a dominant religious motif at Mohenjodaro. Among the male gods, the most remarkable is the figure of a deity regarded by many scholars as a representation of God Siva due to its close resemblance to the description of the God in Hindu literature. According to scholars, the worship of Siva was originally prevalent among the peoples who lived in the Indus Valley and was later adopted by the Aryans. A large number of conical and cylindrical stones have also been regarded as *lingas* or phallic forms of Siva.

Along with the divine images people also worshipped trees and animals, and probably fire and water also. The worship of the sun has been inferred from the representations of the swastika and the wheel on some seals and the Naga cult has been inferred from the figure of a deity with a hooded cobra over the head.

All the three known systems of disposing of the dead— cremation, burial and exposure to be devoured by birds and animals—were prevalent.

The civilisation described above flourished certainly in the third millennium B.C. and probably about 2500 B.C., if not earlier. It was not confined to the Indus Valley, but spread to different parts of north India as far south as the valley of the Narmada river, and Sindh and Baluchistan in the west.

It was inferred from the representation of a ship on a seal found at Mohenjodaro that there was intercourse, for trade or otherwise, between the Indus Valley and seats of ancient civilisation in Western Asia and Egypt. This inference has been confirmed by the discovery of Mohenjodaro seals in very ancient sites in Western Asia.

The discovery of the Indus Valley civilisation in 1922-23 has revolutionised our concept of the beginnings of Indian culture and civilisation. Until then, it was generally an accepted view that the Aryans, whom the Hindus regard as their forefathers, were the first to introduce culture and civilisation in India some time between 2000 and 1500 B.C. Now the general consensus of opinion among the scholars is that the honour must go to the Indus Valley people, especially of Mohenjodaro and Harappa (both in west Punjab, now in Pakistan, where extensive remains of the Indus Valley civilisation have been discovered), who preceded the Aryans. The antiquity of the Indian civilisation is, therefore, pushed back by nearly a thousand years and it may, therefore, be regarded as nearly coeval with the most ancient human civilisations so far known, namely those in Egypt and Western Asia.

# 2

# The Aryans

We know very little of the people, or peoples, whose culture and civilisation has been described in the last chapter. It is agreed that they entered India from the west, probably belonged to the ethnic stock known as the Mediterranean people, and spoke a language which is now represented by Tamil, Telugu, Kannada and Malayalam. In other words, they were the forefathers of the Dravidian races speaking the above languages and now living in South India and the Deccan. It follows, as a corollary, that the Dravidians originally lived in the north-western parts of India and gradually migrated to the south. The main argument in support of this contention is the existence of a tribe called the Brahui in Baluchistan speaking a language akin to the Dravidian. But this is at best a hypothesis, lacking in positive evidence.

How the Indus Valley civilisation came to an end is a problem beset with difficulties and giving rise to a number of hypotheses. The most reasonable view seems to be that a new race of people coming from the north-west overran the country, established their political supremacy and gradually a fusion took place between the cultures of these two peoples. But the newcomers imposed their language on the conquered peoples such that no trace of that language is left, unless we accept the Dravidian language as its prototype. The language of the Aryan invaders is known as Sanskrit and, except the above Dravadian languages and the languages of the small communities of primitive tribes like the Santhals, Mundas, Nagas, Kukis,

Lepchas, Bhutiyas, and others scattered all over India, the languages spoken today by the Hindus all over India are derived from Sanskrit.

The new invaders who spoke Sanskrit are also generally believed to have entered India from the north-west through Afghanistan, and are generally—though not very correctly—designated as Indo-Aryans or simply Aryans (an anglicised derivative of the Sanskrit word Arya, meaning noble). The language of their oldest book—the *Rigveda Samhita*—gives a clue to their origin and early history. The generally accepted view is that the Indo-Aryans who settled in this country belonged to a very ancient stock of the human race, and lived for a long period with the forefathers of the Greek, the Roman, the English, the Dutch, the Scandinavian, the Spanish, the French, the Russian and the Bulgarian nations, who are collectively known as Indo-Europeans. This is best shown by the fact that some words denoting essential ideas of a civilised man are still used in common by their descendants, although removed from one another by hundreds of years and thousands of miles. Thus the Sanskrit words *pitar* and *mata* are essentially the same as *pater* and *mater* in Latin, *pater* and *meter* in Greek, *father* and *mother* in English; and *vater* and *mutter* in German, all denoting the most notable of the earliest notions of mankind, viz., that of the parents. The community of language has led many scholars to suppose that the Aryans, who conquered India, belonged to what may be called the parent stock of the many nations named above, famed in the ancient and modern world. This is not, however, a very logical conclusion, for, the community of language does not necessarily prove the community of blood. The Bengali language, for example, is now spoken by people of diverse nationalities. The only certain conclusion, therefore, is that the forefathers of all these nations lived for long in close intimacy in a certain region. The location of this region and the time when the different groups separated, are alike uncertain and subject of a keen, protracted controversy. The general view is, that they lived somewhere in Central Asia or South Russia. But some would place them still further north, in the Arctic regions, while others locate them in the area now occupied by Austria, Hungary, and Bohemia.

Anyhow, one or more of these groups separated from the rest and proceeded towards India. In course of time some of

them settled in the province now known as Persia, and
developed a civilisation, distinct traces of which are still to be
seen among their descendants, the Parsis of the present day.
The remaining clans crossed the Hindu Kush and occupied the
Punjab after driving away the Dravidians, as has already been
narrated.

In conclusion, it must be mentioned that some Indian
scholars do not accept the view that the Aryans came from
outside. They regard them as indigenous to India, some sections
of whom gradually migrated to different parts of Asia and
Europe. The Greeks, Romans and other peoples, speaking
Aryan languages, were the descendants either of these peoples
or of others upon whom they imposed their language by conquest
or other peaceful means. This view, however, presents difficulties
and is not accepted by many Indians, nor by anybody outside
India.

As our knowledge of the Aryans during the first thousand
years or more of their history in India is derived almost solely
from their literary works, known as the *Vedas,* it would be
convenient for the readers if before proceeding further, we give
a short account of them.

**The Vedas**
The *Vedas* form the oldest literary works not only of Indo-
Aryans, but of the entire Aryan group known as the Indo-
Germans, and, as such, occupy a very distinguished place in the
history of world literature. Besides, for more than three thousand
years, the *Vedas* have been looked upon as revealed words of
God by millions of Hindus, and have formed the basis of their
culture and religion amid continual changes and successive
developments.

The word "Veda" means "knowledge", knowledge *par
excellence, i.e.,* "the sacred spiritual knowledge". It does not
signify either an individual literary work as the *Quran,* or even
a collection of a definite number of books arranged at a particular
time such as the *Bible* or the *Tripitaka.* It is a mass of literature
grown up in the course of many centuries, and was orally
handed down from generation to generation. It consists of three
successive classes of literary productions, to each of which
belongs a number of single works. Some of these still exist, but

many have completely disappeared. These three classes are:

1. The *Samhitas or Mantras*. As the name signifies, these are collections of hymns, prayers, charms, litanies, and sacrificial formulas.

2. The *Brahmanas*. These are massive prose texts which contain "speculations on the meaning of the hymns, give precepts for their application, relate stories of their origin in connection with that of sacrificial rites and explain the secret meaning of the latter. In short, they form a kind of primitive theology and philosophy of the *Brahmans*."

3. The *Aranyakas* and *Upanishads*. These are partly included in the *Brahmanas* or attached thereto, and partly exist as separate works. They embody philosophical meditations of the hermits and ascetics on soul, God, world, and man.

A large number of *Samhitas* must have existed among the different schools of priests and singers. But many of them are only different recensions of the same *Samhita*. There are, however, four *Samhitas*, which are notably different from one another, and each of which has reached us in several recensions. These are:

1. The *Rigveda Samhita* — A collection of hymns.

2. The *Atharvaveda Samhita* — A collection of spells and charms.

3. The *Samaveda Samahita* — A collection of songs mostly taken from the *Rigveda*.

4. The *Yajurveda Samhita* — A collection of sacrificial formulae. (There are two distinct forms of this *Samhita*, viz., the *Samhitas* of the Black *Yajurveda* and the *Samhitas* of the White-*Yajurveda*.)

These four *Samhitas* have formed the basis of four different *Vedas*, and every work belonging to the second and third classes of Vedic literature, viz., the *Brahmanas*, the *Aranyakas* and the *Upanishads*, is attached to one or the other of these *Samhitas*, and is said to belong to that particular *Veda*.

The *Samhitas* and the *Brahmanas* of the four *Vedas* are looked upon as divine revelations and not the compositions of any human authors. They are consequently regarded as eternal and infallible. In other words, their teachings are held to be true for all times and must be accepted as such without question.

Only the *Vedangas*, the last part of the Vedic literature, are attributed to human authors. There are altogether six *Vedangas*. These do not mean six distinct books or treatises, but merely six subjects, the study of which was necessary either for the reading, the understanding, or the proper sacrificial employment of the *Vedas*. These six subjects are *siksha* (pronunciation), *chhandas* (metre), *vyakarna* (grammar), *nirukata* (explanation of words), *jyotish* (astronomy) and *kalpa* (ceremonial). The first two are considered necessary for the proper reading of the *Vedas*, the third and fourth for understanding it, and the last two for employing it at sacrifices. There are various books dealing with these subjects. The *Vedanga* books are also known as *Sutras*.

In addition to the religious literature described above, there was also a mass of secular literature dealing with medical science, military science, music, art and architecture.

It is difficult to determine the time when these different classes of literature were composed. It is generally supposed that the *Rigvedas Samhita* was composed between 2000 B.C. and 1500 B.C. and the other *Samhitas* and the *Brahmanas* between 1200 and 800 B.C. The *Upanishads* are referred to the period 800-600 B.C. and *Vedangas* or *Sutras* to 600-200 B.C.

**Aryan Settlements**

The *Samhita* of the *Rigveda* is the earliest work in Vedic literature. The Aryan settlements at the time of its composition were mainly confined to the Punjab. By the time of the later *Samhitas*, the Aryans had spread towards the east and the south and established kingdoms such as those of Kuru, Panchala, Matsya, Kausambi, Kosala, Videha, Kasi, Chedi and Vidarbha.* By the time of the *Sutras*, the Aryans had thoroughly colonised the whole of northern India and spread over to the Deccan and South India.

---

*(1) Kuru—the region round Delhi (2) Panchala—the upper valley of the Ganges to the north-east of Kuru (3) Matsya—Jaipur (4) Kausambi—Allahabad District (5) Kosala—Avadh (6) Videha—North Bihar (7) Chedi—Bundelkhand (8) Vidarbha—Berar.

### Aryan Polity

The Aryans were no longer nomadic tribes but lived in fixed dwelling houses. There they developed a healthy family life. The family was the foundation of the State. A number of families bound together by real or supposed ties of kinship formed a clan, and a number of clans formed a tribe. The tribe was the highest political unit. The most notable tribes in the early Vedic period were the Bharatas, Tritsus, Yadus and Purus. Later, the Kurus, Panchalas and Kosalas became very powerful. Struggles for supremacy among these tribes were very frequent. A king who could defeat others declared himself a *Rajachakravarti* or a suzerain. There were two ceremonies by which this overlordship was formally established. The first was the *Asvamedha sacrifice,* in which a horse was let loose by the suzerain king together with an army to protect it. The horse roamed at large in various kingdoms, and any king who wished to challenge the supremacy of its owner could seize it. Then followed a struggle between the two and the suzerain had to recover the horse by defeating his opponent. If he thus succeeded in bringing back the horse after defeating all enemies, it was sacrificed in a religious ceremony and the king was recognised as an overlord. The same object was also accomplished by another ceremony called the *rajasuya,* which the subordinate kings had to attend in order to perform menial services at the sacrifice celebrated by the overlord.

The Aryan king was not, as a rule, an absolute monarch. Sometimes, the king was elected by the people, and there were two popular assemblies, called *sabha* and *samiti,* which controlled the authority of the king to a certain extent. Gradually, however, at later periods kingship became hereditary, and the king was invested with almost unlimited powers. But convention, religious injunctions and the influence of ministers and priests, served as a great check to an arbitrary use of royal power. In extreme cases, people rose against a wicked king and dethroned or even killed him. In actual practice, therefore, the king was seldom a tyrant and was often actuated by the highest ideals of duty and justice.

### Food, Drink and Occupation

The Aryans ate both vegetable and meat and used to drink *soma*

juice, an intoxicating liquor. Agriculture formed their chief
occupation. But there were other industries, such as those of
weavers, carpenters, blacksmiths and leather-workers. Trade
and maritime activities were not unknown and the Aryan boldly
navigated in open seas.

## Religion and Society

The religion of the Aryans was at first simple. They believed in
many gods and almost every phenomenon in nature which
impressed their imagination was regarded as a deity. Thus,
Indra was the god of storm, thunder and rain. The brilliant sun
above and fire below were worshipped as gods Surya and Agni.
The beauty of dawn led to the creation of the goddess Usha, and
the vast expanse of heaven, to that of Dyaus.

These gods were at first worshipped in a simple way. A fire
was kindled to which ordinary articles of food and drink, like
milk, ghee, rice, etc., were offered as oblations. This was
accompanied by beautiful hymns addressed to the gods. Later,
the rituals of worship became more elaborate and complicated;
and priests were employed to perform it on behalf of the
worshippers.

It must be noted, however, that the idea of one supreme God
was realised at an early date and some hymns of the *Rigveda*
refer to this sublime conception.

The wife took part in the worship with her husband. In
general, women were held in high honour and occupied a
respectable position in society. They were highly educated and
some of them even composed Vedic hymns. The women not only
performed household duties, but also took part in social gaieties
and amusements. On the whole, both family life and social life
were very pleasant.

The ancient Aryans were gay and light-hearted. They
indulged in various amusements, scuh as race, hunting and
gambling in dice. At the same time they were alive to the serious
side of life and had high and noble moral ideals. The life of an
Aryan was theoretically divided into four *asramas* or stages.
The first was the *brahmacharya* or the student life, when the
young Aryan lived a life of strict discipline with his preceptor.
After finishing this stage the student returned home, married,
and led the life of the householder, that being the second stage
called the *grahasthya*. When he grew old, he left home, retired

to the forest and performed his religious rites there. This was
the third stage, the *vanaprastha*. At a still more advanced age
he gave up all religious rites and simply spent his time in holy
thoughts and contemplations. This was the fourth stage, the
*sanyas*. The rule was meant for all high class Aryans, but of
course, could not have been scrupulously followed by one and
all; nor was it necessary for every Aryan to go through each of
these stages in regular order. The student-life was binding upon
all, but after that an Aryan was at liberty to follow one or the
other of the succeeding stages at his will.

The most characteristic feature of the Hindu society is the
division of the people into a number of castes. No man born in
one caste can change to another; he must marry within his own
caste, and one of a higher caste is precluded from taking cooked
food touched by a member of a lower caste. The caste system in
this rigid form was, however, unknown in the early Vedic
period. There were then only two classes of people, the Aryans
and the *Dasas* (non-Aryans), the fair-skinned conquerors and
the dark-skinned conquered. Gradually, however, class
distinctions arose among the Aryans. When the language of the
*Vedas* became obsolete, and rituals of worship very elaborate,
the ordinary people could no longer perform their religious
ceremonials without the aid of men who had made a special
study of the sacred literature. Thus arose a class of men called
the *brahmanas*. Then with the expansion of Aryan settlements
and growth of new States there arose a new class of military
nobility whose business was to administer the State and protect
it against enemies. This class came to be known as the *kshatriyas*.
The rest of the Aryans who followed trade, industry and various
arts and crafts came to be known as the *vaisyas*. The *dasas* of old
were now called the *sudras* and they were generally employed
in menial work. The society was thus divided into four classes
called the *brahmanas*, the *kshatriyas*, the *vaisyas* and the
*sudras*. But it was long before they were converted into rigid
castes. For, at first a *vaisya* could become a *brahman* or a
*kshatriya* by following the profession of either, and there was
intermarriage among these three classes. A member of any one
of these classes could marry a *sudra* and the latter could even
cook food for a religious ceremony. It is difficult to say when the
restrictive laws about food and marriage were added on to the

old class distinctions, converting them into rigid castes. Even *Manusamhita*, a comparatively late work, permits a member of a higher caste to marry a girl belonging to a lower one. It may also be noted that for a long time, both the *brahmanas* and the *kshatriyas* claimed the position of supremacy among the four castes, and it was only after a pretty hard struggle that the *brahmanas* secured the position of unquestioned supremacy.

# 3

# Rise of Heterodox Religious Sects

After more than a thousand years of growth and development of Aryan religion and society in an even tenor, there was a serious challenge to the current religious thoughts, beliefs, and practices from several quarters which led to the establishment of numerous religious sects. Some of these, like Buddhism and Jainism, questioned the authority of the *Vedas* as divine revelation and laid greater values on the moral character and virtuous life of a man than on observance of rituals and ceremonies. Two others, Saivism and Vaishnavism, did not cut themselves as under from Vedic religion, but chose to accept one personal God, Siva or Vishnu, as the principal object of worship—sincere devotion and absolute surrender to whom was the chief feature of their faith. These four religious sects played a dominant role in the evolution of culture in India. Though Buddhism is no longer a living force, like Saivism and Vaishnavism, it once became a world religion and carried the essential elements of Indian culture to a large part of Asia, and even beyond its frontiers. Jainism is still the faith of a large community, but Vaishnavism and Saivism may be regarded as the two principal religions of India, which have taken the place of the old Vedic religion.

## Buddhism

Gautama, the founder of Buddhism, *was a Kshatriya* of the Sakya clan whose homeland was situated at Kapilavastu in the Nepal Terai immediately to the north of the Basti district in Uttar Pradesh. Gautama shared the growing pessimism and discontent among the people for accepting Vedic sacrifices, with elaborate rituals involving slaughter of a large number of animals, as the proper, not to speak of the only, mode of salvation which is the object of all religions. He felt it so keenly that he left home, wandered from place to place, visited many religious teachers for guidance and ultimately devoted himself to meditation at Gaya in South Bihar. After six years of incessant effort to realise the ultimate truth he formulated some definite principles and declared himself to be Enlightened. Henceforth, he was called Buddha (one who has attained the real knowledge) and he spent the remaining 45 years, of a long life of 80, in preaching his new doctrine, mainly in Bihar and Eastern U.P. A number of followers gathered round him and, before his death at Kusinara, they formed a regular church with definite rules and regulations. According to tradition, his teachings were also formally collected in the *Tripitakas*, the sacred scriptures of Buddhism, shortly after his death.

The fundamental principles of Buddha's teachings are represented by the four Noble Truths (*Arya-Satyani*), viz., (a) that the world is full of sufferings, (b) that thirst, desire, attachment, etc., are the causes of worldly existence, (c) which can be stopped by the destruction of thirst, etc., and (d) that in order to do this one must know the right way. The chain of causes that lead to sufferings are fully explained. There was a way to escape from sufferings. That is the celebrated Eightfold Path (as *angika-marga*) viz., right speech, right action and right means of livelihood; then right exertion, right mindfulness, right meditation; and lastly, right resolution and right view. The ultimate aim of life is to attain *nirvana*, the eternal state of peace and bliss, which is free from sorrow and desire, decay or disease, and, of course, from further birth and death.

The moral doctrines preached by the Buddha are quite simple. Man is the arbiter of his own destiny, not any god or gods. If he does good deeds in this life, he will be reborn in a higher life, and so on, till he attains salvation or the final emancipation from the evils of birth. On the other hand, evil deeds are sure to be punished, and not only will salvation be retarded thereby, but man will be reborn into lower and still lower life. Man should avoid both the extremes, viz., a life of ease and luxury, and a life of severe asceticism—the middle path is the best. In addition to the ordinary moral code such as truthfulness, charity, purity, and control over passions, Buddhism laid great stress on love, compassion equanimity and non-injury to living creatures in thought, word, or deed.

In its negative aspect, Buddhism denied the efficacy of Vedic rites and practices for the purpose of salvation, and challenged the superiority assumed by the *brahmanas*.

Gautama Buddha adopted the life of a religious teacher at the age of thirty-five, and wandered in different places in Magadha, Kosala, and the adjoining territories, preaching his new gospel. The disciples, whom he recruited, were of two categories, the *upasaka* or lay disciple, who lived with his family, and the *bhikshu* or monk, who renounced the world. The Buddha was endowed with a great organising capacity, and the community of Buddhist monks called *samgha*, founded by him, became one of the greatest religious corporations the world has ever seen.

A few striking characteristics of Buddhism may be noticed here. One was the admission of the female members into his church as *bhikshuni* or nun. Buddha was at first opposed to this, but was persuaded by his favourite disciple Ananda to give his consent, though not without much misgivings about the future of his church. Secondly, the members enjoyed equal rights in his church, irrespective of the classes or castes to which they belonged. Thirdly, Buddha introduced the practice of holding religious discourses in the language of the common people, in preference to the highly elaborate Sanskrit tongue, unintelligible to the people at large.

The Buddhist church consisted of the various local *Samghas* of communities of monks. There was no central organisation, coordinating the various local communities, and this defect was sought to be remedied by the convocation of general councils, whenever any occasion arose. In theory, of course, all these local bodies were merely parts of one universal church, and thus any member of any other local body was *ipso facto* a member of any other local community which he might choose to visit. These local bodies were governed on strictly democratic principles. The general assembly of all the monks resident in the locality constituted the supreme authority. Meeting of the assembly was illegal, unless all the members were either present, or, being absent, formally declared their consent. The assembly, whose constitution and procedure would have probably satisfied the ultra-democrats of the present day, had complete authority over the individual monks and could visit their offences with various degrees of punishment. They carried on the necessary secular business of the monastery through the agency of a number of officers appointed by them in due form. The nuns formed a distinct community which was practically subordinate to the community of monks.

How Buddhism gradually spread all over India and a large part of Asia will be told in connection with the great Maurya Emperor, Asoka and the great Kushana Emperor, Kanishka.

According to a tradition current in Sri Lanka which is even now a Buddhist country, Gautama Buddha died in 543 B.C. and an era beginning from that date is still current there. But according to modern scholars, he died in about 487 B.C. and was born in 567 B.C.

## Jainism

According to the orthodox Jaina tradition, the Jaina religion was founded in hoary antiquity and was developed by a series of 24 teachers called *Tirthankaras*. No reliable account, however, is available of the first twenty-two of them. The twenty-third, Parsvanatha, seems to have been a real historical person, but very little is known about his life. About 250 years after the death of Parsvanatha flourished Vardhamana, who was born in a *kshatriya* family in a suburb of the famous city of Vaisali about the year 540 B.C. Like Gautama Buddha, he was married and had a child, but left home and wandered about for twelve years, till, after rigorous asceticism, he attained supreme knowledge and the means of final deliverance from the bonds of pleasure and pain of this world. Henceforth he was called Mahavira, or the Great Hero, and *Jina*, the Conqueror. Like Gautama Buddha, he spent the remaining thirty years of his life in preaching the new doctrine and establishing a church or religious community, till he died at Pawa at the age of 72.

It appears that Vardhamana accepted, in the main, the religious doctrines of Parsva, but reformed them by some additional preachings. Parsva laid stress on self-control and penance as well as on the four great commandments. viz., (1) Thou shalt tell the truth, (2) Thou shalt possess no property, (3) Thou shalt not injure any living being, and (4) Thou shalt not receive anything which is not freely given. To this Vardhamana added another, viz., (5) Thou shalt observe chastity. Mahavira introduced a further innovation by asking his followers to discard the use of clothes, and move about completely naked.

Mahavira was a junior contemporary of Gautama Buddha, and there are striking resemblances in the doctrines of these two teachers. Both started with a frank recognition of the fact that the world is full of sorrows and the salvation of a man means his deliverance from the eternal chain of birth and death; both derived their basic principles from the *Upanishads*, although they denied the authenticity of the Vedas as an infallible authority and the efficacy of the rites prescribed in them for the purpose of salvation; both ignored the idea of God; both laid great stress upon a pure and moral life, specially non-injury to animate beings, rather than the worship of, and devotion to, God as the means of salvation; both emphasised the effects of good and bad deeds upon a man's future birth and ultimate salvation; both decried caste; both preached their religion in the common language of the people, and lastly; both encouraged the idea of giving up the world, and organised a church of monks and nuns. Indeed, the resemblance was so great that many scholars believed that Jainism was merely a branch of Buddhism. This notion is, however, erroneous for, apart from the fact that we can trace the distinct historic origins of the two, they differ in fundamental conceptions about salvation and certain other matters which cannot be explained away as later additions. The Jaina conception of soul, for example, is radically different from the Buddhist. Again, Jainism laid great stress upon asceticism and practised it in a very rigorous manner, whereas Buddha decried it, and asked his disciples to follow the middle path between a life of ease and luxury on the one hand, and rigorous asceticism on the other. Besides, Buddha denounced the practice of going out naked. The Jaina attitude of non-injury to animals was carried to far greater excesses than was ever contemplated by Buddhism. Further, Jainism did not oppose the caste system and was more accommodating to Hinduism than Buddhism.

There can be no doubt that Gautama and Mahavira were founders of independent religious sects. Both of them were products of the prevailing spirit of the time, and no wonder that both travelled the same way, up to a certain distance, in their search after truth. There was, however, a great deal of rivalry between the two sects, even during the lifetime of their founders, and Buddha condemned in no uncertain terms certain aspects of the rival religion. The two religious teachers lived and preached their religion in the same region, and recruited their disciples from the same class of people. So far as can be judged at present, both the religious sects had equal footing in the country at the time when their founders died, within a few years of each other. But it is in their later developments that the two sects differ widely, for, while within five hundred years Buddhism became a world religion, and was destined ere long to count nearly a third of the entire human race as its votaries, Jainism never spread beyond the boundaries of India. On the other hand, while Buddhism practically vanished from the land of its birth more than five hundred years ago, Jainism is still a living force in India, and has got a strong hold upon a large and influential section of the people.

There is no doubt that both Buddhism and Jainism heralded a new era in the religion of India, though both of them were derived from the old Vedic religion, especially the *Upanishads*. It is somewhat singular that about the same time a great transformation of the same nature was taking place in China by the new doctrine of Confucius who lived from 551 to 479 B.C. and was thus a contemporary of both Gautama Buddha and Mahavira.

Both Buddhism and Jainism suffered in the course of time a great split giving rise to two great sects with irreconcilable differences as regards theory, practice and religious texts. There were two Buddhist sects : *Hinayana,* the original, and *Mahayana,* the later form. Apart from new philosophical concepts developed by the latter, they introduced the worship of Buddha as God and gradually the number of gods and goddesses grew.

Among the Jainas also arose the two sects, the *Svetambaras* (*i.e.,* those who put on white robes) and the *Digambaras* (*i.e.,*

those who were stark naked), into which the Jaina community
is still divided. The unfortunate split was followed by other
consequences. The *Digambaras* refused to accept the 12 *Angas*
as authentic. According to the tradition of the *Digambara* sect,
the last man who knew all the *Angas* died about 436 years after
the death of Mahavira, and the knowledge of the *Angas* was
completely lost about 250 years later.

In spite of this internal dissension, the Jaina religion
rapidly spread all over the country. It made headway in South
India also, and ere long it became one of the important all-India
religions.

Besides Buddhism and Jainism, there were other heterodox
religious sects, like the Ajivikas, which exercised considerable
influence for the time being, but ultimately disappeared without
leaving behind any trace whatsoever.

## Bhagavatism

Between the heterodox religions like Buddhism and Jainism at
one extreme, and the orthodox Vedic religion at the other, there
grew up certain theistic religious systems which were destined
to attain considerable power at no distant date. These religious
sects had no faith in the ritualistic system of worship prescribed
in the *Vedas*. But while they agreed with Buddhism and
Jainism to a large extent in this respect, the differences between
them were great. Buddhism and Jainism "discarded, or passed
over in silence the doctrine of the existence even of God, and laid
down self-abnegation and a course of strict moral conduct as the
way to salvation." The new theistic religions, however, centred
round the idea of a supreme God conceived as Vishnu, Siva,
Sakti or some other form. Salvation was possible through His
Grace (*prasada*) alone, and this could be attained by complete
surrender of self to the personal God.

The chief representatives of this new system were
Bhagavatism (known in later times as Vaishnavism) and Saivism.
Originally, Bhagavatism merely laid stress upon the idea of
Supreme God, God of gods, called *Hari*, and emphasised the
necessity of worshipping Him with devotion, in preference to
older methods of sacrifices and austerities. It did not, of course,
altogether do away with either sacrifice or the Vedic literature
which prescribed the same, but regarded them as of minor
importance, and omitted the slaughter of animals, which formed

the principal feature of the brahmanical religion.

Religious reform received a strong impetus from Vasudeva Krishna, son of Devaki, of the Vrishni race, which was probably another name of the Satvatas. He gave a definite shape to the reformed doctrine by promulgating its philosophical teachings in the *Bhagavad Gita*. This led to the regular growth of an independent sect, and ere long Vasudeva was looked upon as the supreme deity, 'The supreme soul, the internal soul of all souls.'

In the ultimate form, as developed in the *Bhagavad Gita,* Bhagavatism stood prominently for two things. It counteracted tendencies to look upon ascetic life as a *sine qua non* of religious elevation, by emphasising the supreme importance of doing one's worldly duties according to one's status in society. Secondly, it sought to turn men's minds away from "dry, moral discourses, and thoughts of moral exaltation, unassociated with a theistic faith. Theistic ideas were, no doubt, scattered in the *Upanishads,* but it was the *Bhagavad Gita* which worked them up into a system of redemption, capable of being easily grasped."

The new religious ideas seem to have been confined to the Mathura district. But by the second century B.C., the new religion had certainly spread far beyond the confines of Mathura. Inscriptions recording the worship of Vasudeva are found in Maharashtra, Rajputana, and Central India. We learn from one of these, that a Greek ambassador of King Antialcidas, called Heliodora (Heliodorus), an inhabitant of Takshashila, styled himself a Bhagavata, and erected a *Garudadhvaja* (a pillar with an image of Garuda at the top) in honour of Vasudeva, the God of gods, at Besnagar, the site of ancient Vidisa, in Gwalior State. It is thus apparent that Vaishnavism, like Buddhism, made converts of the foreigners, and was distinguished enough in the second century B.C. to attract the most civilised nation among them. A Syrian legend further informs us that the cult of Krishna worship was prevalent in Armenia as early as the second century B.C.

The development of the local sect of Mathura into what promised to be an all-India religion, in the second century B.C., seems to be due, at least partially, to an event of far-reaching importance. This was the adoption of the new sect into the fold of orthodox Brahmanism. The reconciliation between the two is clearly demonstrated by the fact that Vasudeva-Krishna was

successively identified with the two prominent Vedic gods, viz.,
(1) Vishnu, originally a satellite of the Sun, but recognised to be
a great god in the later Vedic period, and (2) Narayana, probably
a deified sage, who however appears later as Hari and the deity
Eternal, Supreme and Lord. That this identification was completed
before the second century B.C. is evidenced by the dedication of
Garudadhvaja by Heliodorus, in honour of Vasudeva, the God of
gods, for Garuda was the recognised bird vehicle of Narayana-
Vishnu, these two deities being ultimately regarded as one.

The reconciliation of Bhagavatism with orthodox Brahmanism
not only assured a permanent position to the former, but gave
an altogether new turn to the latter. Henceforth Bhagavatism,
or as it may now be called by its more popular name, Vaishnavism,
formed with Saivism, the main plank of the orthodox religion in
its contest with Buddhism. It was mainly due to its influence
that the worship of images, unknown in the Vedic period,
gradually dominated the Brahmanical religion. The sacrificial
ceremonies prescribed in the *Vedas* no doubt survived, but
gradually receded into the background.

## Saivism

The origin of Saivism may be traced to the conception of Rudra
in the *Rigveda*. Rudra represented the malignant and destructive
phenomena in nature, which destroyed the cattle and caused
diseases to the people. His wrath was sought to be appeased by
offerings and prayers. "Rudra, however, occupies a minor position
in the *Rigveda*," though, like many other gods, he is occasionally
described as possessing supreme power. It has been suggested
that he represents the storm, "not the storm pure and
simple, but rather its baleful side, in the destructive agency of
lightning."

The conception of Rudra is further developed in the *Yajurveda*.
In the famous *Satrudriya*, where his benevolent characteristics
are emphasised in addition to the malevolent ones. "When his
wrathful nature is thoroughly appeased he becomes *Sambhu* or
benignant, Sankara or beneficent, and Siva or auspicious."
These three names, which occur at the end of the *Satrudriya*,
were destined to become famous at no distant date.

The supreme God, Rudra-Siva, was at first the object of
worship, not of a particular sect, but of the Aryans in general all

over India, and this character it has retained down to the present day in spite of the rise of innumerable Saiva sects.

The existence of Saiva sects may be traced as early as the second century B.C. It is probable that a definite Saiva system or school was established, in imitation of the Bhagavata sect, by a person, called variously Lakulin, Lakutin, Lakulisa and Nakulisa. The Saiva sects were at first generally known as Lakula, Pasupata or Mahesvara after the name of their God or historical founder. Before the end of the period under review, however, four important schools arose, viz., Pasupata, Saiva, Kapalika and Kalamukha.

The Saivas, like the Buddhists and Bhagavatas, attracted foreigners to their creed. Wema Kadphises, the Kushana conqueror of India, adopted the new religion and the 'reverse' of his coins depicts the figure of Siva with a long trident leaning on Nandi, or the bull, behind him.

It must be noted here that the image of Siva, as an object of worship, was soon replaced by the Linga or the Phallus. Many eminent scholars think that this element of phallic worship, and probably also the whole idea of Siva as a God, were borrowed by the Aryans from the Sindhu Valley civilisation. But the Linga cult obtained wide currency, and almost completely ousted the likeness of Siva as an object of veneration.

In addition to Vaishnavism and Saivism, other minor religious sects, of more or less the same general character, flourished during the period under review. These were the followers of Sakti, Ganapati, Skanda or Karthikeya, Brahma and Surya. Sakti was the wife of Siva, while Ganapati and Karthikeya, at first leaders of Ganas or hosts of Rudra-Siva, came to be regarded as his sons. Surya or the Sun was one of the principal deities in the Vedic age.

Brahma, who later formed with Vishnu and Siva the famous Trinity, is not a Vedic God. He was derived from Prajapati who occupied a very high position as the Creator of gods in the *Brahmanas*, and was identified with Brahman, the impersonal absolute of the *Upanishads*. From this the theists derived the name Brahma.

As to the Vedic gods other than those mentioned above some were still remembered, though occupying a distinctly inferior position, while others almost completely disappeared.

In order to complete the picture of religious condition, it is necessary to add that primitive belief in the spirits of the earth and mountains, in Yakshas, Gandharvas, and Nagas, and worship of all these, as well as of animals like elephant, horse, cow, dog and crow still retained a hold on the popular mind.

# 4

# The Maurya Empire

Reference has been made to the rise of a large number of tribal states in the Vedic age and their struggle for supremacy leading occasionally to the establishment of mighty empires. But we do not know anything definite about the history of these states or empires. The first definite picture of the political condition of India is furnished by the Buddhist scriptures. According to these, there were sixteen more or less powerful States in northern India about the time Gautama Buddha was born. Some of these were ruled over by kings, while others were *Ganas* or Republics. Among the kingdoms, the most powerful were Magadha (South Bihar), Kosala (Avadh), Avanti (Malwa) and Vatsa (Allahabad region) with their capitals, respectively, at Rajagriha (Rajgir), Sravasti, Ujjain and Kausambi. Among the republican clans, the most well-known were the Lichchavis of Vaisali and Sakyas of Kapilavastu (where Gautama Buddha was born). There were struggles for supremacy among these States out of which Magadha rose as the most powerful under a dynasty whose king Bimbisara was a contemporary of Gautama Buddha. He laid the foundations of an empire which, under a new dynasty founded by a *sudra* named Mahapadma Nanda, extended from Bengal to the borders of the Punjab.

About the time of Gautama Buddha, a very pwerful empire was established in Persia by the Achaemenids whose king Darlus (522-486 B.C.) conquered Sindh and a part of the Punjab. But the Achaemenid Empire was destroyed by Alexander the Great, ruler of Macedonia, to the north of Greece in Eastern

Europe. His father had conquered Greece and now Alexander
resolved to conquer the whole world. With this object, he started
towards the east, conquered Egypt and the Persian Empire and
then invaded the Punjab. He advanced as far as the river Beas,
but did not advance further to the east for fear of the Nanda
Emperor, though the Greek historians attribute his retreat to
the unwillingness of the Greek soldiers to proceed beyond the
Beas. But the brave resistance offered to the army of the world-
conqueror Alexander successively by a number of small republican
States like the Kathaioi (Kathas?), Malloi (Malavas), Oxydrakai
(Kshudrakas), and the valiant king called Porus, by the Greeks—
all of whom ruled in the western Punjab—made a deep impression
upon Alexander and he made friends with Porus after defeating
him in battle, not only by restoring to him his kingdom but also
adding to it some of the territories conquered by him. He left his
own generals to rule over the other dominions conquered by him
and left India in 325 B.C. after a campaign of two years in the
course of which he devastated many towns and massacred many
thousands of people, irrespective of age or sex.

Alexander no doubt hoped to make the conquered territories
in India an integral part of his vast empire extending over
Europe, Asia and Africa, but his death in 323 B.C. on his way back
home was a signal for the disruption of his vast empire which
was ultimately divided among his great generals. One of these,
Seleucus by name, acquired the eastern portion, including
India, but before he could consolidate his authority, the Greek
territories in India were conquered by Chandragupta.

The origin of Chandragupta is uncertain, but later legends
represent his as the son of a Nanda King of Magadha, by a low-
born woman named Mura. It is generally believed that the royal
dynasty founded by Chandragupta, known as Maurya, was so
called after the name of his mother Mura. But most probably,
Maurya is derived from the name of an old *kshatriya* republican
ruling clan called the Moriyas of Pippalavana in Buddhist
literature. In any case, there is no doubt that Chandragupta
rose from a humble position and began his career as a brave
adventurer. His own military genius, aided by the statesmanship
of a *brahman* named Kautilya or Chanakya, enabled him first
to drive the Greek garrison from the Punjab and Sindh and then
to ascend the throne of Magadha by uprooting the Nanda

dynasty about 322 B.C. By a series of brilliant military conquests he established a vast empire in northern India from the back of the Sindhu to the mouth of the Ganga. Seleucus, the greatest general of Alexander, who had obtained possession of the Asiatic dominations of his master extending from Syria to Afghanistan, proceeded to recover the Indian dominion of Alexander from Chandragupta. Unfortunately for him, the Punjab and Sindh were no longer divided among a number of petty kings and republican clans unable or unwilling to make a common cause against a foreign invader, thus falling a prey to Alexander. These two provinces, which Seleucus came to reconquer, now formed parts of a well-organised empire at the head of which stood a great military genius and farsighted politician. The Greek historians have not given a detailed account of the campaign, if any, of Seleucus, but merely state that Seleucus concluded peace with Chandragupta by not only abandoning all claims upon the Punjab and Sindh, but also ceding to him three rich provinces of Afghanistan with capitals, respectively, at Kabul, Kandahar and Herat and also a part of Baluchistan. In return, Chandragupta presented him five hundred elephants and probably also married his daughter. The Greek writers regard the five hundred elephants as the price of the provinces which Seleucus gave to Chandragupta, which is of course absurd, and it is legitimate to hold that Seleucus was worsted in his fight with Chandragupta and forced to buy peace by ceding those rich territories. It is a sad commentary on the lack of historical sense of the ancient Indians that we possess no account of the life and achievements of Chandragupta beyond a statement in a later Jaina text that in his old age Chandragupta abdicated the throne, became a Jaina monk, and in approved Jaina fashion, starved himself to death at Sravanabelagola in Mysore. How far this account is correct we cannot say, but we know from other sources that he ruled for 24 years (324-300 B.C.) and was succeeded by his son Bindusara who ruled from about 300 to 273 B.C. It appears from some Tamil accounts that during the reign of these two kings not only the whole of the Deccan but also a considerable part of any South Indian peninsula formed parts of the Maurya Empire which now extended from Herat in Afghanistan to Madurai in the south, with the exclusion of a few isolated pockets like Kalinga which was conquered by the next ruler. The Maurya Empire is thus the first historical All-India Empire the like of which was witnessed only twice during the next two thousand two hundred years, namely under the Mughal Emperor Aurangzeb in the seventeenth and the British during the nineteenth century. After the unsuccessful military expedition of Seleucus, friendly relations were established between the Maurya and the Greek rulers of the Western countries in Asia, Africa and Europe, some of whom sent ambassadors to the Maurya court. One of them, Megasthenes, sent by Seleucus to Chandragupta, lived for some years at Pataliputra, the Maurya capital city now represented by the ruins at Kumrahar near Patna in Bihar. Megasthenes wrote a very detailed and interesting account of what he saw and heard. The book is lost, but the quotations from it by later Greek writers, which are fortunately preserved, give us a fair idea of the life of the people and the administrative system during the last decade of the fourth century B.C. Reference to it will be made later.

Bindusara was succeeded by his son Asoka, who is justly regarded as the greatest king, in every sense of the term, not only in India, but even in the whole world, according to some Indian and European writers of modern times. As usually happens in the case of a great man, a number of legends have gathered round his name from remote antiquity, but fortunately he has left quite a large number of records of his life and reign engraved on rocks an stone pillars from which we are in a position to describe his reign with authentic detail. It may be said without any hesitation that no figure in ancient Indian history is more familiar to us, and none leaves a more abiding impression of a towering personality than this immortal son of Bindusara.

Asoka ascended the throne in or about 273 B.C., and added to the vast empire he had inherited, the province of Kalinga (roughly modern Orissa), which he conquered after a terrible war in the course of which "150,000 were captured, 100,000 were slain and many times that number suffered in various ways," as we learn from one of his records.

Asoka, who led the campaign in person, was profoundly moved by the scenes of horrible carnage in the battlefield, and the woes and miseries that it brought upon the people. He vowed

never to make war in future, and adopted the Buddhist doctrine
of non-injury to living beings.

He was soon formally initiated into Buddhism by a monk
called Upagupta. He undertook a pilgrimage to the Buddhist
holy places and everywhere preached the gospels of the new
religion. He devoted the remaining part of his life to propagate
the teachings of Buddha to the whole world. For this purpose,
he organised a network of missionaries who not only visited
different parts of India, but also various countries in Western
Asia, Africa and Europe. He sent his son and daughter, Mahendra
and Sanghamitra, to preach the new religion in Ceylon. In order
to bring home to the people the simple moral teachings of
Buddha he had them engraved on rocks and pillars throughout
his dominions. He convoked a Council of the Buddhist monks at
Pataliputra to reconcile the different Buddhist sects. Besides,
he appointed a special class of officers called *Dharma-Mahamatras*
to look at the morals of the people.

**Asoka, The Great**
The emperor himself set an example of the pious benevolent life
that he expected others to lead. He established hospitals for men
and animals, and planted medicinal plants and herbs, not only
in his own dominions, but in the neighbouring countries as well.
Formerly hundreds of animals were daily killed for the royal
kitchen, but Asoka put a stop to it by adopting vegetarian diet
and laid down regulations prohibiting wanton slaughter of
animals. He also made arrangements for alms-giving on a large
scale, and provided for the comforts of travellers by digging
wells, planting trees and building rest-houses along the roads.
Asoka was a great patron of arts. He built fine palaces at
Pataliputra and erected numerous religious structures, such as
pillars and *stupas*. Most of these have perished, but even the few
that have reached us are regarded as marvellous works of art
and show the wonderful progress of the Indians in this direction.
He also arranged religious processions to impress the imagination
of the people. He preached that the followers of one religious sect
should not abuse or ill-treat the followers of any other religious
sect. Asoka himself set an example of this great virtue of
toleration, for although he was a Buddhist, he behaved kindly
with the followers of other sects, and looked to their comforts
with equal care.

*Asoka, an Ideal King*

Asoka was also great as a king. He repeatedly declared that he looked upon his subjects as his own children and was always anxious to do good to them. He worked hard and personally supervised the details of administration. His rule was eminently just and benign. He had an ideal character and lived and died as a simple, pious Buddhist monk.

*Greatness of Asoka*

Asoka is justly regarded as one of the greatest kings of the world. When he ascended the throne, Buddhism was merely a local sect, but at the time of his death, it had already developed into a world religion. Few other kings can show equally brilliant success in uplifting the moral condition of the vast masses of people. The fact that even today one-third of the entire human race follows the doctrines of Gautama Buddha, is the most striking proof of the greatness of Asoka as a man and as a king.

## The End of the Maurya Empire

Asoka died in about 232 B.C. At the time of his death his empire included Afghanistan, Baluchistan, Makran, and nearly the whole of India. But the Maurya empire did not flourish for very long after his death. The Andhras revolted in the Deccan, and established an independent principality under a ruling family called the Satavahanas. Kalinga too followed suit. The Greeks who had established an independent principality in Bactria on the other side of the Hindu Kush seized the opportunity and sent plundering raiders into India. When confusion had thus set in the Maurya empire, Pushyamitra, the commander-in-chief of the last Maurya king Brihadrath, killed his master and declared himself king. Altogether ten kings of the Maurya dynasty ruled for 137 years (321-184 B.C.).

## Megasthenes

As mentioned above, Megasthenes, the Greek ambassador of Seleucus who lived in the court at Pataliputra (Patna, the capital of the Mauryas) wrote a very interesting account of the people and the administrative system, of which only a portion has reached us. This is supplemented by the *Arthasastra*, a book on polity, by Kautilya, from which we learn that the king was not an autocrat. He was advised by a number of ministers and a council, representing various classes of people, and on all important questions of policy the king was guided by the decision arrived at in a joint meeting of the ministers and members of this council.

Megasthenes says: "The inhabitants of India have abundant means of subsistence and famine never visits the country. The country is very rich in minerals and precious stones and the Indians are fond of finery and ornaments. But otherwise they lead plain lives. They are honest and truthful, and theft is of very rare occurrence. Truth and virtue are highly prized by them and they never drink wine except at sacrifices. Personal freedom is greatly valued and slavery is unknown. The people are divided into seven classes such as philosophers (*i.e.,* Brahmanas and Buddhist religious teachers), husbandmen, shepherds, artisans, soldiers, civil officers and ministers."

Megasthenes also supplies interesting information about the administrative system of Chandragupta Maurya: "It was highly organised and the country enjoyed peace and prosperity. The business of the State was carried on by a number of departments, each efficiently managed by one or more officials. Criminal law was very severe and mutilation of limbs was an ordinary punishment. The emperor took special interest in the system of irrigation. The means of communication were excellent and there was a royal road from the Punjab to Pataliputra, the capital city. Pataliputra was strongly fenced by walls and ditches. The municipal administration of the city was vested in a council of thirty members. These were divided into six Boards, each consisting of five members. Each of these Boards was entrusted with a special duty, such as: (1) taking proper care of foreigners, (2) registration of births and deaths, (3-5) supervision of manufacture, trade and industry, and (6) collection of taxes.

The military organisation of Chandragupta was equally efficient. A commission of thirty members, divided into six Boards, each with five members, controlled the army. Each of the six Boards was in charge of a separate department, such as (1) Admirality, (2) Infantry, (3) Cavalry, (4) Chariots, (5) Elephants, and (6) Transport Commissariat etc. The army was composed of six lakhs of infantry, nine thousand elephants, and thirty thousand cavalry, the number of chariots being unknown. Altogether there must have been about 700,000 regular fighting men in the army whose salary and equipments were provided by the State.

**Asoka's Empire**

The Empire of Asoka was not only vast in extent, but was closely knit together as an administrative unit. One imperial writ ran from Peshawar to Bengal, and Kashmir to Mysore. Asoka's inscriptions further prove that there was one common language for the whole empire, and the same script was current except in a small region in the extreme north-west. The Asokan Empire thus brought about political and cultural unity which is the dream of modern India, symbolised by her emblem of the capital of an Asokan Pillar.

Several other circumstances make the reign of Asoka a memorable one. The earliest written records of India date from his reign. His inscriptions are written in the earliest Indian alphabet known to us. Similarly, the history of Indian art practically begins from Asoka's reign. For, excluding the prehistoric examples found in the Sindhu Valley, no other specimen of fine art has come down to us which may be definitely dated before the time of Asoka. Asoka seems to have introduced the art of building in stone, and although only a few specimens of his numerous works have survived, they form the first, though a brilliant chapter in the continuous history of Indian art. Indeed his monolithic stone pillars, with their remarkable polish and still more wonderful animal sculptures on the top, hitherto remain not only unsurpassed, but even unapproached anywhere in the world.

# 5

# The Gupta Age

Pushyamitra, who usurped the throne of the Maurya successfully resisted the Greek invaders and fought them on the banks of the Sindhu river, most probably the Indus. He was a powerful king and performed two *Asvamedha* sacrifices. The royal dynasty founded by him is known as the Sunga and its ten kings ruled for a period of 112 years (185-73 B.C.). The last king's minister Vasudeva usurped the throne and founded the Kanva dynasty, four kings of which ruled for 45 years when the Satavahanas of the Andhra country in the Deccan overthrew the dynasty.

During the rule of these dynasties a number of foreign invasions took place in North India. The first were the Greeks who, as a result of Alexander's conquest, became masters of Bactria on the other side of the Hindu Kush mountains. After the decline of the Maurya Empire they occupied the Punjab and Afghanistan and established a number of principalities. Some of them were powerful and carried on raids far into the interior of North India. They were overpowered by two other foreign tribes, the Sakas and Kushanas, who originally lived to the north-west of China. The Kushanas conquered a large part of northern India and their empire stretched from the western border of China to Banaras (Varanasi), if not further east. The greatest Kushana emperor was Kanishka who adopted Buddhism and erected a tower over the remains of Gautama Buddha at his capital city Purushapura (modern Peshawar) which attracted visitors from distant countries as the Taj Mahal of Agra does now. The Kushana Empire came to an end in India in the second century A.D., but the Sakas ruled in Malwa at Kathiawar Peninsula for 300 years.

The break-up of the Maurya empire was followed not only by these successive foreign invasions but also by the rise of a large number of States ruled over by kings and republican clans all over north India. After this political disintegration lasting for more than five hundred years from about 150 B.C. to 350 A.D. north India was once more politically united by the powerful dynasty known as the Guptas. During this long period the Deccan saw the rise of a great power, the Satavahanas who ruled over the region, successfully defending it from the foreigners who had established their rule in northern India. The far south was still divided into a few independent States, the more prominent being the Cholas on the east coast, the Cheras on the west and the Pandyas in the south midway between the two. The Guptas ruled over one of the petty States in eastern India towards the end of the third century A.D.

The first two kings of the dynasty were merely local chiefs, but Chandragupta, the third king, married Kumaradevi, a Lichchhavi princess, and raised the power and prestige of his family. He extended the boundaries of the kingdom as far as Allahabad in the west, and made Pataliputra his capital. His succession in 320 A.D. established a new era known as the Gupta era.

## Samudragupta

Chandragupta was succeeded by his son Smudragupta, the greatest king of the dynasty. He was a great military genius, and is justly regarded as one of the greatest heroes of ancient India. By a series of brilliant military campaigns, he transformed the small Gupta kingdom into one of the mightiest empires. He first conquered a large number of kingdoms that flourished in northern India and incorporated them into the Gupta dominions. He then led a brilliant campaign in the south, along the eastern coast, and advanced as far as Madras, defeating all the kings on his way. These kings were, however, reinstated, probably as tributary kings.

The territory directly administered by Samudragupta was bounded by the Yamuna and the Chambal on the west, the Narmada on the south, and the Brahmaputra on the east. But a large number of States, both monarchical and non-monarchical, just outside this area, paid tribute to the great Gupta emperor. Among these were Samatata or Lower Bengal, Kamarupa or Assam, Nepal and the tribal states of the Malavas, the Yaudheyas and the Arjunayanas in the Punjab and Rajputana.

After these brilliant conquests, Samudragupta performed an *Asvamedha* sacrifice with due pomp and ceremony. The sacrifice is a sign of the revival of Brahmanical religion, for Buddhism, which was very influential up to the time of the Guptas, prohibited the slaughter of animals.

Samudragupta had a unique personality. He was a poet and a musician, and some of his gold coins represent him playing on a lyre. Although a votary of Brahmanical religion, he revered the other religious sects. Meghavarna, the Buddhist king of Ceylon (Sri Lanka), sent an ambassador to him asking for permission to build a monastery at Bodh Gaya, and this was readily granted. Samudragupta, who has been styled the Indian Napoleon, must in any case be regarded as one of the greatest kings of ancient India.

## Chandragupta II "Vikramaditya"

Samudragupta was succeeded by his son Chandragupta (A.D. 375 c.).* His reign is memorable for the conquest of Malwa and Gujarat from the Saka chiefs called the Western Satraps. The Gupta empire thus extended to the Arabian Sea.

Chandragupta II assumed the title of *Vikramaditya.* This title means 'powerful like the sun', and was adopted by more than one Indian king. Probably Samudragupta had also assumed the title. As noted above, according to an old tradition, there was a king Vikramaditya at Ujjain who defeated the Sakas and he started the famous Vikram Era (Samvat) beginning in 58 B.C. His court is also said to have been graced by *Nava-Ratna* or nine jewels, *i.e.*, nine learned men including Kalidasa, the greatest poet that India has ever produced. It is now generally believed that this legendary Vikramaditya is no other than Chandragupta II of the Gupta dynasty, who defeated the Sakas of Malwa and Gujarat. It is also probable that Kalidasa graced that court of the great Gupta emperor.

---

* An elder brother of Chandragupta named Ramagupta ruled for a short period before him.

The Gupta empire remained intact during the reign of the two successors of Chandragupta II, namely Kumaragupta (A.D. 413-455) and Skandagupta (A.D. 455-468). The Huns, a barbarian tribe, originally living in Central Asia, invaded India but were defeated by Skandagupta. But at the beginning of the sixth century A.D. the Huns under Toramana and his son Mihirakula conquered the Punjab, Malwa and a part of Central India. But the latter was defeated by Yasodharman, originally a local ruler of Malwa, who had overrun the whole of north India. The rise of this great adventurer indicates the fall of the Gupta empire. Though Yasodharman founded another empire, it perished with his death shortly after A.D. 530 and the entire Gupta empire was divided into a number of independent States by the middle of the sixth century A.D.

The Gupta age was one of the most brilliant periods in Indian history. It witnessed a resurgence of intellectual activity manifested in various forms. Sanskrit poetry reached its high watermark of glory, while mathematics, astronomy and other sciences were highly developed. Architecture, sculpture and painting received their due share of attention and made remarkable progress. As noted, there was revival of Brahmanical religion, and this was accompanied by a revival of Brahmanical literature. The two epics, the *Ramayana* and the *Mahabharata*, were finally recast, and the *Puranas* and the *Smriti* works were composed during this period.

Fa-hien, a Chinese pilgrim, visited India during the reign of Chandragupta II, and has left an interesting account of the country. The administration was just and liberal, and the magnificent palaces of the city of Pataliputra (Patna), some of them dating back to the days of Asoka, excited Fa-hien's wonder and admiration. There were hospitals all over the country, and Fa-hien was extremely pleased with the manners and customs of the Indians. The people were humorous and happy, the criminal laws were liberal. The low caste (*chandalas*) were, however, regarded as outcastes and they had to live outside the city.

# 6

# The Struggle for Empire

Yasodharman was followed by a few other military adventurers who sought to establish an empire, and their success was also shortlived like that of Yasodharman. The first was Sasanka, king of Gauda (Bengal) who conquered territories as far as Kanauj in the west and the Ganjam district in the south during the first quarter of the 7th century A.D. Next was his great adversary Harshavardhana (A.D. 606-47), the king of Kanauj who also conquered a great part of northern India. We possess an interesting account of his life and reign from his biography written by Banabhatta and the accounts of the Chinese pilgrim Hiuen Tsang who travelled all over India between A.D. 629 and 645. About the beginning of the eighth century A.D., Yasovarman, another king of Kanauj, conquered a large part of north India and sent a minister to China in A.D. 731. He was defeated by Lalitaditya, king of Kashmir, who also led a victorious military expedition across the whole of northern India. But none of these empires survived the death of the founders.

About the middle of the eighth century A.D. two great powers arose in northern India, the Palas in Bengal and Gurjara-Pratihars in Malwa.

## The Palas of Bengal
After the death of Sasanka, Bengal passed through evil days. It came under the later Guptas, and was successively conquered by Yasovarman, Lalitaditya and many other kings. These repeated external conquests destroyed the solidarity of this

kingdom, and anarchy and confusion prevailed everywhere. There was no central authority, every petty landlord behaved like an independent chief, and everywhere the strong oppressed the weak. Unable to bear this miserable state of things any longer, the people of Bengal at last elected an experienced man called Gopala to be their king. Gopala at once restored order, gave peace to the country and left a happy, united and prosperous kingdom to his son Dharmapala.

Dharmapala was the greatest king of the Pala dynasty. He carried his conquests far and wide, and made his suzerainty acknowledged by almost all the important States of northern India. In particular, he defeated Indrayudha, king of Kanauj, and placed his own nominee Chakrayudha on the throne. The great *durbar* which he held at that famous city was attended by the vassal kings of Bhoja, Matsya, Madra, Kuru, Yadu, Yavana, Avanti, Gandhara, and Kira and the imperial ambitions of the Pala kings of Bengal were thus fully realised. Dharmapala enjoyed a long reign of more than 32 years and was succeeded by his son, Devapala. Devapala defeated the Gurjaras and the Huns and conquered Utkala and Kamarupa. He was thus the undisputed master of nearly the whole of northern India. Devapala ruled for more than 39 years, and his name and fame reached even the distant islands in the Indian archipelago. Balaputradeva, king of Sumatra and Java, sent an ambassador to Devapala and the latter granted five villages for the upkeep of the monastery which Balaputradeva had built at Nalanda.

With Devapala ended the most glorious period of Pala history. His successors were weak; during their rule the Pratiharas rose to great power and the Pala empire declined. The Palas, however, continued to rule in Bengal as a local power for nearly three centuries more.

## The Gurjara-Pratiharas

The Gurjara-Pratiharas probably entered India along with the Huns. The most important section of them, called the Pratiharas, had carved out independent kingdoms in Rajputana and Malwa as early as the seventh and eighth centuries A.D. The Pratihara king of Malwa rose into prominence by resisting the inroads of the Arab rulers of Sindh. The two most prominent kings after him were Vatsaraja and Nagabhata. They both made extensive conquests but, being defeated by the Rashurakutas, could not achieve any lasting result. They were also constantly engaged in war with the Pala kings. After the death of Devapala, the Pratihara king Bhoja restored the fortunes of his family by rapid conquests. Under him and his son Mahendrapala, the Pratihara power reached its zenith and their capital, Kanauj, became a flourishing city. The Pratihara empire included Magadha and even a portion of Bengal, and extended to Kathiawar peninsula in the west. But with Mahendrapala ended the glory of the dynasty. Shortly after his death, the Rashtrakuta king Indra III defeated the Pratihara king Mahipala and even sacked his capital Kanauj. Mahipala recovered his kingdom within a short period, but the prestige of the Pratiharas received a severe blow from which they never recovered.

As usual, the decline of the Pratihara empire was followed by the rise of new local powers. The feudatory States, one after another, declared their independence, and within a short time the Pratihara kingdom was confined to Kanauj and its neighbourhood. The most important among the powers that thus arose out of the disintegration of the Pratihara empire were the Chandellas.

**The Chandellas**

The Chandellas rose into prominence in the ninth century A.D. and established a kingdom called Jejakabhukti in the Bundelkhand region. They were at first feudatories of the Pratihara emperors, but Yasovarman threw off the allegiance and ruled as an independent king. He fought successful wars against various powers from Kashmir to Bengal and conquered the fort of Kalanjara which henceforth became the stronghold of his kingdom. The Chandella power rapidly advanced under Dhanga, the son and successor of Yasovarman. He defeated the Pratihara king of Kanauj and extended his power up to the Jamuna in the north and Gwalior in the north-west. In the course of his long reign covering the latter half of the tenth century A.D. Dhanga extended his power as far as Banaras. The Chandella kings were great builders. They built many beautiful temples and constructed lovely lakes and massive embankments.

The success of the Chandellas was a signal for the final disruption of the Pratihara empire. The Kalachuris who dwelt in the neighbourhood of the Jabalpur district followed the example of the Chandellas. Their king Lakshmanaraja flourished in the middle of the tenth century A.D. and consolidated his kingdom by extensive conquests. About the same time the Chalukya Mularaja established the independent kingdom of Anhilawara in Gujarat, which included parts of southern Rajputana. In the west, Jaipal, the king of the Shahi dynasty of Kabul, extended his power over almost the whole of the Punjab. Other powers also rose on the ruins of the Pratihara empire, the most notable of them being the Paramaras of Malwa and the Chahamanas or Chauhanas of Sakambhari and Ajmer.

# 7

# Sultan Mahmud—the Beginning of the Muslim Conquest

## Kingdom of Ghazni

While political disintegration was thus taking place in India, Alaptagin, a Muslim Turkish slave of the Samani kings, carved a principality in the Sulaiman hills around Ghazni. The kingdom passed, some time after his death, to one of his Turkish slaves, named Sabuktigin. Around A.D. 977. Sabuktigin led several expeditions against India and conquered some forts.

## Jaipal

Jaipal, the Shahi king, who, as already related, ruled over extensive territories in Afghanistan and the Punjab, naturally took alarm and invaded the kingdom of Sabuktigin. The two armies met between Ghazni and Jalalabad, but before there was any serious engagement, a furious thunderstorm broke out, and induced Jaipal to retreat after concluding a treaty with Sabuktigin. Once safely back in his kingdom, Jaipal refused to observe the treaty. Thereupon, Sabuktigin assembled an army with a view to invading his dominions, and ravaged some territories on his frontier. Jaipal, who foresaw the danger of a Muhammadan invasion of India, did not underrate its gravity and appealed to other Indian chiefs to save the honour of their motherland. The appeal was immediately responded to by the king of Kanauj as well as the Chahamana, the Chandella, and various other kings.

The Indian chiefs met the hostile army beyond the Indus and bravely fought in defence of their faith and country. But Sabuktigin gained the day. He levied a heavy tribute and made himself master of all the territories up to the Indus (A.D. 991).

## Sultan Mahmud

Sabuktigin died in A.D. 997. He had nominated his younger son Ismail to the throne of Ghazni, and the latter caused himself to be proclaimed king immediately after his father's death. But he was defeated by his elder brother Mahmud who conquered Ghazni and declared himself king. Mahmud refused to pay homage to the Samani kings and called himself Sultan.

Sultan Mahmud was undoubtedly the best general of his age. Master of extensive territories from the heart of Persia, he was determined to pursue the policy of his father towards India on a much bigger scale. In A.D. 1001 he marched towards India with 10,000 chosen horses. The old king Jaipal met his adversary near Peshawar, but was defeated and taken prisoner. Although Jaipal was released on promise of paying tribute, he did not choose to survive the disgrace, and burnt himself to death in a pyre which he set on fire with his own hands.

What followed took the breath of India away. Almost every year Sultan Mahmud repeated his incursions into India. He directed his march against a notable place, plundered everything that came his way, destroyed the temples within reach, broke the idols, and returned home with immense booty.

In A.D. 1004 Mahmud crossed the Indus and attacked the city of Bhera on the banks of the Jhelum. Its chief Biji Raj fought bravely and Mahmud's position became critical. But the Sultan ultimately gained victory and annexed the principality to his dominions. Next year he advanced against Multan and reduced it to submission.

## Anandapal

The chief of Multan had appealed for aid to Anandapal, the son and successor of Jaipal. Anandapal refused to allow Mahmud to march through his kingdom and sent an army against him. The Ghazni army was defeated and pursued as far as the Chenab.

In A.D. 1009 Mahmud advanced against Anandapal to punish his treachery. But the Indians were not insensible to the danger

which threatened their country and religion. Anandapal organised
a confederacy in which the kings of the principal states of
western and central India took part. It was the last desperate
struggle to retain freedom; and so profoundly did the cause
impress the heart of the Hindus that even their "women sold
their jewels, melted down their golden ornaments, and sent
their contributions from a distance to furnish resources for this
holy war."

Sultan Mahmud was alarmed at the preparation of his
enemy and took up a defensive position, fortified by trenches.
But the Indians attacked his camp with 'astonishing fury', and
cut down three to four thousand soldiers in a few minutes.
Sultan Mahmud sheathed the sword. But suddenly one of those
unfortunate incidents that have again and again decided the
fate of Indian battles snatched away the victory which was
almost within the grasp of the Hindus. The elephant, on which
the Hindu general* was mounted, took fright and fled from the
battlefield. The Indians lost heart at what they took to be the
desertion of their general and fled. Sultan Mahmud at once
charged home with 10,000 select horse. It was then pure
butchery, and thousands of Indians lay dead on the field. In
spite of the stubborn courage of Indian soldiers, the field was lost
for lack of discipline and generalship.

The sultan followed up his victory by the plunder of Nagarkot
(Kangra). There was no garrison to protect it, as they had joined
the late war, and it is said that 700,000 golden *dinars*,** 700
*mans**** of it gold and silver plates, 200 *mans* of pure gold
ingots, 2,000 *mans* of unwrought silver and twenty *mans* of
various jewels, including pearls, corals, diamonds and rubies
fell into the hands of the victor. Shortly afterwards Anandapal
bought peace by promising an annual tribute to Mahmud.

---

* Most probably Anandapal himself, but accounts differ.

** Dinar is equal to about 10s. The statement is probably
exaggeraton.

*** The weight of the *man* varies from 2 lbs. to 8 lbs. in different
parts of Arabia and Persia. Indian *man* is about 80 lbs. It is
difficult to say which measures are adopted by Ferishta, our
authority for this information.

**Expeditions of Sultan Mahmud**

Henceforth the Sultan met with hardly any serious opposition
in his periodical excursions into India. Altogether about seventeen
expeditions are set to his credit and Kanauj, Mathura, Multan
and Thaneswar were among the more important cities sacked
by him. The Pratihara king submitted to Mahmud after a
struggle. The Chandella king opposed bravely at first, but
afterwards bought peace by offering presents. Trilochanapala,
the successor of Anandapala, again opposed Mahmud. The
Sultan defeated him, and in order to put an end to all future
trouble, annexed the whole of the Punjab to his kingdom (A.D.
1021).

The last important expedition of Mahmud was directed
against the celebrated temple of Somnath in A.D. 1024 or 1025.
The Indians offered brave resistance, and for two days repulsed
the Muslim army from the walls of the city. The king of Gujarat
and the neighbouring chiefs joined the defence and in the battle
that ensued on the third day, the Muhammadan army was
almost beaten back. But the stubborn courage and superior skill
of Sultan Mahmud reversed the fortunes of the day. When the
Sultan entered the temple he was struck with awe by the
grandeur and magnificence of the structure. The treasures
which he secured at this place were incalculable and are said to
have exceeded all his former captures. On its way back to
Ghazni, the Sultan's army suffered great miseries in the desert
of Rajputana. It is said that a priest of Somnath, in order to
avenge its destruction, assumed the role of a guide to Mahmud's
army and lured it to what he thought would be sure destruction.

The Sultan, however, extricated his army and reached
Ghazni in safety. His attention was now drawn to western
territories and he conquered the greater part of Persia, extending
his dominions as far as the Caspian Sea. Soon after this brilliant
achievement the Sultan died at Ghazni in A.D. 1030.

**Character of Sultan Mahmud**

Sultan Mahmud was undoubtedly one of the greatest military
geniuses that the world has ever seen. His intelligence, courage,
prudence, military skill, and many other qualities of head and
heart command universal respect and admiration. But from the
point of view of India, he can only be regarded as a ruthless
conqueror like Alexander, Timur and Nadir Shah. He inflicted

great miseries on the people of India and wounded their religious sentiments by indiscriminate destruction of temples and idols. His avarice knew no bounds and most of his military expeditions were undertaken with the sole object of plunder. He was a great patron of arts and letters in his own dominions, but his ruthless conquests did not advance the cause of Islamic religion or civilisation in India.

# 8

# The Last Days of Hindu Independence in Northern India

### The Rajput States

The invasions of Sultan Mahmud destroyed the political solidarity of India. Thenceforth we only find a large number of States in India, mostly ruled over by Rajput tribes, quarrelling with one another until all of them were involved in a common ruin. The history of the more important of these States may be told in brief.

**Kanauj:**  The sack of Kanauj by Sultan Mahmud dealt a death-blow to the Pratihara power. In the last quarter of the eleventh century, Chandradeva of the Gahadavala clan established a new kingdom and assumed the proud title of *Maharajadhiraja*. The most famous king of the dynasty was Maharajadhiraja Govindachandra who ruled for nearly half a century and extended his rule over Magadha. His grandson Maharajadhiraja Jayachandra ascended the throne in A.D. 1170 and is described by the Muhammadan writers as a great sovereign.

**Bengal:** The Palas ruled in Bengal, but they were continually troubled by hostile powers. Towards the close of the tenth century, Kamboja chief occupied the throne, but Mahipala (A.D. 980-1030 c.) recovered the paternal territories. About the beginning of the eleventh century A.D., the Chola king Rajendra

Chola invaded the Pala kingdom. It must be said to the credit of Mahipala that he not only defended his country against the Cholas, but extended his dominions up to Banaras before A.D. 1025.

Mahipala II, the great-grandson of the first king of that name, ascended the throne about the middle of the eleventh century A.D. During his reign a rebellion broke out in North Bengal (Varendra). The leader of the successful revolt, Divya (also known as Dibboka), was a Kaivarta by caste, and hence the episode is referred to as Kaivarta rebellion. Divya defeated Mahipala and occupied the throne. He was succeeded by his son and brother. The latter, named Bhima, was defeated by Ramapala, the youngest brother of Mahipala. But although Ramapala regained the throne, the power and prestige of the family were gone for ever.

About the end of the eleventh or the beginning of the twelfth century, we find a new power in Bengal, the Senas. The first notable king of the new dynasty was Vijaya Sena who defeated the Pala king and conquered Bengal. He pushed his conquests to Assam and Mithila and probably also occupied a part of Magadha, although some Pala kings still reigned in a corner of this province. Vijaya Sena was succeeded by his son Ballala Sena. Lakshmana Sena, son of Ballala Sena, carried his victorious arms to Kalinga in the south and Banaras and Allahabad in the west. The Sena period is associated with important social changes like the introduction of Kulinism, the effect of which is to be seen to this day. The Sena rulers were great patrons of arts and letters. Ballala Sena was the author of two famous works *Danasagara and Adbhutasagara*. The court of Lakshmana Sena was graced by Jayadeva, the author of *Geeta Govinda,* and many other poets like Dhyoi and Umapati.

**Central India:** The Kalachuris, Haihayas and the Chandellas were, as before, the chief political powers in Central India. Gangeyadeva Kalachuri was one of the greatest kings of his dynasty. He and his son *Maharajadhiraja* Karna raised the power and glory of the family to an extent unknown before, and their suzerainty was established as far as Banaras. Karna tried his strength with the Pala king of Magadha and defeated Bhoja, the Paramara king of Malwa. But he himself was defeated by the Chandella king Kirtivarman in the latter half of the eleventh century A.D. The Chandellas remained in power for nearly a century more.

**Malwa:** The Paramaras founded the kingdom at Malwa in the ninth century, with its capital at Dhara. The most important king of this dynasty was Bhoja, who ascended the throne in about A.D. 1018, and his glorious reign of more than forty years is still remembered in numerous Indian legends. Popular tradition has invested him with all the qualities of an ideal king, and even today the name of Bhoja stands for all that is good and great in an Indian king. He was a great patron of learning, and was himself an author of considerable reputation. He established a Sanskrit college within the precincts of the temple of Saraswati, and his wide range of knowledge included diverse subjects, such as architecture, astronomy and poetry. As already related, he was defeated by Karna, king of Chedi, and with him departed the greatness of the dynasty.

**Gujarat:** Karna was helped by the king of Gujarat in his expedition against Bhoja. The Chalukya (Solanki) kingdom was founded by Mularaja about the middle of the tenth century. The capital was situated at Anahilapataka, better known as Anhilwara, which rapidly rose to be one of the most important cities. The kings of the dynasty successfully fought with Sultan Mahmud and other Muhammadan invaders, and continued to rule till the middle of the thirteenth century.

**Ajmer:** But by far the most important power in India subsequent to the invasion of Sultan Mahmud was that of the Chahamanas (Chauhans) and the most famous king of this dynasty was Prithviraja. He defeated the Chandellas and captured Mahoba, and was looked upon as the greatest king in northern India. The Gahadavala king Jayachandra of Kanauj was however, his sworn enemy, and the hostility between the two paved the way for the destruction of Indian independence. The stories explaining the enmity between the two chiefs read more like romance than history. We are told that Jayachandra invited all notable kings to *Rajasuya* a sacrifice which was to be followed by a *Svayamvara* ceremony for the marriage of his daughter Samyukta. Prithviraja, who refused to attend, was represented by a stone statue, Samyukta, however, placed the nuptial wreath round the neck of the statue, and Prithviraja, who was present in the city in disguise with his retinue, carried her off

with great difficulty. This story sounds a fairytale. The hostility
between two neighbouring kingdoms is very nutural and we
need not invent any excuse for explaining it.

## The Kingdom of Ghor

But the true fame of Prithviraja rests upon his fight with the
Muhammadan invaders from Ghor, a mountainous country to
the east of Heart. It was conquered by Sultan Mahmud and was
a dependency of the kingdom of Ghazni. About the middle of the
twelfth century, hostility arose between the two States, and was
accompanied by unusual acts of cruelty and treachery. At last
Beharam, the king of Ghazni, was defeated, and his kingdom
fell into the hands of his rival, who for seven days sacked the city
of Ghazni with fire and sword.

Khusru Malik, son of Beharam, now found shelter in the
Indian province of the Punjab, but hostility continued with the
house of Ghor. That kingdom shortly passed into the hands of
Ghiyasud-ud-din bin Sam who appointed his brother Shihab-
ud-din (also known as Muhammad and Muiz-ud-din) Ghori as
ruler of Ghazni and Kabul with the title of Sultan. Shihab-ud-
din advanced to the Punjab and took Multan and Uch, but was
disastrously defeated in an expedition to Gujarat by the Chalukya
king. He was, however, more successful in Sindh and in about
A.D. 116 wrested the Punjab from Khusru Malik who was taken
prisoner and put to death.

## First Battle of Tarain

The conquest of the Punjab brought the dominions of the Ghori
kings to the confines of the kingdom of Prithviraja, and a
struggle between the two was inevitable. Prithviraja organised
a confederacy of Hindu kings and marched against
Shihab-ud-din. The armies met at Tarain or Talawari* in 1191.
Shihab-ud-din, being wounded had to be carried away from the

---

* It was within two miles of the present south bank of the
Chitang, between Thaneshwar and Karnal, 13 miles south of
the former and north of the latter. The battles were fought
near Azimabad-i-Talawari or Talawari, otherwise Tarain
Garh, the Turaoree of the maps (Raverty *J.A.S.B.*, 1869,
p.418, footnote 451). Some, however, locate the sale between
Bhatinda and Sirsa.

field and this caused a panic among his soldiers who fled in all
directions. Prithviraja gained a complete victory and routed the
army of his opponent.

## Second Battle of Tarain

Shihab-ud-din never forgot this great insult. Burning for revenge,
he collected a vast army of the hardy mountaineers of Central
Asia, and, the next year, again marched towards India. Prithviraja
met him in the same field, and was joined by the contingents of
a number of other Indian kings who displayed once more their
sense of unity in the face of a common danger. Prithviraja sent
a message to Shihab-ud-din asking him to retire, and the latter
complacently replied that he was referring the matter to his
brother, the king. Having thus allayed the suspicions of the
Indians, who were encamped quite close by, Shihab-ud-din
suddenly attacked them at about daybreak and threw them into
confusion. But order was at last restored in the Indian camp,
and the Indians advanced to attack. Shihab-ud-din divided his
army into five or six units, which attacked the Indian army on
all sides and then pretended to retire, with the Indian army
following them in hot pursuit. Thus, the battle raged fiercely the
whole day and when the Indian army was tired and also
probably scattered and disorderly, he charged home with 12,000
chosen horses, and completely routed the Indian hosts. A
number of Indian chiefs lay dead on the field. Prithviraja
himself was taken prisoner and killed in cold blood.

## Muhammadan Conquest

Shihab-ud-din followed up his victory by the conquest of Ajmer
which became a tributary state under an Indian chief. On his
return to Ghazni, Qutub-ud-din Aibak, whom he left in charge
of his Indian dominions, conquered Delhi, Ranthambhor, Koil,
and other places. Next year Shihab-ud-din himself defeated
Jayachandra of Kanauj at Chandawar and thereby carried the
banner of Islam to Banaras. The Eastern conquests were completed
by Muhammed bin-Bakhtyar Khalji,* a soldier of fortune, to
whom Qutu... ud-din had presented a robe of honour. By frequent
raids in va.... s parts of Bihar, he amassed rich booty and with

---

* Muhammad Khalji, son of Bakhtyar.

its help collected a large army. He then suddenly attacked Nadia where Lakshmana Sena, king of Bengal, resided. Taken unawares the old king fled from the city. Muhammad conquered western and northern Bengal, but Lakshmana Sena, and after his death his two sons, continued to rule in East Bengal. Thus the Muslim dominion extended to the frontiers of Assam.

# 9

# The Deccan

Except during rare intervals when it formed a part of an Empire, such as that of the Mauryas and the Guptas, the Deccan, *i.e.*, the region lying between the Narmada and the Vindhya hills in the north and the Krishna and the Tungabhadra rivers in the south, formed a separate political unit unaffected by the events of the regions to its north and south, generally, though occasionally, coming into conflict with both.

The oldest powerful kingdom in this region was that of the Andhras who gave the name to this region, still called Andhradesa. The Andhras lived in this region at least as early as 800 B.C. Five hundred years later they had established a powerful kingdom containing thirty towns, defended by walls and towers and possessing an army of 100,000 infantry, 2,000 cavalry, and 1,000 elephants. They had to acknowledge the suzerainty of the Mauryas but threw off the yoke after the decline and fall of the Maurya empire and became a powerful kingdom under the rulers belonging to the Satavahana dynasty, whose name, slightly altered, still lives in legends about the great king Salivahana. They ruled over the whole of the Deccan and for some time also conquered some regions to the north of the Vindhyas. One of the most powerful rulers of this dynasty was Gautamiputra Satakarni, who stood as a bulwark against the incursion of the foreigners, the Greeks, the Sakas and the Kushanas, who overran north India, and saved the Deccan from subjection to these foreigners. A later ruler of this dynasty, Yajnasri Satakarni, issued coins with figures of ships, probably indicating that they were also a naval power. The family ruled till about the middle of the third century A.D. They had two capitals, Pratishthana (modern Paithan on the Godavari) in the west and Dhanyakataka near Bezawada on the Krishna, in the east.

The next powerful ruling family were the Vakatakas who were contemporaries of the Guptas and a daughter of the Great Gupta Emperor Chandragupta II was married to a Vakataka king. The greatest king of this dynasty was Pravarasena who assumed the title *Samrat* and ruled over the extensive region extending from Bundelkhand in the north to Hyderabad in the south. Narendrasena, a later king of this family, took advantage of the decline of the Gupta empire to extend his dominions to Central Indian and Malwa. The rule of the dynasty came to an end in the sixth century A.D.

The next powerful ruling family in the Deccan, the Chalukyas, carved a small principality with Vatapipura (Badami) as their capital. The greatest king of the dynasty was Pulakesi II, who made extensive conquests in the north and the south. He defeated the great emperor Harshavardhana, probably on the bank of the Narmada, and established his suzerainty over Malwa and Gujarat. He inflicted a crushing defeat upon the Pallava king Mahendravarman, and advanced within a few miles of his capital. He then established his suzerainty over the Cholas, the Cheras and the Pandyas. These great victories made Pulakesi the master of nearly the whole of India, south of the Vindhyas. His reputation also travelled beyond India, and he is said to have exchanged embassies with Khusru II, king of Persia. The Pallava king Narasimhavarman defeated and killed Pulakesi II, and plundered and devastated the Chalukya capital (A.D. 642) The fortunes of the Chalukyas were, however, restored and the dynasty ruled till A.D. 753.

The Rastrakutas succeeded the Chalukyas in the Deccan (A.D. 753). Their capital was at Manyakheta, modern Malkhed, in Hyderabad. The dynasty became very powerful under Dhruva, who carried a victorious campaign in the north and defeated the Gurjaras. Early in the ninth century his son Govinda III again overran the Gurjara territory, and proceeded up to the Himalayas in his career of conquest. The rise of the Pala power put a stop to the aggrandisement of the Rashtrakutas in the north, but they remained a great power in the Deccan till the middle of the

tenth century when they were overthrown by a new Chalukya
dynasty in about A.D. 973. These later Chalukyas were also
called Chalukyas of Kalyan from the name of their capital city.
The most important king of this dynasty was Vikramaditya. He
had a glorious reign of fifty years (A.D. 1076-1126) in the course
of which he led victorious expeditions against various countries
in northern and southern India including Bengal and Malwa.
Shortly after his death the power of the dynasty declined, and
it came to an end by about A.D. 1190.

The decline of the later Chalukyas was followed by the
tripartite struggle between the Yadavas of Devagiri (Daulatabad),
the Kakatiyas of Warangal in Hyderabad and the Hoysalas of
Doarasamudra in Mysore. The Yadava king Bhillama (A.D.
1185-93) conquered the greater part of the dominions of the
later Chalukyas, but was defeated by the Hoysalas. He defeated
the kings of Malwas and Gujarat.

Bhillama's son and successor Jaitrapala of Jaitugi (A.D.
1193-1200) was also a great conqueror. He successfully fought
with the Kakatiyas, the Gangas and the Cholas in the south and
the Paramaras and Chalukyas in the north. Jaitugi's son and
successor Singhana was the greatest ruler of the family. He
defeated the Hoysalas, wrested back the territories acquired by
them from his grandfather, and established the undisputed
supremacy of the family in the Deccan. He made extensive
conquests in the north. He successfully invaded Gujarat several
times and conquered Lata. He also defeated the king of Malwa,
a Muhammadan ruler of the north, and the Kalachuris or
Chedis of Chattisgarh and Jabalpur. The Silaharas of Kolhapura,
the Kadambas of Goa, and various other petty principalities in
the Deccan submitted to him. In commemoration of his victorious
expedition against the Hoysalas he erected a column of victory
on the bank of the Cauvery. Thus during the long reign of
Singhana (A.D. 1200-1247) who assumed the full titles of a
paramount sovereign, the Yadavas of Devagiri ruled over an
extensive empire which not only embraced nearly the whole of
the Deccan, but also a part of southern India beyond the
Krishna.

Singhana was succeeded by his two grandsons, Krishna
(A.D. 1247-1260) and Mahadeva (A.D. 1260-71). They maintained
the empire intact and fought successfully with the powerful
neighbouring kings in the south and the north, as well as with

the petty chiefs in the Deccan. Some territories beyond the Tungabhadra were wrested from the Hoysalas, and Northern Konkan was annexed by Mahadeva. His minister was the famous Hemadri who credits his minister with decisive victory against the Vaghelas of Gujarat, the Paramaras of Malwa and the Kakatiyas of Telangana (Warangal). The next king Ramachandra, son of Krishna, was the last independent king of the dynasty and concluded a peace on condition of an annual tribute, cession of certain territories, and immediate payment of 600 maunds of pearls, two of jewels, 1,000 of silver, 4,000 pieces of silk and other precious things.

### The Kakatiyas

The Kakatiya traced their descent from one Karikala-Chola, *sudra* by caste and belonging to Durjaya family, who settled in Kakatipura. The earliest known king of this family was Beta I who took advantage of the confusion caused by the invasion of Rajendra Chola and carved out a small kingdom in Nalgonda district (Hyderabad). His son and successor, Prola I, rendered distinguished service to his suzerain Chalukya Somesvara I and received as reward Anmakonda-Vishaya (Hanamakonda in Warangal, Hyderabad). The next king Beta II (A.D. 1079-90) received further territories from Vikramaditya and established his capital at Anmakonda.

Mahadeva's son Ganapati, who ascended the throne in A.D. 1178 was the most powerful ruler of this family. The disintegration of the Chola empire led to a triangular fight between the Pandyas, the Hoysalas and the Kakatiyas. Ganapati conquered nearly the whole of Andhra, Nellore, Kanchi, Kurnool and Cuddapah district and thus ruled over a vast empire, though sometime after A.D. 1250. Jatavarman Sundara Pandya defeated him and wrested Nellore and Kanchi from him. Ganapati transferred his capital to Orungallu (Warangal).

Ganapati was succeeded by his daughter Rudramba sometime after A.D. 1261. Marco Polo, who visited Motupalli, the important seaport of the Kakatiyas, in A.D. 1293, has highly praised the administrative qualities of the queen. Rudramba was succeeded by her daughter's son Prataparudra. The invasion of Kafur in A.D. 1309-10 forced him to buy peace by paying a vast amount of treasure. Yet, instead of exploiting his resources against Muslim invasion in future, he resumed his southern campaign, conquered

both Nellore and Kanchi, and even carried his victorious arms
as far as Trichinopoly. In spite of these brilliant achievements
he was ruined by his own folly. As could be easily foreseen, his
kingdom was invaded by the Muslims in A.D. 1323. Ulugh Khan
(afterwards Muhammad Tughluq) defeated Prataparudra and
took him prisoner, and the Kakatiya kingdom formed part of the
Delhi Sultanate.

**The Eastern Gangas**

The only region in the Deccan that resisted the onslaught of the
Muslims for more than two centuries was the eastern Deccan
under the Eastern Gangas. One Ganga dynasty had ruled in
this region as far back as the 6th century A.D., but another very
powerful Ganga family ruled in this region in the 11th century
whose rulers are called later Eastern Gangas to distinguish
them from the earlier one. The greatest king of the dynasty was
Anantavarman who conquered Orissa, and pushed his conquests
up to the Ganga in the Hoogly district. Anantavarman had a
long reign and ruled at least up to A.D. 1150. He left a vast empire
which extended from the Ganga to the Godavari. He built the
famous temple of Jagannatha at Puri.

The successors of Anantavarman could not retain south-
west Bengal which passed into the hands of the Senas, and the
Sena king Lakshmanasena even claimed to have planted a
pillar of victory at Puri. But the Senas were soon overwhelmed
by the invasion of Muhammad Bakhtyar who occupied north
and west Bengal and thus advanced up to the border of Orissa
in about A.D. 1200. In A.D. 1250 Bakhtyar sent an army against
Orissa which failed to achieve any success against Rajaraja III,
grandson of Anantavarman Chodaganga, who then occupied
the throne. His son and successor Anangabhima III, whose
known dates are A.D. 1216-1235 also repulsed the invasion of
Khalji. Ghiyas-ud-din I was the Muslim ruler of Bengal. He also
fought successfully with the Kalachuris of Tummana, but was
disastrously defeated by the Kakatiya, Ganapati.

Narasimha I, son and successor of Anangabhima III,
distinguished himself by boldly invading the Muslim dominions
in Bengal in A.D. 1243. His general defeated the Muslim governor
at Katasin, captured Lakhnor by defeating and killing its
commander, and even advanced up to the very gate of the
capital, Lakhanauti (Gauda), but he returned on hearing that a

large Muslim contingent from Avadh was coming to help the ruler of Bengal. He fought four more battles, but was defeated in the last one whereupon the Muslims occupied some territories of the Gangas. Narasimha I, who thus offered a heroic resistance to the Muslims, was the builder of the famous temple of Konarak, near Puri.

Narasimha II, the grandson of Narasimha I, not only recovered the territories conquered by the Muslims, but drove them from south-west Bengal and advanced as far as the Ganga, from the banks of which he issued some landgrants in A.D. 1296. The Muslims of Bengal now remained quiet, but Ulugh Khan, after conquering Warangal in A.D. 1323 invaded the Ganga kingdom from the west. He was, however, repulsed by Bhanudeva II, son and successor of Narasimha II.

The Muslim attacks continued throughout the 14th century. To make matters worse, the Gangas had also to defend themselves from the aggressions of Vijayanagar. Bhanudeva III (A.D. 1353-1376), grandson of Bhanudeva II, suffered greatly from the invasions of Shams-ud-din Iliyas, Shah of Bengal, Bukka of Vijayanagar, and lastly of Firuz Tughluq Sultan of Delhi. Bhanudeva III, submitted to the Sultan who remained in Orissa for two years and a half, but declared independence after his departure. During the reign of his son Narasimha IV (A.D. 1379-1424) Muslim rulers of the Deccan, Jaunpur, and Malwa led expeditions against Orissa. It may be said to the credit of Narasimha IV that he survived these shocks and maintained his hold on Orissa and Kalinga. But soon after his death the minister Kapilendra usurped the throne and founded a new dynasty called Suryavamsa in A.D. 1434.

The Gangas thus achieved the unique distinction of being the only Indian royal dynasty that successfully resisted the Muslim onslaught for more than two centuries and maintained its independence to the very end after the Muslims had conquered the rest of India, literally from the Himalayas to Cape Comorin.

# 10

# Southern India

From the earliest times of which we possess any record, three important kingdoms flourished in South India, *i.e.*, the region south of Krishna and Tungabhadra. To the east were the Cholas and to the west were the Chera kingdoms, while to the south in Madurai region was the Pandya kingdom. According to Tamil tradition, the sage Agastya came from the north and civilised the land. These three kingdoms together with Satyaputra are mentioned in the inscriptions of Asoka as independent kingdoms just south of the Maurya empire.

The most important Chola king of the early period is Karikala who defeated the joint forces of the Chera and Pandya kings and conquered Ceylon. According to the traditions he defeated at Veni, 15 miles to the east of Tanjore, a confederacy of about a dozen rulers headed by those of Chera and Pandya and established his supremacy over the whole of Tamil land. He is said to have constructed big irrigation channels by controlling the waters of the Cauvery and fortified the famous seaport of Puhar through which a brisk trade was carried on between South India and Southeast Asia. He was a great patron of Tamil literature and established his capital at Uraiyur.

Another distinguished figure is that of Nedunjeliyan, the Pandya king. The rulers of Chera, Chola and five other minor states combined against him and advanced to his capital Madurai. Nedunjeliyan drove them away and obtained a decisive victory at Talaiyalanganam. This great victory was long remembered and is even mentioned in an inscription of the tenth century A.D.

Nedunjeliyan also conquered Kongu and other minor states and increased the extent of his kingdom. He is eulogised by many poets whom he patronised, and was himself a poet of no mean order. He is also said to have performed many Vedic sacrifices.

Although not as distinguished as either Karikala or Nedunjeliyan, the Chera ruler Imaiyavaramban Nedunjeral Adan also occupies a high position in the annals of the country, He conquered Kadambu near the sea. This is perhaps the region which was later known as Kadamba, with its capital at Vanavasi (near Goa). He is also said to have defeated the Yavanas and brought some of them as prisoners, "their hands being tied behind and oil being poured on their heads." The reference is probably to the Greek or Roman traders who came to India in large numbers and set up colonies in south India, as we learn from both old Tamil poets and the classical writers of the west. There was an extensive maritime trade between south Indian ports and the Roman empire in the early centuries of the Christian era, and possibly even before that. This seaborne trade greatly enriched all the three kingdoms, some of whose rulers are known to have maintained diplomatic relations with Rome.

## The Pallavas

A new power, known as the Pallavas, arose in the south in the third century A.D. Their origin is obscure. Some think that they belonged to the Parthian stock, but this view is not generally accepted. They soon became very powerful, and conquered the northern part of the Chola territory. Their capital Kanchi (now known as Kancheepuram) was a famous city of ancient India. The Pallavas gradually extended their power over a large part of the State of Tamil Nadu.

At the end of the sixth century A.D., the Pallava king Simhavishnu conquered the whole of the south Indian peninsula and even the island of Ceylon. His son Mahendravarman and grandson Narasimhavarman had to fight with the Chalukyas, as noted above. Narasimhavarman conquered Ceylon and maintained diplomatic relations with China. By his great victories over the Chalukyas, the Pallavas, who were the dominant power of the south, also became powerful in the Deccan for the time being. The Chalukyas recovered their kingdom, but the struggle continued. The Pallava power declined in the middle of the eighth century A.D., and finally disappeared one hundred years later making room for the Cholas. The Pallava kings were great builders and the name of Narasimhavarman will ever be remembered in connection with the 'Seven Pagodas' at Mamallapuram, each of which is cut from a great rock boulder.

## The Cholas

The Cholas rose again as a power under Aditya I (A.D. 871-907). But it was Rajaraja I (A.D. 985-1018) who first adopted an aggressive imperial policy. He defeated the Kerala ruler, destroyed his ships at Kandalursalai (Trivandrum), and attacked Kollam (Quilon); he defeated the Pandya king and seized Madurai; and he took possession of the stronghold of Udagai in Kudamali (Coorg) which gave him a position of vantage against both the Pandyas and the Cheras. He also conquered the Maldive lands by means of his powerful navy. To crown it all, he invaded Ceylon and annexed the northern part of the island.

Rajaraja was one of the greatest rulers of south India, and fully deserved the title, "The Great", that is usually applied to him. He was a great conqueror and laid the foundation of the mighty Chola empire. He also made excellent arrangement for the administration of his vast dominions. The great land-survey, which he commenced in A.D. 1000, and the growth of local self-government constitute great landmarks in the administrative history of India.

Rajaraja was a great builder, and the famous temple of Tanjore, named after him as Rajarajesvara testifies to the glory of Chola art. Rajaraja was himself a Saiva but he also erected temples for Vishnu and helped the Sailendra king of Java, Maravijayottungavarman, to construct and endow a Buddhist *vihara*.

Rajendra ascended the throne on his father's death in A.D. 1018, but his reign was held to commence from A.D. 1012, when he was crowned a *yuvaraja* and associated with the government of his father. Rajendra followed the practice adopted by his father and crowned his son Rajadhiraja as *yuvaraja* in A.D. 1018.

Rajendra, usually known as Rajendra Chola, was the worthy son of a worthy father and raised the Chola power to the high watermark of greatness. His extensive conquests are referred to in his records, and may be briefly enumerated. In the south he not only conquered the Pandya and Chera countries, as well as Ceylon, but ruled all these provinces of his empire.

Two military expedition of his reign deserve special notice. One, sent along the eastern coast, passed through Kalinga, Odra (Orissa) and south Kosala to Bengal, and defeated not only three petty rulers of west and south Bengal, but even the great Pala king, Mahipala. The avowed object of the expedition, which proceeded up to the bank of the Ganga, was to bring the sacred water of that river, and it is said that the defeated kings were made to carry it on their shoulders. But in any case, it was of the nature of a raid, and did not lead to any addition to the empire. The other expedition may be regarded as unique in the history of India. It was a big naval expedition, equipped on a scale unknown before or since in ancient India, with the object of conquering the Sailendra empire which comprised the Malaya Peninsula, Java, Sumatra, and many other neighbouring islands. The Sailendras were on friendly terms with Rajaraja, and the reasons for the hostility of Rajendra are unknown. But he achieved brilliant success. His fleet crossed the Bay of Bengal and landed an army which conquered successively a number of feudal principalities in Sumatra, and possibly also in Java, and then crossing over to Malaya Peninsula, conquered Kataha or Kadaram (Keddah), the chief stronghold of the Sailendras. The mighty Sailendra empire, the biggest naval power in the east, lay prostrate before the victorious Chola army, and Rajendra Chola had the proud satisfaction of seeing his banner flying from the Ganga to the island of Ceylon, and across the Bay of Bengal over Java, Sumatra, and Malaya Peninsula.

Rajendra Chola was without doubt one of the greatest conquerors in Indian history and was justified in assuming the proud titles of *Kadarangonda* and *Gadgaikonda* in memory of his great victories. He also built a new capital called Gangaikondasolapuram and lavishly decorated it with temples and palaces. One of his greatest achievements was a magnificent irrigation tank sixteen miles in length. He also established a big college for teaching various branches of the Vedic study. Rajendra Chola was thus not only a great conqueror, but also excelled in the arts of peace. Like his illustrious predecessors he improved the efficiency of administration to an extent unknown before.

The power and prestige of the Cholas were maintained by two other great kings, Virarajendra (A.D. 1003-70) and Kulottunga (A.D. 1070-1118). Their successors were weak and the Chola empire declined in the thirteenth century owing to internal dissensions and the constant fights with the Kakatiyas in the north and the Pandyas in the south. For some time the Chola ruler was a protege of the Hoysalas, and then Jatavarman Vira Pandya defeated the Cholas, Hoysalas and the Kakatiyas until all these kingdoms were swept away by the Muslim invasion under Malik Kafur during the reign of Ala-ud-din Khalji. It is a sad lesson of Indian history that with the impending Muslim invasion staring in the face of these great powers of the south, they, instead of uniting against a common danger, frittered away their energy in fighting among themselves till they were all reduced to a common ruin.

### The Hoysalas

The Hoysalas were feudatories of the later Chalukyas in the Mysore region till Bittideva or Vishnuvardhana (A.D. 1106-41) established an independent *de facto* kingdom which comprised the whole of Mysore with its capital first at Belur and then at Doarasamudra. His grandson Vira Ballala II (A.D. 1173-1220) formally declared independence. As mentioned above the kingdom was constantly at war with the neighbouring powers and was further weakened by internal dissensions till it was invaded by the Muslim forces under Malik Kafur in 1310. Though defeated, the ruling king Vira Ballala III fought valiantly for thirty years, first against the Khaljis and then against Muhammad Tughluq as well as the Muslim kingdom of Madurai. He died in a battle at Trichinopoly in 1342.

### The Pandyas

As mentioned above, the Pandyas ruled in the southern tip of Indian peninsula from very early times, at least from the 3rd century B.C. Their history is a long record of fights with the neighbouring powers with alternate successes and reverses. A series of victories by Rajasimha (A.D. 735-65) and his successor Jatila Parantaka (A.D. 735-815) extended the boundaries of the Pandya kingdom so as to include Trichinopoly, Tanjore, Salem and Coimbatore districts. The next king Srimara

Srivallabha (A.D. 815-862) defeated at Kumbakonam a hostile confederacy consisting among others, of the Gangas, Pallavas, Cholas, Kalingas, and Magadhas, and also led an expedition against Ceylon and sacked its capital. But internal dissensions and the counter-invasion of Ceylon, probably aided by the Pallavas, led to his downfall and the end of the First Pandya Empire.

Jatavarman Sundara Pandya I (A.D. 1251-68) established the Second Pandya Empire. He defeated the Chera king, overthrew the Hoysala power in the south, and completely destroyed Chola power as mentioned earlier. He also conquered northern Ceylon, and put down the turbulent chiefs that rose to power on the decline of the Cholas. He captured Kanchi, defeated Ganapati Kakatiya, and advanced triumphantly as far as Nellore. He annexed both the Chola kingdom and Kongudesa, and ruled over a vast empire that included the whole of south India (excluding Mysore) as far as Nellore in the north, and also northern Ceylon. He lavished the enormous wealth he had plundered from the conquered countries in decorating and endowing the temples, particularly those of Srirangam and Chidambaram which were provided with golden roofs.

His successor Maravarman Kulasekhara (A.D. 1268-1310) maintained intact the vast empire he had inherited. He captured Kollam (Quilon) and sent a victorious expedition to Ceylon which returned with the famous tooth relic of Buddha. Parakramabahu, the king of Ceylon, however, offered submission and regained the relic.

The Venetian traveller, Marco Polo, who visited the Pandya country in 1293, has left a detailed account of the power, wealth and grandeur of all the empire which he calls "India, the greatest, best of all the Indias", and "the finest and the noblest in the world." It contained a number of ports which were the great centres of world trade, a detailed account of which we get also from Muslim historians, specially Wassaf.

Maravarman had two sons, a legitimate one named Jatavarman Sundara Pandya and an illegitimate one named Jatavarman Vira Pandya. As the latter was chosen heir apparent, the former killed his father and ascended the throne in A.D. 1310. But Vira Pandya soon expelled the patricide who thereupon appealed for help to Malik Naib Kafur who had invaded the

Hoysala kingdom. Kafur was only too glad at this invitation, for Vira Pandya had helped the Hoysala ruler against him, and the quarrel between the two brothers gave him an excellent opportunity to extinguish the last Hindu kingdom in the extreme south of India.

# 11

# Retrospect and Review

India constitutes a definite geographical unit with its natural boundaries of hills and seas. Perhaps with the exception of China, it is the only well defined region in the whole world where the regular evolution of a distinct human culture and civilisation may be traced in an unbroken continuity for a period of four thousand years or even more. Civilisation probably flourished earlier in the valleys of the Nile, the Tigris and the Euphrates. But the continuity was rudely disturbed from time to time so that there is a complete break between the earliest and the latest civilisations of these regions. It would be as difficult to trace a continuous cultural link between the pyramid-builders and the people of present day Egypt as between the peoples who inhabit today the region between the Tigris and the Euphrates and those whose society was based on the code of Hammurabi. On the other hand, the hymns of the *Rigveda* which were sung on the banks of the Sindhu and the Saraswati four thousand years ago are still recited on the banks of the Ganges and the Cauvery rivers. The well-defined stages through which the Vedic Aryan culture has passed into modern Hinduism have been indicated already in broad outlines, but this fascinating subject could not be dealt with in detail within the brief compass of this book. Fortunately, there are many scholarly works available on the subject.

The cultural development of a more or less uniform type forms today the sole basis of the unity of the Hindus. A political unity was forged by the great Maurya Emperor Asoka when the people of nearly the whole of India obeyed the command of a single ruler, spoke a common language and wrote in a common script and, broadly speaking, were nourished by the same culture. But such an integration was of short duration and soon became a thing of the past, never to return again, leaving behind a perpetual hope, a fond but unrealised dream and despair. Except for the occasional short intervals, India always presented the spectacle of a congeries of independent states fighting with one another for supremacy; for the highest ideal of a ruler was to establish an empire, and the basic political principle was to regard the neighbouring state as the greatest potential enemy.

The theoretical conception of India as a geographical and cultural unit was, perhaps, never altogether absent, for we find echoes of it in literary works. But apart from the inspiring ideal of imperialism, mentioned above, there was no sign of a popular impulse, to a political, not to speak of national integration.

The reason is not far to seek. The barriers of language, different ways and degrees of cultural progress, and vital matters affecting economic interests — difficulties which are apt to increase as time passes — have kept India divided into a large number of independent States. This will be evident from the history of the ancient period narrated above and of the medieval period to be described later. The normal state of affairs is neither unexpected nor unnatural as many are apt to think. They generally contrast the disunion of India with the stable States of Europe. It is forgotten that in point of area India is comparable with Europe, with the exclusion of Russia, and a proper comparison should, therefore, be with the whole of Europe minus Russia and not with any single European State.

How far the political disunity of India has adversely affected her cultural progress is a debatable question. It has not been possible to review the cultural progress in detail within the short compass of this work, but enough has been said to indicate its nature. An Indian author would not perhaps be accused of a parochial spirit if he maintains that ancient India may justly feel proud as regards the developments in religion, philosophy, art, literature, social and political institutions, moral and spiritual life either of individuals or of people as a whole, and material progress indicated by trade, industry and commerce, leading to accumulation of wealth, a high standard of living without its accompanying evil, namely miserable condition of the masses, and above all, a spirit of toleration and assimilation which allowed all types of religions to flourish without hindrance and absorbed millions of diverse foreign peoples from Europe and different parts of Asia into her society without leaving any mark of distinction (except for the small bands of Parsis driven out of their homeland by Islam to find refuge on the hospitable shores of India).

But this bright picture is marred by a few black spots which a modern historian feels bound to hold up for public scrutiny. The first is the invidious distinction of caste in its later developments, particularly the iniquitous system of untouchability, which made it impious for a *brahmana* to cross even the shadow of a *panchama* (one belonging to the lowest caste).

The second is the gradual growth of a narrow spirit of self-adulation which made the Indians feel that they were superior to the rest of mankind and averse to gain knowledge of the outside world under the false pride that they had little to learn from an outsider. It is perhaps not a mere accident that while we have accounts of India written by Greek, Roman, Arabic and Chinese travellers to India, we have no record about any foreign country written by a Hindu traveller in ancient times.

Thirdly, the Hindus showed a lamentable lack of interest in writing their own history. With the exception of the *Rajatarangini*, a local history of Kashmir, written in the twelfth century A.D. we have not a single book deserving the name of history though the literary efforts of the Hindus were directed towards subjects like the art of thieving or love-making.

The defects mentioned above seem to have been inherent in Hindu culture, and even a close and intimate contact with the Muslims for a period of six hundred years did not remove them in the least though the Muslims held before the Hindus a shining example of freedom from every one of these drawbacks. The Muslims did not allow the observance of distinctions among one Muslim and another in social rules and practices; they visited foreign countries and wrote their own history and accounts of foreign peoples. The wonderful ideal of Islamic fraternity failed to produce any impression upon their Hindu neighbours. As will be related later, instances are on record

when a Muslim State engaged in hostile operation against
another Muslim State in India, suspended all hostilities so long
as the other was engaged in the pious work of fighting with an
'infidel', *i.e.* Hindu State, whereas a Hindu State would take
advantage of the invasion of the neighbouring Hindu State by
the Muslims and invade it from the rear to serve its own
interests.

The Hindus had to pay dearly for these shortcomings. The
lack of historical literature kept the Hindus ignorant of their
glorious past. The caste distinctions stood in the way of national
or political solidarity. Ignorance of foreign countries made the
Hindus an easy prey to foreign invasions as they were usually
ignorant of the latest developments in the art of warfare. The
brave Rajput Rana Sangram Singh had to fight with spear and
sword against Babur's artillery.

In conclusion, reference should be made to one aspect of
Hindu civilisation which is little known even to the Hindus, but
constitutes a brilliant chapter in its history of which every
modern Hindu may justly feel proud. An unerring testimony to
the greatness of a people is furnished by the nature and extent
of their contribution to the material, moral and spiritual welfare
of mankind, living outside their country. India's contribution in
this respect is perhaps second to none in the history of the world.
It has not been possible to treat this fascinating subject within
the small compass of this book, but attention may be drawn to
two facts to which there is no reference in Indian literature. The
first is the civilising influence of Buddhism over a large part of
humanity outside India, which is testified to be the fact that
though Buddhism as such has practically disappeared from
India, one-fifth of the entire human race still follows the religion
which originated in India and was deliberately propagated in
distant regions by an Indian Emperor, Asoka. The second fact
is that notwithstanding the general aversion of the Indians to
contact foreign countries in later times, a large number of
Indians—traders, artisans, religious missionaries, *kshatriya*
adventurers and others—visited Central Asia, Burma, Indo-
China and Indonesia, and settled in these regions. It may be said
without such exaggeration that the culture of Indo-China and
Indonesia did not pass beyond the neolithic stage in most

regions when the Indians settled there and they were mainly instrumental in creating and developing the wonderful culture, language, literature, script, religious and social institutions, and art which has been immortalised in monuments like Borbudur and Angkor Vat of worldwide fame and Indo-Javanese literature which compares favourably with the greatest poetical works of the classical period, and established empires richer and larger than those of the Dutch and the French in modern times. The hundreds of temples and many hundreds of Sanskrit inscriptions written in flawless *kavya* style in all the known metres of Sanskrit prosody—some of them containing 50 to 100 verses and three of which contain respectively, 108, 218 and 298 verses— still exist as mute witnesses of Indian culture in those regions. Even in the distant Vietnam and Laos, the names of which were unknown to 99 per cent of Indians before the grim struggle in recent times, there are numerous Sanskrit inscriptions, referring to a capital city named Champa and the establishment by a pious ruler of a second Kurukshetra, as a place of pilgrimage whose very dust, we are told, was holy. India may thus rank with Greece as the creator of civilisation.

# II
# Medieval Period

# 1

# Muslim Invasion of India

The Muslim conquest of India is one of those epochmaking events which have left a permanent impression on the subsequent stages of her history. It was the most important episode in the history of India since the invasion of the Aryans, and it has radically changed the whole aspect of it such as no other event has yet done or is likely to do in future.

The story begins with the appearance of the Prophet Muhammad in the dreary desert country of Arabia at the western extremity of Asia, far away from the frontiers of India. The spirit of martial energy which the great Prophet had infused into the Arabian people produced remarkable results. At the time of his death in A.D. 632 he had established his political and spiritual authority over nearly the whole of the Arab peninsula. Within six years, Syria and Egypt were subdued by his successors. Northern Africa was conquered between A.D. 647 and 709, and nearly the whole of Spain was subjugated by A.D. 713. Within a century of the death of the Prophet, the Muslims, as his followers are called, advanced to the heart of France when their further progress was checked by Charles Martel in A.D. 732.

The Muslims achieved equally brilliant success in the east. The mighty Persian empire was laid low in A.D. 636 and within eight years the whole of Persia as far east as Herat was annexed to the growing empire of the Caliphs, the successors of the Prophet to the pontificate. By A.D. 650 its northern frontier was advanced to the Oxus river in Central Asia and all the countries

between it and the Hindu Kush mountains were included in the
mighty Muslim Empire.

The Arab invaders had thus reached the border of the Hindu
dominions. Immediately to their east lay the Hindu kingdom of
Kapisi to the east of Bamian, including the Kabul region; the
kingdom of Zabulistan lay immediately to the south, and the
kingdom of Sind further south extending up to the sea.

It is hardly a matter of surprise that the Arabs, the world-
conquerers, stopped at the gate of India and failed to enter into
India proper. There is little wonder that they had to fight for a
length of time to overcome Hindu resistance and make a
permanent conquest of Indian borderlands. All the three border
kingdoms were simultaneously attacked, but these kingdoms
fought valiantly and there were alternate brilliant victories and
very serious reverses on either side both in Kabul and Zabulistan.
Though the first raid took place in A.D. 649, the efforts of half a
century enabled the Arabs only to impose a nominal suzerainty
over Kabul and Zabul. But even this could not be maintained for
more than fourteen years, after which Kabul and Zabul maintained
their authority practically unimpaired for a century and a half.
Kabul was finally conquered by the Arabs only in A.D. 870.

Sind also put up a brave struggle under the *brahman* king,
Chach. It became a very great and powerful kingdom, extending
up to the borders of Kashmir and Kanauj on the north and east
and to those of Kirman to the west. During his rule (A.D. 622-62),
several raids were carried by the Arab army from A.D. 637
onwards against the coastland of Sind and Bombay but the
Arabs could not gain any appreciable success and in the battle
at Debal, the main harbour of Sind, they were defeated and their
leader was killed. Successive failures of coastal raids induced
the Caliph to send a great expedition by land about A.D. 660. But
it was disastrously defeated. This was followed by no less than
six expeditions against the frontier post of Kikanan during the
next twenty years, but the only notable success was the conquest
of Makran.

During the next 25 years the kingdom of Sind obtained
respite from repeated Muslim aggressions on its frontier. But
about A.D. 712 Al-Hajjaj, the Governor of Iraq, made elaborate
preparations for the conquest of Sind. He appointed Muhammad-
bin Qasim commander of the expedition and provided him with
soldiers, arms and ammunition on a most lavish scale. Muhammad

besieged the port of Debal. There was a great Buddhist temple
in the city. According to the *Chachnama*, our principal source of
information, a *brahman* told Qasim that according to the
*Sastras* Sind will be conquered by the army of Islam, but so long
as the flagstaff remains over the dome of the temple it cannot
take the fort. The flagstaff was broken by throwing stones from
the catapult. This demoralised the besieged and the fort was
taken by assault. Similarly, Muhammad was helped by the
Buddhists in his onward march. The Buddhist priest had
already entered into a treasonable correspondence with Hajjaj
and openly received Muhammad and supplied him with provisions.
In many towns the Buddhist party welcomed the Arabs and
entered into a pact with them against their own governor,
partly, it is said on account of their aversion to the slaughter and
bloodshed, and partly due to their belief in the prophecy of their
sacred texts about the conquest of India by Islamic forces. It is
interesting to note that such beliefs on the part of the people of
Bengal at the other remote frontier of north India have been
recorded by Muslim chroniclers to explain the easy victories of
Muslim conquerors. Even on the eve of the final and decisive
battle between Muhammad and Dahir, the king of Sind, it was
the betrayal of the Governors of Dahir that enabled Muhammad
to cross the lake that lay between him and the enemy and to
obtain a position of vantage from which he could command both
the front and rear of Dahir's army and cut off its supply. Dahir
then went to the fort of Raor and a pitched battle was fought
near it. In spite of desertion and treachery, Dahir fought with
valour and on the second day, the Muslim army was nearly
routed, when the renegade Indian chiefs came to the aid of
Muhammad and he rallied his army. But the death of Dahir who
had been charging the Muslim army from the back of an
elephant was followed by a complete route of his army. Jai
Singh, the son of Dahir, retreated to the strong front of
Bahmanabad while the widowed queen was left to defend Raor.
The queen put up a brave resistance, and when conditions
became hopeless, burnt herself along with other ladies to escape
the infamy of falling into the hands of the Muslims. Jai Singh
strongly fortified Bahmanabad and the capital city Alor, and
began to harass the Muslim army. But once more treachery
played its part. The Wazir of Sind joined Muhammad and some
leading citizens of Bahmanabad, which had stoutly resisted

Muslim attack for six months, entered into a secret covenant with Muhammad and betrayed the fort. The fate of Alor and Multan was also decided by similar treachery on the part of their residents. Thus Sind was conquered and its people and king embraced Islam. The Muslim conquest of Sind has been treated in some detail as this first important Islamic conquest may be taken as the pattern of other conquests that followed.

# 2

# India under the Turks

Qutb-ud-din, the founder of the first Muslim ruling dynasty in India, was originally a slave and so were many of his successors. The royal dynasty founded by him is, therefore, known as the Slave Dynasty. By merciless military campaigns he silenced the opposition of most of the Hindu rulers and firmly laid the foundations of Muslim rule in India. Iltutmish, originally a Turkish slave of Qutb-ud-din but later his son-in-law, was the greatest ruler of the dynasty (A.D. 1210-36), and he consolidated Muslim rule in north India. His task was completed by another ruler, Ghiyas-ud-din Balban (A.D. 1266-86) who efficiently organised the administration and enhanced the dignity, honour and majesty of the throne. His name and fame spread all over Asia and fifteen Muslim rulers of Central Asia found shelter in his court from the ravages of the Mongols. The incapacity of his successor, a boy of 18, led to the overthrow of the dynasty in A.D. 1290.

Jalal-ud-din Firuz who usurped the throne in A.D. 1290 and murdered the boy-king was a nobleman of the Khalji tribe, which was akin to, but different from, the pure Turk to which belonged the preceding Muslim rulers as well as those of the next dynasty. He proved to be a kind ruler, but not very strong in action, and was murdered by his nephew and son-in-law, Ala-ud-din Khalji.

Ala-ud-din Khalji, who thus ascended the throne in A.D. 1299, was perhaps the most remarkable Muslim Sultan in India before the Mughals. Both the good and bad ingredients in his character were displayed in his treatment of the Mongols who made repeated incursions into India and on one occasion advanced even to the precincts of Delhi. Ala-ud-din always repulsed them with heavy losses and massacred thousands of them. Mongol commanders were trampled under the feet of elephants and towers were built of their heads. Some of the Mongols who invaded India in A.D. 1292 became Muslims and settled near Delhi. Once they hatched a conspiracy against the Sultan, and under his orders the entire colony of twenty to thirty thousand "New Musulmans" were killed in a single day. But such barbarous cruelty proved effective and the dreaded Mongol invasions were stopped.

Ala-ud-din extended Muslim rule to the southern extremity of India. He conquered Gujarat and Ranthambhor. His conquest of Chitor in A.D. 1303 is associated with the famous episode of the beautiful queen Padmini whose image in a mirror is said to have captivated him. The truth of this story is, however, doubted by many modern historians. But in any case Chitor was recovered by Rana Hammir of Mewar which became ag, in the premier State of Rajputana (Rajasthan) within 15 years. 1 vo years later Ala-ud-din conquered Malwa and then turned his attention to the Deccan.

The military expeditions to the south were led by Malik Kafur, who was originally a slave but became a great favourite of the Sultan. He defeated the Kakatiyas of Warangal, the Yadavas of Devagiri and the Hoysalas of Doarasamudra and advanced as far as Ramesvaram. One by one all the ancient Hindu kingdoms fell, and by the year A.D. 1313 the Muslim empire extended to cover nearly the whole of India.

Sultan Ala-ud-din, who ruled over a vast empire, did not possess the high qualifications befitting such a position. He was a stern despot, paying little heed to religious principles or any moral consideration. By his military organisation and over-centralisation of State authority he maintained peace in the country. He even made people happy by strictly enforcing such unusual regulations as fixing the price of necessaries of life. But he was illiterate, uncultured and given to excessive drinking. He was cruel, licentious, and tyrannical to the extreme, and was also vain, capricious and whimsical to a degree. He regarded himself as a second Alexander, and dreamed of conquering the whole world. He forbade public meeting and even social gatherings at private residences. He employed spies on an extensive scale and maintained his authority by inflicting ferocious punishments not only on the offenders, but sometimes also on their wives and children. But the Sultan lived long enough to see the total breakdown of State authority. All classes of people were discontented and there were conspiracies and revolutions on all the sides, in the midst of which he died in A.D. 1316. Some say that he was poisoned by Malik Kafur.

The five years that followed the death of Ala-ud-din was a period of anarchy and confusion, taking advantage of which Ghiyas-ud-din Tughluq ascended the throne and founded the Tughluq dynasty in A.D. 1320.

His son, Muhammad Tughluq, was one of the most eccentric sovereigns that ever ruled. He was regular in his devotions, abstained from wine and conformed to all the moral precepts of Islam in private life. He, however, imposed such oppressive taxes that the peasants were ruined and fled to the jungles. He changed his capital from Delhi to Devagiri. Delhi was practically deserted and ruined—but after some years shifted it back to Delhi.

The king now thought of an experiment to recoup his loss. This was the introduction of something like currency notes of the present day; only he used copper tokens instead of paper. In other words, the copper coins were made to carry the same value as the silver coins. But such a system can work only when due precautions are taken against forgeries. But no such precautions were taken and "every house was turned into a mint and people manufactured lakhs and crores of coins." The system was an utter failure. Foreign merchants refused to accept his copper tokens, trade was brought to a standstill, and confusion and distress prevailed everywhere. To the credit of the Sultan it must be said that he paid the face-value of all these coins at a tremendous loss to the treasury.

The Sultan's grand schemes of conquests were equally disastrous. He planned the conquest of Persia and collected a large, strong army of 3,70,000. After paying the salary of the soldiers for one year he gave up the project as impossible. He also sent a large expedition to the mountainous country between

India and China. But the hill-tribes closed the passes and the entire force was destroyed.

The wild career of Muhammad Tughluq produced its inevitable results. The internal administration of the country was completely ruined and rebellions broke out in every part of the empire. Some of these were put down by the Sultan, and their leaders were beheaded or cruelly flayed alive. But some provinces were finally lost to the empire. Thus Bengal, Madurai, and Warangal declared themselves independent, while the rest of the Deccan and south India were lost by the foundation of two independent kingdoms, viz., the Hindu kingdom of Vijayanagar founded in A.D. 1336 and Bahmani kingdom founded in A.D. 1347.

The reign of the next Sultan Firuz Shah Tughluq was famous for his public works of great utility, such as the foundation of towns, forts, mosques, colleges, hospitals, inns and many other buildings, besides bridges, embankments and canals. He also built a New Delhi called Firozabad and laid out 1,200 gardens in the neighbourhood. He was, on the whole, a good ruler and introduced many reforms in the administration. He restored the *jagir* (grant of land as remuneration for service) which was abolished by Ala-ud-din Khalji. He put to an end the barbarous practice of mutilating the limbs of offenders and other forms of torture, and abolished many vexatious taxes. He was a pious orthodox Muslim and a patron of learning. But he was narrow-minded and a fanatic. He encouraged the Hindus to embrace the Islamic faith and promised to exempt them from *Jiziya*, a poll-tax, which all non-Muslims had to pay. He died in A.D. 1388 at the advanced age of 79.

A number of puppet kings followed Firuz Shah in quick succession. While the petty Sultans were quarrelling with one another, India was visited by a terrible calamity—the invasion of Timur.

Amir Timur, popularly known as Tamerlane, was the head of the Chughtai Turks and king of Samarkand. In A.D. 1398 he invaded India and perpetrated incredible atrocities all along his way till he reached the neighbourhood of Delhi. He easily defeated the feeble force of Sultan Mahmud and then entered Delhi and proclaimed himself king. He was one of the most cruel and ferocious tyrants that the world has ever seen. He put to death a lakh of prisoners whom he had captured on his way to Delhi. Delhi itself was sacked and plundered for three days. The streets of Delhi were dyed with the blood of her innocent citizens. Similar dreadful scenes were repeated in the city of Meerut.

The invasion of Timur dealt a death-blow to Turkish rule in India. Two other Muslim dynasties followed: one, founded by Khizri Khan, Timur's deputy in Hindustan, ruled over Delhi and a small territory adjoining it for 37 years (A.D. 1414-51); and the other founded by Bahlol Lodi, ruling for a longer period (A.D. 1451-1526) over a larger kingdom. Khizri Khan claimed to be a descendant of the Prophet and hence his dynasty of four rulers, including himself, is known as the Sayyid. The Lodis were Pathans, though curiously enough, all the Turkish Muslim rulers of India preceding them are popularly, but wrongly, designated as Pathans. Bahlol and his two successors, Sikandar and Ibrahim, made a vain effort to restore the Indian empire built up by the Turks. The Afghan nobles broke out into open rebellion, and two of them, Alam Khan, an uncle of the third and last Lodi king, Ibrahim, and Daulat Khan Lodi, Governor of the Punjab, invited Babur, the Mughal ruler of Kabul to invade India in order to place Alam Khan on the throne of Delhi. Though both Lodi nobles ultimately backed out, Babur pursued his plan of conquering India. In November A.D. 1526 Babur marched against India and met the forces of Ibrahim at Panipat, the famous battlefield where the fate of India was decided no less than three times. Ibrahim Lodi was defeated and killed (A.D. 1526), and Babur established the Mughal rule in India.

The defeat of Ibrahim Lodi, however, did not mean the conquest of north India, far less the whole of India, by the Mughals. For, as mentioned above, the Muslim empire of the Turks in India had broken up into a number of independent States and the Lodi dominions of which Babur came into possession by defeating and killing Ibrahim Lodi consisted only of Delhi, Agra and the territories around them.

The various independent States that arose on the break-up of the Sultanate of Delhi may be divided into four groups. First, the northern belt of Muhammadan powers comprising Sind, the Punjab, Delhi, Jaunpur and Bengal which sweeps in a semicircle from the mouth of the Indus to the Bay of Bengal. Second, the southern belt of Muhammadan powers, viz., Gujarat, Malwa, Khandesh and the Bahmani kingdoms. Wedged in between these two lay the third group, the Rajput States, fast regaining their lost power and supremacy; while to the south and east of the southern Muhammadan belt lay the Hindu kingdoms of Vijayanagar, Kalinga and the Koch and Ahom kingdoms. There were thus two great groups of Muhammadan powers, each threatened by formidable Hindu powers. It is not possible to give a detailed account of these States but a brief reference must suffice.

### Bengal

Iliyas Shah established an independent kingdom about A.D. 1345. He levied a tribute on Orissa and Tirhut. The Tughluq Emperor Firuz Shah recognised the independence of Bengal. His son and successor Sikandar died in A.D. 1393 after a prosperous rule of 36 years. The Emperor of China sent an embassy to the court of Sikandar's son Azam Shah who also sent an embassy to China. Shortly after his death in A.D. 1410 a Hindu Zamindar Ganesh seized the sovereignty of Bengal and probably ascended the throne under the name of Danujamardanadeva, for the coins issued by a Hindu ruler of this name show that he ruled over nearly the whole of Bengal. His son Jadu succeeded him but took the name of Jalal-ud-din on becoming a Muslim. Chaos and confusion followed after his death when the Hindu and Muslim chiefs elected Ala-ud-din Husain Shah to the throne in A.D. 1493. He restored peace and prosperity and conquered south Bihar, Cooch Behar and portions of Tippera. His son Nusrat Shah conquered north Bihar and attacked Babur in alliance with the brother of Ibrahim Lodi. An honourable treaty was concluded with the Mughal Emperor.

### Jaunpur

During the period of chaos and confusion by the invasion of Tamerlane an independent kingdom was founded by the Vizir of the Tughluq Emperor, Khwaja Jahan, who was given the title of *Malikushsharq* or Lord of the East, by his master, and placed in charge of the territory extending from Kanauj to Bihar. The capital of this new kingdom was Jaunpur, a new city founded on the bank of the river Gomti by Firuz Tughluq. The rule of the Sharqi dynasty came to an end in A.D. 1476 when the Lodi Emperor of Delhi, reconquered it.

## Gujarat and Malwa

The Governors of Gujarat and Malwa declared independence after the invasion of Timur. Ahmed Shah, a powerful king of Gujarat, founded a beautiful city known after him as Ahmedabad and moved his capital there. His grandson Mahmud Begarha, who ascended the throne as a boy and ruled from A.D. 1458 to A.D. 1511, was a remarkable person and his peculiarities or eccentricities were carried by travellers in a legendary form to Europe. He allied himself with the Sultan of Turkey for driving away the Portuguese from the Indian seas. The combined fleet of Turkey and Gujarat defeated the Portuguese fleet near Chaul in A.D. 1508 but next year the Portuguese fleet defeated the fleet of Gujarat and re-established its supremacy in the Indian seas. The next important king, Bahadur Shah, annexed Malwa, and stormed the famous Rajput fort of Chitor. His contest with the Mughal emperors will be related later.

## The Rajputs

The Rajputs were distinguished for their military spirit, bravery, love of independence and the spirit of self-sacrifice, and their annals form a brilliant chapter in the history of medieval India. Their origin is obscure but they claimed to be Kshatriyas and sustained this claim by many legends which cannot be regarded as historical truth. The Chauhans, Paramaras, Chalukyas and the Pariharas or the Pratiharas to whom reference has been made above as powerful ruling clans during the Hindu period, all claimed to be Rajputs during the medieval period. But the most distinguished among them during this period were the Guhilots of Mewar who also ruled as a minor clan during the Hindu period. The name Guhilot is derived from Guhila, the traditional ancestor who is said to have lived about A.D. 600. They are better known as the Sisodiyas, the name of the royal section of the clan founded by a hero called Bappa Rawal, who conquered Chitor about A.D. 628.

But it was Samar Simha who really raised it to an important position towards the close of the 13th century. In the 14th century, Ala-ud-din Khalji invaded the kingdom and conquered Chitor, its famous capital, as has already been related. But the glory of the kingdom was again revived by Hammira. During the reign of Hammira and his two successors, which covered the latter half of the 14th century, the kingdom was extended in all directions by a number of brilliant victories including one against the Sultan of Delhi.

The next important king of the dynasty is Maharana Kumbha (A.D. 1433-68). He was a great warrior and repeatedly defeated the Muhammadan chiefs of Malwa, Gujarat and Nagor. In A.D. 1440 he marched with 100,000 horse and foot soldiers and 1,400 elephants against the combined forces of Malwa and inflicted a crushing defeat upon them. He commemorated this victory by building a lofty tower which exists in Chitor. Kumbha built 32 forts in Mewar of which Kumbhalgarh was the most famous. He was a good poet. He was murdered by his own son about A.D. 1468. Sangram Singh or Rana Sanga (A.D. 1509-28), the grandson of Kumbha, was another notable king of the dynasty. He, too, fought successfully against the Muhammadan chiefs of Malwa and Gujarat, and captured the kingdom of Malwa. He was truly a hero of hundred battles, and under him Rajput power reached the high watermark of its glory. He gained victories no less than 18 times against the king of Malwa and Delhi and was unquestionably the most powerful king in India at the time. The Rana was seized with the ambition of freeing Indian from the Muhammadan yoke. The defeat of Ibrahim Lodi at the hands of Babur seemed to offer a good opportunity to the Rana, and he organised a confederacy of Rajput chiefs against the Mughal conqueror. Although lacking an eye and an arm, crippled by a broken leg, and scarred by eighty wounds from lance or sword, he led the immense host of the Rajput army, including 80,000 horses and 500 war elephants, against Babur. Babur realised the gravity of the danger, while a regular consternation seized his entire army. At last the two armies met at Khanua near Fatehpur Sikri. The superior military tactics of Babur, aided by a powerful artillery, carried the day and the rout of the Rajput army was complete (A.D. 1527). The Rana himself escaped, but died soon after. With him ended the dream of Rajput supremacy in India.

## The Bahmani Kingdom

During the dark days of Muhammad Tughluq's reign, the foreign Amirs of the Deccan revolted and established an independent kingdom. In A.D. 1347 they elected as king a brave soldier named Hasan. On ascending the throne, he assumed the name of Ala-ud-din Hasan Bahman Shah. It is popularly supposed that the title Bahman was assumed by him out of respect for an old Brahman master, under whom he had served in his youth. The fact, however, seems to be that he traced his descent from a Persian king called Bahman Shah and hence assumed the title. The kingdom founded by him came to be known as the Bahmani kingdom.

The new Sultan rapidly extended his kingdom and when he died in A.D. 1358 its boundaries reached the Pen Ganga on the north and the Krishna in the west, and included the ports of Goa and Dabhol, while its eastern frontier was marked by Bhonagir, a town in the Nizam's dominions. The capital of this extensive kingdom was established at Gulbarga, which was named Ahsanabad or Hasanabad.

Altogether, fourteen Sultans ruled over this kingdom between A.D. 1347 and 1518. The annals of their reigns contain little more than horrible accounts of bloodshed and savage wars against neighbouring kingdoms, notably those of Vijayanagar and Warangal, palace revolutions and strifes among different factions in the court leading to indiscriminate massacres.

Firuz Shah (A.D. 1397-1422) the most notable among the later rulers, has been called the Akbar of the south. He was a talented king and beautified his capital Gulbarga with many fine buildings. He twice defeated the king of Vijayanagar, but was himself defeated in the third battle. He married a daughter of the king of Vijayanagar and ruled with justice and moderation. He was succeeded by his brother Ahmad Shah who finally conquered Warangal in A.D. 1424, and also founded the city of Bidar, to where the capital was soon transferred. But the southern expansion of the Bahmani power was effectively checked by Vijayanagar. It is not necessary to give a detailed account of the kings of this dynasty. Of the fourteen kings, four were murdered and two others were deposed and blinded.

Thus at the time when Babur gained his victory over Ibrahim Lodi, the extensive Bahmani kingdom was divided into five independent principalities: (1) The Imad Shahi kingdom of Berar, (2) The Nizam Shahi of Ahmadnagar, (3) The Adil Shahi of Bijapur, (4) The Qutb Shahi of Golconda, and (5) the Barid Shahi of Bidar. This history of their struggles with, and their final absorption into the Mughal empire, will be related in conection with the history of the latter.

## Kingdom of Vijayanagar

The origin of the kingdom of Viyaanagar is shrouded in obscurity. It appears, however, to be most likely that two brothers, Harihara and Bukka, who were forced to embrace Islam and appointed Governor of Kampili in the Deccan, declared independence and were taken again into the Hindu fold. Harihara reigned from A.D. 1336 to A.D. 1356 and was succeeded by Bukka. When Bukka died in A.D. 1377, nearly the whole of the peninsula, south of the Krishna was included in the kingdom of Vijayanagar. Harihara II (A.D. 1377-1404), the next king, formally assumed the royal title, and consolidated his dominions over the whole of South India.

The next important king was Deva Raya (A.D. 1406-22). The establishment of a Hindu kingdom in the neighbourhood had already provoked the jealousy of the Bahmani kings, and from the very beginning, they led several expeditions against it. The reign of Deva Raya and his successors is also one long story of struggles between the two powers, which were often accompanied by cruel barbarity of the worst type. Deva Raya gave his daughter in marriage to the Muslim king. But it did not end the hereditary war which went on as usual for generations.

In A.D. 1485 the throne was usurped by Saluva Narasimha, the governor of Chandragiri. The usurper, however, proved a capable ruler and made extensive conquests in the Tamil country. The Bahmani kingdom was now tottering, but its hereditary role of fighting with Vijayanagar devolved on the independent State carved out of it, notably the sultanate of Bijapur. Narasimha, as usual, had to engage in constant fighting with the Muhammadan States. He died in 1490 and shortly afterwards the kingdom of Vijayanagar passed into the hands of a new dynasty founded by his Tuluva minister, Narasa Nayaka. The greatest king of the dynasty was Krishnadeva Raya whose long rule of 20 years (A.D. 1509-29) shed lustre on the kingdom. He gained repeated victories over the State of Bijapur and even temporarily occupied the city of Bijapur itself. He also stormed and destroyed the fortress of Gulbarga, once the capital of Bahmani kingdom. Krishnadeva Raya was a hero in peace as well as in war. In an age marked by bigotry and cruelty, he was distinguished for his catholicity and humanity. From the ghastly stories of rapine and massacre that invariably followed the military campaigns of those days, we turn with relief to "Krishna Raya's kindness to the fallen enemy, and his acts of mercy and charity towards the residents of captured cities." The king was a patron of letters and was famous for his religious zeal and charity. He is justly regarded as the greatest of the Vijayanagar monarchs. Under him the kingdom of Vijayanagar comprised nearly the whole of the south Indian peninsula, south of the Krishna.

Krishnadeva Raya's successors were weak and tyrannical. They pursued the policy of joining one Muhammadan State against another, which soon provoked the wrath of the Muhammadan States against the kingdom of Vijayanagar. At last the kings of Bijapur, Ahmadnagar, Golconda and Bidar formed an alliance and marched against Vijayanagar. The allied army assembled at Talikota to the north of the Krishna, but though the battle is known in history as the 'Battle of Talikota' the actual battle took place about thirty miles south, on the other side of the river in the plain near Mudgal.

Sadasiva Raya was the nominal king of Vijayanagar, but the actual power was in the hands of his minister, Rama Raja. The latter, confident of victory, led an immense army against the Muslim invaders. The battle was fought on January 23, 1565. The Hindus at first gained some advantages but the capture and death of Rama Raja was followed by the complete route of his army. By an incomprehensible folly, Rama Raja had staked everything upon a single battle, and when that was lost, the kingdom and its magnificent capital lay at the mercy of the victors. The Muslim forces destroyed the city completely so that nothing remains now but a heap of ruins to mark the spot where once stately buildings stood.

There are several accounts of the kingdom of Vijayanagar from the pen of foreign travellers, who visited it in its day of glory. All of them refer in glowing terms to the grandeur and magnificence of the capital city and the power and resources of its kings. The Italian traveller, Nicolo Ponti, who visited Vijayanagar in A.D. 1420 estimated the circumference of the city to be sixty miles, and considered its king to be more powerful than any other monarch in India. The other travellers refer to a number of temples, palaces and strong forts which adorned the mighty Hindu kingdom. Art and literature flourished, and the famous commentator Sayanacharya occupied a high position in the kingdom.

## Orissa

Reference has been made to the Eastern Gangas and their fight with Muslims. Kapilendra Deva who founded the Solar Dynasty in A.D. 1434 defeated the Bahmani king and the king of Vijayanagar and extended his kingdom from the Ganges to the Cauvery. During the reign of his son Purushottama (A.D. 1467-97) the king of Vijayanagar occupied the lands south of Krishna and Bahmani, conquered the territory between the Krishna and Godavari; but Purushottama recovered all this territory and extended his conquests up to Guntoor. Purushottama was succeeded by his son Prataparudra (A.D. 1497-1540). As a result of three successive wars with Vijayanagar he lost all the territories south of the Godavari. The Sultan of Golconda also invaded Orissa. King Prataparudra was a disciple of Chaitanya, who lived in his dominions for a long time.

The great task facing Babur after the Battle of Panipat (A.D. 1526) and the occupation of the Lodi dominions was to bring all these independent States under the sovereignty of the Mughals. This was accomplished in stages by his successors before the end of the seventeenth century. The successive conquest of north India, the Deccan and finally the whole of south India made the Mughal emperor the sovereign of practically the whole of India, a task accomplished once before, by the Mauryas, about two thousand years ago and later by the Khaljis for a brief period. But before narrating that story of the glorious period of Mughal

rule in India, it is necessary to make a brief survey of the first
phase of Muslim rule in India covering a period of nearly three
centuries and a half intervening between the second battle of
Tarain (A.D. 1192) and the second battle on the historic ground
of Panipat in A.D. 1556, to which reference will be made later.

# 3

# Pre-Mughal Muslim Rule:
# A Broad Survey

The rapid conquest of the greater part of India by the Turks after the Second Battle of Tarain in A.D 1192. offers a striking contrast to the slow progress of the Arabs and Turks during the period of nearly five hundred years that elapsed from the conquest of Sind. The causes usually suggested for this phenomenon, viz., the enervating climate of India, lack of unity, caste system, etc. cannot be accepted as sufficient as these factors were prevalent during the earlier period also, to a large extent. Apart from internal conditions in the Muslim world which might have reduced the incentive opportunity to conquer far away lands like India, the difference must be attributed to normal decline in the political insight and moral spirit of Indians such as normally occurs in the history of nations which, like individuals, have to pass through successive stages of adolescence, youth, old age and decay. There were also probably some inherent defects in the national character to which reference has already been made. We may note an additional factor, namely, the spirit of aloofness and superiority-complex which made the Hindus averse to travel in foreign lands and kept them ignorant of the advances made in military organisation, equipment and tactics by other nations. There is probably a great deal of truth in the following statement of Alberuni, the Arab traveller, who accompanied Sultan Mahmud to India and made a careful study of the literature, religion and social institutions of the Hindus:

"The Hindus believe that there is no country but theirs, no nation like theirs, no king like theirs, no religion like theirs, no science like theirs. Their haughtiness is such that, if you tell them of any science or scholar in Khurasan and Persia, they will think you to be both an ignoramus and liar. If they travelled and mixed with other nations they would soon change their mind, for their ancestors were not as narrow-minded as the present generation is." In support of Alberuni it may be pointed out, that while the Greeks, Romans, the Chinese and the Muslims wrote accounts of India, no Indian account of any of them has yet reached us.

There may be something in the soil of India to account for this. For even the Turks and Pathans, after they had settled in India, imbibed the exclusive spirit of the Hindus and proved inferior to the Mughals who followed them. For example, in the First Battle of Panipat, the Mughals used firearms which revolutionised the art of warfare of which the Muslim and the Hindu rulers of India were quite ignorant, although the Portuguese had introduced it a short while ago, and a few Indian rulers had learnt the use of it.

We may now pass on to a broad review of some major effects of the Muslim rule in India—of the Turks from the 13th to the first half of the 15th century and of the Pathans or Afghans during the second half of the 15th and first quarter of the 16th century. Associated with these were the Persians and the Arabs and also Muslims from other foreign countries, particularly the Muslim refugees from Central Asia towards the end of the 13th century. Throughout the 13th century the Turks monopolised all political power and had nothing but supreme contempt for non-Turks, and even the Indian Muslims were completely bereft of all power and pelf. Ala-ud-din Khalji, for the first time, associated Indian Muslims with the administration. It was perhaps necessary as the successes of the Mongols stopped the flow of Central Asian Turks into India and it was impossible to carry on the administration without the help of the Indians who consisted mostly of Hindus of low castes who, for various reasons embraced Islam in gradually increasing number. But "the Indian Muslims were not only not admitted into the aristocracy of the conquerors but were not even given a share in the social and economic privileges. The soldiers were mostly foreigners, mainly Turks, while non-Turkish foreigners were mostly appointed to civil and ecclesiastical posts."

The lot of Hindus was unenviable. They had to suffer a lot during and after the invasions of the Turks. Thousands of them were killed during the process of conquest or subjugation, massacred after wars and many of them were converted to Islam. The upper and middle class Hindus suffered the most, particularly in the field of employment, both civil and military. They had to suffer personal indignities and religious persecution. There were, however, exceptions but we hardly find a Hindu enjoying the post of a governor or a minister or even that of a secretary. There are many passages in the historical narrative written by Muslim authors such as Ibn Batuta (14th century A.D.), a learned Muslim traveller from Africa and others which leave no doubt of the cruelties perpetrated by early invaders.

In view of the difference between the religious ideas and the social practices of the Hindus and Muslims in respect of food, dress, ideas of purity and many other things which have persisted down the ages, it is no wonder that the two communities lived apart in two strongly guarded citadels. The Hindus could and often did become Muslims, but none of them could re-enter the Hindufold.

From time immemorial many people with diverse types of civilisation have settled permanently in India such as the Greeks, Sakas, Parthians, Huns, etc., but they completely merged themselves with the local people that today we cannot find any trace of these foreign elements in the Indian population. But the Muslims—Arabs, Turks, Persians—have retained their separate cultural identity for 1,200 years or more. This is due to the radical, one may say, fundamental differences between the two cultures. As long ago as the beginning of the eleventh century, Alberuni noticed and gave forceful expression to it as follows: "They (Hindus) totally differ from us in religion, as we believe in nothing in which they believe, and vice versa... . All their fanaticism is directed against those who do not belong to them—against all foreigners. They call them *mleccha, i.e.,* impure, and forbid having any connection with them, be it by intermarriage or any other kind of relationship, or by sitting, eating or drinking with them, because, thereby, they would be polluted. They consider as impure anything which touches the fire and the water of foreigners; and no household can exist without these elements. They are not allowed to receive anybody who does not belong to them, even if he wished it, or was inclined to their religion. This too renders any connection with them quite impossible, and constitutes the widest gulf between us and them.

"In all manners and usages they differ from us to such a degree as to frighten the children with us, with our dress, and our way and customs, and as to declare us to be the devil's breed and our doings as the very opposite of all that is good and proper."

It would be idle to deny the existence of fundamental differences between the two communities or to ignore the most outstanding historical fact of the medieval age that for the first time since the dawn of history of which we have definite knowledge, India became the homeland of two categories of peoples with distinct cultures of their own.

It is thus evident that the main current of Indian history after A.D 1200 flowed through two distinct channels. However, many sects arose which tried to harmonise Islam and Hinduism and to find common ground for the devotees of both the creeds in which their differences of ritual, dogma and external marks of faith were ignored. Ramananda, Kabir, Nanak, Dadu and Chaitanya were some of the leaders of the movements. The teachings of the Bhakti saints played an important role in weakening the distinctions between the higher and lower castes.

It must, also, be remembered that conversion of Hindus to Islam was not by force alone, but partly due to the evils of Hindu society. The low-caste Hindus had to lead a very degraded life, but as soon as they adopted the Islamic faith, they were placed on an equal footing with the highest grandees in the realm. Islam has carried into practice the ideas of equality and fraternity to a far greater extent than any other religion and caste is the worst offender in this respect. Not that the Hindus adopted the faith of Islam in large numbers.

Perhaps another cause of the conversion of the Hindus is to be sought in the humiliating treatment, meted out to them by some Muhammadan rulers. It is scarcely a matter of surprise that a large number of Hindus should try to get rid of their humiliating position by conversion to Islam. It is only fair to remember in this connection that some Muhammadan rulers followed this policy against the Hindus because they regarded it as their religious duty and they are no more guilty in this respect than many Hindu kings who justified their barbarous treatment to the *Sudras* on the same ground. The main teachings of these saints of Bhakti Movement were a belief in the unity of God, stress on moral character, and a disbelief in the ceremonials of worship and distinctions of caste and creed. These ideas were not, of course, new. The first is traceable, to the time of the *Rigveda,* and the second and the third formed the essence of Buddhism and Jainism. But the long contact between the Hindus and the Musalmans gave fresh impetus to these views, and some of the foremost religious teachers of the period gave a forceful expression to them. The most prominent of these were Ramananda, Kabir, Mirabai, Namdev, Nanak and Chaitanya.

## Ramananda

In the 14th century, Ramananda, the famous Vaishnava preacher, introduced a radical reform among the Vaishnava sect. "He made no distinction between the *brahmanas* and members of the degraded castes, and all could even dine together." He preached the gospel of unity of God and unity of men all over northern India.

## Kabir

One of the disciples of Ramananda was Kabir, a Muhammadan weaver. He flourished in the 15th century, and is famous for his beautiful poetic stanzas containing philosophical gems in the most popular garb. He preached that there is no real distinction between the Hindus and the Muhammadans, the God of the Hindus being also the God of the Muhammadans.

## Mirabai

According to tradition she was the queen of Raja Kumbh of Mewar (15th century) but renounced the world as a devotee of Lord Krishna. Her devotional songs in *Brajabhasha* (a dialect of Hindi) are full of beauty and breathe deep emotions of love and surrender to God. Even now they are very popular throughout northern India.

### Namdev

He was a tailor by profession but preached throughout Maharashtra that devotion to God was the only way to salvation and there was no need for rituals or worship. His disciples included both Hindus and Muslims. He was probably born at the beginning of the 15th century.

### Nanak

Nanak founded the Sikh sect in the Punjab on the same principles. He flourished in the 15th century. He had a large number of Hindus and Muslims as his followers. The Sikhs rose to be one of the most important factors in Indian history and more will be heard of them hereafter.

### Chaitanya

One of the greatest reformers in the Vaishnavaite sect was Chaitanya. He was born at Nabadwip in Bengal in A.D 1486. He was a great scholar, and preached his emotional doctrine of "love and faith" in God. He did away with distinctions of caste, and one of his principal followers was a Muhammadan. He died before he was fifty in A.D 1533.

The teachings of these reformers profoundly affected the life of the people. The policy of Sher Shah and Akbar could be regarded as a translation of these theories into practice.

The six reformers named above rendered another great service to India by giving an impetus to vernacular literature. Like the old reformers, Gautama Buddha and Mahavira, they preached to the people in the popular language of the day, and thus the vernacular literature was enriched by their efforts. The Hindi literature was improved by Ramananda and Kabir, while the Bengali and the Punjabi literature were similarly influenced by Chaitanya and Nanak. Two other writers, Vidyapati and Chandidas enriched the vernacular literature of Bihar and Bengal with their melodious poems. Both Bengali and Maithili were patronised by the Muslim kings. Krittivasa, the author of the Bengali *Ramayana*, Maladhar Basu (Gunaraj Khan), the author of *Srikrishnavijaya* based on the *Bhagavata* and *Vishnu Puranas*, and Bijayagupta, the author of *Manasamangala*, were all patronised by Muslim kings. The great epic of *Mahabharata* was translated into Bengali for the first time by Kavindra Paramesvara (Srikara Nandi) at the instance of

Paragal Khan, the General of Hussain Shah, and a portion of it was again translated by the same author by the order of the General's son Chhuti Khan (Nasrat Khan). Vidyapati also received the patronage of more than one Muslim Sultan.

The Muhammadans added a new branch to Indian literature, viz., history. The Hindus, for some reason or the other, were not fond of historical writings, and Sanskrit literature, although very rich in many respects, contains very few historical works. The Muhammadans, however, were very fond of history, and many good works were written by them. Minhaj-ud-din wrote a history of Muhammadan rule in and outside India up to the reign of Nasir-ud-din. His book is called *Tabaqat-i-Nasiri* after that king. Zia-ud-din *Barni* began where Minhaj-ud-din had stopped and continued his account up to the time of Firuz Tughluq.

A new vernacular, Urdu, came into existence as a result of the interaction of the Hindus and Muhammadan. Persian literature was highly developed. The great poet Amir Khusrau (A.D 1253-1325), who lived in India, wrote in Persian as well as in Hindi.

### Foreigner's accounts

The information supplied by Muslim historians about the Muhammadan period is supplemented by the accounts of foreign travellers who visited India. Ibn Batuta, an African traveller, visited this country during the reign of Sultan Mohammad-bin Tughluq. The prosperous economic condition of India at this time may be realised from the following list of prices noted by him:

|                                    | Rs | As | Ps |
|------------------------------------|----|----|----|
| Paddy per maund of present day     | 0  | 2  | 0  |
| Ghee per maund of present day      | 1  | 7  | 0  |
| Sugar per maund of present day     | 1  | 7  | 0  |
| Til oil per maund of present day   | 0  | 11 | 6  |
| Fine cotton cloth 15 yds           | 2  | 0  | 0  |
| A milch cow                        | 3  | 0  | 0  |
| A fowl                             | 0  | 0  | 3  |
| A ram                              | 0  | 4  | 0  |

There were easy means of communication. The capital was connected with all the chief cities by posts placed at regular distances of about a mile. Runners with a whip in hand to which small brass balls were tied, ran from one post to the next, where other runners waited in readiness for the incoming mail.

## Art and Architecture

The Muhammadan rulers were all patrons of art, and many fine buildings—tombs, mosques and palaces — were erected during their rule. The most characteristic feature of these buildings is the extensive use of arches and domes.

The earliest monuments of the Muslim period are the mosque at Ajmer, the Qutb Mosque and Minar, and the tomb of Sultan Iltutmish at Delhi. The Qutb Minar, about 253 ft. high is one of the most beautiful examples of detached minarets erected near mosques for the use of *Muazzins,* whose duty is to summon the faithful to prayer at stated times by uttering a loud and prolonged call. The Qutb Mosque had a screen of eleven pointed arches, eight smaller and three larger, Muslim in form, but Hindu in construction; for the early Muslim rulers were obliged to employ Hindu artists and utilised materials of Hindu temples destroyed by them.

The most important monument of the Khalji period is the magnificent gateway, erected in A.D 1300 by Ala-ud-din Khalji to the south of Qutb Mosque. True or radiating arches, as against the pointed arches of the Hindus, were used in this structure, showing an advance in Indo-Muslim architecture, but many details still showed the influence of Hindu tradition.

The Sultans of the Tughluq dynasty introduced a new style which shows no trace of Hindu influence. Their buildings were massive, but the decorations were simple and austere. The most remarkable example of this style is the tomb of Ghias-ud-din Tughluq in Delhi.

Special reference should also be made to the groups of fine buildings erected by the various local dynasties, notably those of Bengal and Gujarat, Jaunpur, Bijapur and the Hindu kingdom of Vijayanagar. The Adina Masjid, the two Sona Masjids, Qadam Rasul Masjid, Dakhil Darwaza and other buildings of Gaur and Pandua testify to the grandeur of art in Muhammadan Bengal.

# 4

# The Mughal Empire

Zahir-ud-din Muhammad, surnamed Babur, the Tiger, was the direct descendant of the Turkish Chief Tamerlane, whose invasion of India has been already described. Inheriting from his father at the tender age of eleven the small principality of Farghana, the upper valley of Syr Darya, he conquered Samarkand, lost each of them in turn, was finally driven from both and ultimately became king of Kabul, invaded India more than once, and defeated Ibrahim Lodi in A.D. 1526 and the Rajput hero Sangram Singh in A.D. 1527 as mentioned earlier. These two great victories, followed by many others, notably one against the combined Afghan chiefs of Bengal and Bihar made him master of a vast territory extending up the frontiers of Bengal in the east and Gwalior in the south. The prospects of establishing a big empire over north India loomed large, but were shattered by his death in A.D. 1530 and the rise of an Afghan Chief Sher Shah, the son of a petty *jagirdar* who gradually became powerful and drove away after a series of battles, Babur's son Humayun from India.

Sher Shah was a brilliant conqueror and successful administrator and there was every chance of his restoring Afghan rule in India. During his brief rule of five years (A.D. 1540-45), he placed the administration of his Indian empire on a sound basis which none of his Turkish predecessors could do. Though his son and successor, Islam Shah, maintained the Empire, his death in A.D. 1553 was followed by a period of chaos and confusion caused by internal dissensions in the royal family and the discontent and turbulence of the Afghan chiefs of the court. There arose several contenders to the throne and the empire was divided among them. Humayun, who had been a refugee in the court of the Persian king, seized this opportunity to return to India, and with the help of the Persian king, recovered Kabul, Kandahar and the Punjab. Sikandar Suri the Afghan ruler opposed him but was defeated, and Humayun occupied Delhi in A.D. 1555. But once more fate was against the Mughals. Humayun died in January A.D. 1556, and his young son Akbar, a lad of 14, had to face an opponent of sterner stuff in Sikandar Suri. This was the Hindu General of the Afghan Emperor Islam Shah, and the Prime Minister of his successor Mahammad Adil Shah. His name was Hemchandra but he was nicknamed Hemu by the Mughal historians and is generally known as such. His romantic career from a grocer to an emperor will be related later. On hearing of the death of Humayun and the absence of Akbar in the Punjab, Hemu advanced with an army and captured both Delhi and Agra after defeating the Mughal army. After seizing Delhi, Hemu won over the Afghan soldiers, and with their help, ascended the throne with the imperial canopy raised over his head, issued coins in his name, and assumed the historic name of Vikramaditya or Vikramjit. He then advanced to meet the Mughal army sent against him. Once more, in 1556, the throne of Delhi was won and lost on the battlefield of Panipat. The battle began with a bold charge by Hemu and victory was almost within his grasp when an arrow pierced his eye and he became unconscious. This decided the fate of the battle, as his soldiers, thinking him dead, fled pell-mell in all directions. Akbar killed Hemu in cold blood under the directions of Bairam Khan, his guardian.

The foundations of the MughalEmpire were well and truly laid at Panipat, not in A.D. 1526 but in A.D. 1556 After the defeat and death of Hemu, the Mughal rulers of Delhi never faced any real danger till after the death of Aurangzeb in A.D. 1707. It is somewhat singular that its duration was more or less the same as that of the two preceding empires in India, namely those of the Mauryas and the Guptas, and in all these three instances the empire was built up by a succession of three or four great monarchs—Chandragupta, Bindusara and Asoka in the first, Samudragupta, Chandragupta II, Kumaragupta and

Sikandagupta in the second, and Akbar, Jahangir, Shah Jahan and Aurangzeb in the third case. Two other analogies also easily occur to our mind, namely, the building up of a good administrative machinery and the wonderful efflorescence of art and architecture.

It is not necessary to narrate in detail the thrice told tale of the gradual extension of the Mughal Empire till it reached the Himalayas, on the north, the Hind Kush on the west and the geographical boundaries of India in the east and south. Only a few special features need be stressed. After having defeated the Afghan rulers, Akbar adopted an aggressive policy from the very beginning and established his authority almost all over northern India, Afghanistan, Baluchistan and Kandahar during the period between A.D. 1560, when he sent an expedition against Malwa, and A.D. 1595, when he conquered Kandahar. His conquests included those of Gondwana (1564), Rajputana (1569), Gujarat (1572), Bengal (1576), Kashmir (1586), Kabul (after his brother, who was its Governor revolted in 1581), southern Sindh (1591), Orissa (1592), Baluchistan (1595), and Kandahar (1595).

Having thus established a vast empire which included the whole of northern India together with Kabul, Kandahar, Ghazni and their dependencies, Akbar turned his attention towards the Deccan. He invaded both Ahmadnagar and Khandesh but had only partial success, having acquired Berar (1596) and small portions of the two kingdoms (1601).

Reference may now be made to a few special features in connection with these conquests, before turning to those of his successors.

The conquering expedition of Akbar had brought into relief the figures of two queens who shed lustre on the Medieval Age. Rani Durgavati, the regent for her son, the young ruler of Gondwana, showed exemplary courage and military acumen in fighting with the Mughal forces at the head of her army and when no hope remained, stabbed herself and the other ladies burnt themselves to death.

Another heroic lady was Chand Sultana, popularly known as Chand Bibi, the queen of Ahmadnagar. Dressed in full armour, she moved about encouraging the troops who defended the besieged city, and when the Mughal guns made a breach in the wall and while supervising repair work of the same she was shot dead by Akbar.

But the most interesting episode in the military career of Akbar is his fight with Rana Pratap of Mewer which has been immortalised by ballads of the Rajput bards and *The Annals and Antiquities of Rajasthan* by James Tod. The Rajputs had been the chief bulwark of Hinduism against the intrusion of Islam in India. Most of the Pathan rulers had to fight against the Rajputs who, though often defeated, again asserted their independence whenever any opportunity arose. Akbar decided to win them over by matrimonial alliances. The first fruit of that policy was Akbar's marriage with the daughters of the Rana Ambar (Jaipur) and Raja Bahari Mal, and as a result thereof both Bhagwan Das and Man Singh, son and grandson, respectively of those rulers were "enrolled amongst the nobility and received high commands." There were two other marriage alliances of that nature (with Bikaner and Jaisalmer) with similar obligations. This policy endeared Akbar to the Rajput princes, who, became the strongest champions of the Mughal empire, Man Singh and Jaswant Singh, for example, may be said to have been the pillars of the Mughal empire during the reigns of Akbar and Aurangzeb. But the new policy of Akbar failed in the case of Mewar, the premier State in Rajputana, whose rulers prided themselves as the Sisodiyas and descendants of the famous, almost legendary hero, Bappa Rawal.

The policy of peace having succeeded with most of the Rajput clans and States, Akbar turned his attention to the Rajput kingdom of Mewar. The Rana of Mewar refused to submit to the Mughal emperor. Akbar besieged the capital city of Chitor. Rana Udai Singh, son of the famous Sangram Singh, took refuge in the hills and the defence of Chitor was organised by two brave chiefs, Jaimal and Patta. The siege continued from October 20, 1567 to February 23, 1568, when the death of Jaimal by a chance shot disheartened the defenders. The heroic Rajputs saw their wives, daughters and sisters burnt on funeral pyres according to the custom of *Jauhar*, and then rushed upon the Mughal soldiers. They perished fighting almost to a man, but the fame of their heroic resistance survives to this day. It must ever remain an indelible stain on the character of Akbar that far from appreciating the heroism of his brave foes, he massacred

30,000 persons taking part in the defence of the city. It should be noted, however, that Akbar gave evidence of his appreciation of Rajput heroism by placing the statues of Jaimal and Patta at the main entrance to the fort of Agra.

Though most of the Rajput states such as Marwar, Ambar (Jaipur), Bikaner and Bundi acknowledged the suzerainty of Akbar, Mewar refused to submit. Bereft of the capital city, the brave sons of Mewar rallied under Pratap Singh, the heroic son of Udai Singh, who had died in A.D. 1572. With great difficulty Pratap organised an army and met the Mughal forces at the famous Haldighat Pass. The Rajput chief Man Singh of Ambar led the Mughal forces against this last pillar of Rajput fame and glory. A sanguinary battle followed, in which the soldiers of Pratap displayed the highest courage and skill. Pratap himself was in the thick of the fight, and was saved only by the heroic self-sacrifice of one of his followers. But nothing availed. The superior number of the Mughal forces carried the day (June 1576). Pratap again took shelter in the Aravali Hills of his kingdom. But in spite of privations and sufferings, he never ceased to carry on the struggle for liberating his country.

The story of Pratap's bravery, heroism and untold sufferings for the cause of liberation of his kingdom has become almost proverbial, and even today no name is held in greater honour in Rajputana than that of the brave Pratap. Flying from hill to hill before the superior forces of the Mughals he suffered extreme want and privation together with his wife and children, but still his brave heart refused to yield.

His gallantry and patriotism were at last rewarded and he recovered most of his possessions before his death in 1597. But he could never recover Chitor, the far-famed capital of his ancestors. He had vowed that he would take food only on a leaf and sleep on a straw-bed, until he recovered Chitor. He kept this vow till his death, and during the last year of his life, he often kept gazing at Chitor from a neighbouring hill, while tears rolled down his cheeks. It is fair to add that Akbar fully appreciated the heroism and patriotism of his mighty opponent and paid glowing tributes to his character.

The death of Akbar did not arrest the progress of conquest, and expansion continued during the reigns of the next three emperors, Jahangir, Shah Jahan and Aurangzeb, who ascended the throne, respectively, in A.D. 1605, 1628 and 1658, and each

of whom was the son and successor of the preceding king.
Jahangir captured the fortress of Kangra, which had defied
even Akbar and completed the conquest of Bengal and Mewar.
Rana Amar Singh, son of Pratap Singh, submitted to the
Mughals in A.D. 1614. With the exception of the fact that Mewar
never had any matrimonial relations with the Mughals, it was
reduced to the same subordinate position as the rest of Rajputana.
Bengal was completely subdued and Cooch Behar became an
integral part of the Mughal Empire. The fortress of Ahmadnagar
also surrendered. Shah Jahan and Aurangzeb completed the
conquest of the Sultanates of the Deccan. Both Bijapur and
Golconda and the rest of Ahmadnagar formed integral parts of
the Mughal empire. Even distant Tanjore and Trichinopoly
were conquered by Aurangzeb.

But the Mughals met with failure in three cases. In spite of
the repeated attempts and despatch of costly expeditions they
failed to capture the fort of Kandahar which remained a part of
Persia. The greatest failures were, however, in respect of the
Rajput States of Mewar and Marwar, and the rising power of the
Marathas in the Deccan which require a more detailed
consideration.

Aurangzeb was a religious fanatic. His cruel persecution of
the Hindus led to the rise of two military powers, the Marathas
and the Sikhs, which undermined the mighty fabric of the
Mughal empire and caused its fall. The Marathas had already
grown into a great power and sapped the vitality of the Mughal
empire during the lifetime of Aurangzeb while the Sikhs completed
the work of destruction during the rule of his successors. Viewed
in this light, the growth of the Maratha power constitutes a
momentous event which must be considered in some detail
before we proceed further with the history of the Mughals.

## Shivaji

Shivaji, the founder of the Maratha power, was born in A.D. 1627
in the fort of Shivner in Maharashtra and was brought up by his
mother Jija Bai, as his father Shahji, served under the Sultan
of Bijapur and lived with another wife. The small *jagir* assigned
by Shahji for the maintenance of Shivaji and his mother extended
over the regions known as the Mavals, namely, the long stretch
of valleys to the west of Poona. From his boyhood Shivaji liked
military ventures and gathered round him a number of brave

young men of the locality sharing his temperament. The group
of young Mavalis under the leadership of Shivaji, a boy of 19,
captured the hill fortress of Torna and other fortresses in quick
succession and thus came into possession of a fairly large estate
protected by a number of hill forts. He obtained by treachery the
principality of Jaoli (1653) and gradually seized the whole of the
Konkan which formed part of the dominions of the Sultan of
Bijapur, who sent a strong force under Afzal Khan with orders
to "bring back the rebel (Shivaji) dead or alive."

But before any serious fighting took place, an interview was
arranged between the two chiefs to settle terms of peace. Shivaji
and Afzal Khan, each accompanied by two attendants, accordingly
met in the neighbourhood of Pratapgarh. As soon as they met,
the Khan, on the pretext of embracing Shivaji, held him tight
and struck him with a dagger. But as Shivaji had put on a coat
of armour, he remained unhurt, and soon "tore the Khan's
bowels open with a blow of the *Baghnakh* or tiger claws which
were fastened to the fingers of his left hand." Then with the right
hand he drove a thin sharp dagger called *Bichwa* (scorpion) into
Afzal's side. The Khan's hand was then cut off by Shivaji's
followers. The Khan's hand was taken by surprise and routed.
Some historians deny that Afzal Khan first struck Shivaji with
a sword, and it is difficult to decide which version is true. But in
any case the defeat of Afzal's army was decisive and Shivaji
could now justly regard himself as an independent chieftain,
free from any fear from the Bijapur side.

### Shivaji and Aurangzeb

The growing power of Shivaji and his plundering raids into
Mughal territories in A.D. 1657 brought him into conflict with
Aurangzeb, then Mughal viceroy in the Deccan. In 1660 Aurangzeb
appointed Shayista Khan, governor of the Deccan with a view
to crush Shivaji. But the latter overtook Shayista Khan at Poona
by a night attack (1663). Aurangzeb then replaced him by his
son Prince Muazzam. Shivaji, growing bolder, plundered Surat
and Ahmadnagar and assumed the title of king (1664). Aurangzeb
then sent Jai Singh of Ambar and Dilir Khan against Shivaji. Jai
Singh was one of the ablest generals of the emperor. He allied
himself with Bijapur and other minor powers and closely
besieged the hill-fort with Purandar. Shivaji was then forced to
come to terms. By the Treaty of Purandar, Shivaji surrendered

all his forts, except twelve, and accepted the suzerainty of the Mughal emperor (1655).

The victorious Jai Singh then proceeded against Bijapur and received the help and cooperation of Shivaji. Aurangzeb appreciated the valuable services rendered by Shivaji in the campaign, and not only sent him presents but also invited him to come to the court. Jai Singh having guaranteed his personal safety, Shivaji accepted the invitation of the emperor.

When Shivaji presented himself at the Imperial Court he felt humiliated and degraded at the insulting manner of his reception by Aurangzeb. Even while in court he openly gave vent to his feelings and at last, overpowered with emotion, fell senseless on the ground. The emperor dismissed him without conferring any distinction and placed guards round his residence to prevent his escape (1666).

Shivaji asked for permission to return to the Deccan with his attendants. The emperor allowed the attendants to return, but Shivaji was kept under close surveillance. In vain did Shivaji remind the emperor of the promise of Jai Singh and his own services to the emperor in the Bijapur campaign. The crafty Aurangzeb had his enemy within his grasp and would not let him go.

Shivaji then thought of a cunning artifice to effect his escape. He feigned illness, and sent sweetmeats to Brahmans, mendicants and nobles in huge baskets. When the gatekeepers were accustomed to the state of things, Shivaji put himself and his son in two of these baskets and got out of Agra. He safely reached his own land in December 1666, after an absence of nine months.

Shivaji now resumed hostilities against the Mughal emperor. Jai Singh died in 1667, and was replaced by Prince Muazzam, but the latter was unable to achieve any success against the Maratha leader. In 1668, a peace was made with Shivaji, and Aurangzeb recognised his title of Raja. But hostilities broke out again in 1670, and Shivaji plundered Surat and levied regular *Chauth* or fourth part of the government revenue, on Khandesh. Shivaji also recovered some of the forts, and forced the imperial armies sent against him to retreat with loss. In 1674 Shivaji formally crowned himself at Raigadh with solemn ceremonies. He also allied himself with the Sultans of Bijapur and Golconda

against the Mughals. In 1677 Shivaji made a daring raid to the
south, and captured Jinji in South Arcot together with Vellore,
Bellary and other places. The victorious career of the
great hero was, however, brought to a close by his death in A.D.
1688.

### Shivaji's Character and Achievements

Shivaji must be reckoned as one of the greatest heroes of Indian
history. From the humble position of a leader of the Mavalis he
rose to be the master of an independent kingdom. He established
a Hindu kingdom in the teeth of the opposition of the bigoted
Mughal emperor at a time when that emperor was at the height
of his greatness. But the greatest credit of Shivaji lies in the fact
that he brought about the regeneration of the Maratha nation,
which long survived him, and played a prominent part in Indian
history for more than a hundred years after his death. Shivaji
was a superman in every sense of the term. His daring
resourcefulness, endurance, and above all his wonderful military
skill are worthy of the highest praise. His intense piety and
devotion, and a scrupulous regard for the honour of women and
sanctity of religion, irrespective of race or creed, distinguished
him from the other military adventurers of his age. He conceived
the noble idea of liberating his 'country and religion' from
foreign yoke, and nobly did he carry it out by consecrating his
whole life to the sacred cause. He was occasionally led to adopt
questionable methods in achieving his purpose, but in spite of
this his people looked upon him as a great hero, patriot and
nation-builder.

   The growing power of the Marathas was not, however, the
only concern of Aurangzeb. He was soon involved in a war with
the Rajputs. When Raja Jaswant Singh of Marwar died (1678)
at Jamrud, near the Khyber Pass, in the service of the emperor,
the latter immediately seized his kingdom. The event was
signalised by the imposition of *Jizya,* and the destruction of
temples and idols. The emperor even made an attempt to
capture Ajit Singh, the infant son of Jaswant Singh, but was
foiled in this design by the heroic and gallant efforts of the
Rajput chief Durgadas. The emperor sent forces to ravage
Marwar and formally annexed it to the Mughal empire. The
Rajputs, however, rallied round Ajit Singh. Maharana Raj
Singh of Mewar also took up his cause. He was alienated by the

anti-Hindu Policy of Aurangzeb and knew quite well that the
annexation of Marwar was sure to lead to the conquest of
Mewar. War broke out between the emperor and the Rajput
kingdoms of Mewar and Marwar (1679). Both sides sustained
many serious reverses, and at last a treaty was arranged with
Mewar in A.D. 1681, by which the emperor withdrew the hated
tax *Jizya*, on condition of receiving certain territories. The war
with Marwar continued beyond the emperor's reign, and was
terminated in 1709 when the right of Jaswant Singh's son, Ajit
Singh to succeed was formally recognised.

Aurangzeb next turned to the Deccan. He reached the
Deccan in 1681 and spent there the remaining 26 years of his
life. His most notable achievements during this period were the
final conquest of Bijapur and (1689) and Golconda (1687), the
remnants of the mighty Bahmani kingdom. This was followed a
few years later by the establishment of Mughal authority as far
south as Tanjore and Trichinopoly (1694), and the Mughal
empire reached its greatest extent. The dream of the Mughal
emperors since the days of Akbar was realised.

But Aurangzeb failed to crush the Marathas. After the
death of Shivaji, the Maratha throne was occupied by his son
Shambhaji, a dissolute young man under whom the entire
government was thrown into confusion. In 1689 he was captured
by Mughal troops, and was executed together with his attendants.
Shambhaji's son, Shahu, a boy of seven years was kept in the
imperial camp.

The capture and execution of Shambhaji did not mean the
fall of the Maratha power. Shambhaji was succeeded by his
brother Rajaram, and when the latter died in A.D. 1700 his
widow Tara Bai ably administered the State as the regent for
her son Shivaji III. Aurangzeb continued the campaign against
the Marathas till his death, but although he secured possession
of many forts, mostly by bribery, he could not achieve any
permanent success. Between A.D. 1699 and 1706 the Marathas
crossed the Narmada and entered Malwa. They overran Khandesh
and Berar, and penetrated into Gujarat. At the time of the
emperor's death, the Marathas were plundering close to the
imperial camp.

Aurangzeb, with all the resources of the Mughal empire,
could not subdue the mountain rats, as he used to call the

Marathas. The reason for his failure lay in the peculiar nature of the Marathas. Whenever they were pressed hard by the Mughals, they would seemingly yield, abandon warfare, and return to the cultivation of their fields; but as soon as the Mughals turned their backs, the Marathas would return to the army. They had no need of heavy equipments, and could easily turn into a fighting force. It has been well remarked that a defeat to the Marathas was like a blow given to water, which offers no resistance to the stroke, and retains no impression of its effect.

After an unsuccessful campaign of 26 years in the Deccan, in the course of which the imperial army endured untold sufferings and the immense treasures of the Mughal empire were squandered in a most reckless manner, the old emperor died broken-hearted at Ahmadnagar in February 1707. It has been well remarked that the Deccan was the grave of his reputation as well as his body.

The death of Aurangzeb closes the most glorious period of Mughal rule in India and marks the beginning of its decline and downfall. Before dealing with it, it would be convenient to refer to some of the special features of the Mughal period.

**Great Personalities**
The period of 150 years (A.D. 1556-1707) witnessed a number of great personalities who played a dominant part in the political field. A detailed account of two of them Rana Pratap Singh and Shivaji has been given above, the others are Sher Shah, Hemu and Aurangzeb.

**Sher Shah**
Sher Shah must be recognised as one of the greatest figures in Indian history. By his courage, ability, prudence and military skill, he rose from a humble position to be the emperor of Hindustan. He is usually regarded as an usurper, but if we bear in mind that he was an Afghan chief born and brought up in India, whereas the Mughals had conquered India from the Afghans only about 14 years earlier, his claim to the throne of Agra would appear as hardly less valid than that of Humayun. Indeed, he should rather be regarded as an Afghan hero who recovered the Afghan empire from the hands of the Mughal conquerors.

The fame of Sher Shah, however, mainly rests upon his administrative reforms. He divided the provinces of his empire into well-organised administrative units, called *sarkars* which were again subdivided into *parganahs,* and appointed an executive and judicial officer in each. He made a survey of the land, and marked out the holding of each tenant. The revenue was fixed at one-fourth of the gross produce, and the peasants were allowed to pay either in cash or in kind. He introduced the system of *kabulyiat* and *patta* by which each tenant was furnished with a written document containing a record of the area of his land and the total amount of revenue due from him.

Sher Shah greatly improved the means of communication. He made the Grand Trunk Road which runs from Bengal to the Punjab, and planted trees and established inns for the Hindus and the Muhammadans on the roadside.

He recognised the fact that India was the land of both the Hindus and the Muhammadans, and made an attempt to reconcile the two elements. He improved the system of coinage, issuing abundant silver coins and used Hindi characters along with Persian on his coins. He reformed the army and kept strict discipline over his soldiers. He administered justice with strict impartiality, and was particularly solicitous for the rights and interests of the tenants. He was a great builder, and his mausoleum at Sasaram is a noble piece of architecture.

If we remember all that Sher Shah was able to accomplish within a brief period of five years, we are filled with admiration for his genius untiring industry. His character is no doubt stained by occasional treachery, but he was one of the greatest sovereigns in the medieval period of Indian history.

### Hemu
Hemchandra, referred to in history as Hemu—either a nickname or an abbreviated form contemptuously used by the Mughal historians who had no love for this arch-enemy of Akbar—was an adventurer of the type of Sher Shah though he had a still humbler origin.

Historians, both medieval and modern, have failed to show due appreciation of the unique personality and greatness of Hemu who, during the heyday of Muslim rule in India, worked his way from a grocer's shop to the throne of Delhi, and but for an accident in a battle, which turned victory into defeat, might have founded a Hindu empire on the ruins of that of the Afghans in India. He furnishes the only example of a Hindu born and brought up in medieval India who once dominated the political stage of north India by sheer merit and personality without any advantage of birth or fortune. Badaoni calls him "the greengrocer of the township of Rewari in Mewar whom Islam Shah had gradually elevated from the position of the Police Superintendent of the bazaars by degrees into a trusted confidant." When Adil Shah ascended the throne murdering the minor son of Islam Shah, rebellions broke out in all quarters and the Governors of Bengal, Agra and Lahore assumed royal titles. In this grave crisis, Hemu was appointed Prime Minister, and he defeated the rivals of his master Adil Shah in a series of battles more than twenty in number. When after the death of Humayun, his son Akbar was proclaimed Emperor, Hemu advanced and "inflicted a severe defeat on the Mughal forces and gained possession of both Delhi and Agra." It was at this stage that Hemu thought of abandoning his worthless and incompetent master and making a serious effort to re-establish his *raj* by defeating the Mughals. He enthroned himself under the title of Vikramaditya and issued coins in his own name.

When Hemu met Akbar at the Battle of Panipat on November 5, 1556, he succeeded in throwing both the wings of the Mughal army into confusion and was almost on the point of winning a decisive victory, but suddenly he was struck by an arrow which pierced his eye and made him unconscious. As usually happened in those days, on the death of the general, Hemu's soldiers at once scattered. Eminent writers have held the view that it was merely an accident that deprived Hemu of victory, throne and life. V.A. Smith thinks that Hemu had every chance of winning the battle; Sir Wolsley Haig asserts that the Mughal forces "would certainly have been overpowered had not Hemu's eye been pierced by an arrow." More or less the same view has been held by others.

## Akbar

Apart from the extensive conquests already mentioned, Akbar's greatness rests on the organisation of the administration on a sound and stable basis, the brilliance of his court, the enunciation of a sound policy towards the Hindus, and above all, his remarkable personality.

## Akbar's Administration

Akbar organised the administration on a sound basis. He divided the whole empire into 15 *Subahs* or provinces viz., Delhi, Agra, Ajmer, Lahore, Kabul, Multan, Ahmedabad (Gujarat), Malwa, Khandesh, Berar, Ahmadnagar, Allahabad, Oudh, Bihar and Bengal. A more or less uniform administrative arrangement was made in each. A *Subedar\** corresponding to the modern Governor, was placed at the head of each province, with almost unlimited authority over civil and military affairs. A *Dewan* was placed under him to supervise the revenue department. Officers called *Miradls* and *Kazis* were appointed to administer justice, and law and order was maintained by the police officers called *Kotwals*. Among other important officials may be mentioned *Bakshi* (Pay Department), *Mir Bahr* (Shipping, Ports and Ferries), *Wakia-Navis* (Record Department), and *Sadr* (Ecclesiastical and Grants Department). Akbar also introduced regular gradation of military officers, called *Mansabdars,* and reformed the whole military administration. He introduced the system of paying his officers in cash in place of the old system of Jagir (grant of land). He reformed the revenue system with the help of Todar Mall. He was the first to make a correct measurement of all the lands dividing them into three classes according to their fertility. The revenue was fixed at one-third of the produce, and could be paid either in cash or in kind. In this respect Akbar is said to have improved the system originated by Sher Shah, but it conferred lasting benefits upon the people.

## Akbar's Court

Akbar had the capacity and good fortune to draw around him some of the best talents of his age. The most notable among them were the two brothers Faizi and Abul Fazl. Faizi was a man of letters, while Abul Fazl combined in himself the 'parts of a scholar, author, courtier and man of affairs'. Abul Fazl was the trusted friend and adviser of Akbar, and to him we owe the most detailed account of the reign of his imperial master. His assassination by Prince Salim caused intense grief to the

---

* This officer was called *Sipahasalar* or commander-in-chief in Akbar's time, but he was known by the more familiar name of *Subedar* in later days.

emperor. Raja Man Singh, the Rajput chief of Ambar (Jaipur), was the great general of Akbar. He was put in charge of the most difficult campaigns and ruled over considerable territories as the deputy of the emperor.

Raja Todar Mall offers a typical instance of Akbar's power of selecting men. He rose from a humble position by his merit, ability and untiring industry. He was a good general, but his fame chiefly rests upon his knowledge and skill in revenue administration. The great revenue reforms of Akbar's reign was conducted under his personal guidance.

Among other notable persons that graced the court of Akbar, mention may be made of Raja Birbal, famous for his wit and humour, and Tansen, the celebrated musician.

### Akbar's Policy towards the Hindus

Akbar formulated a policy of his own with a view to consolidate the Mughal empire in India. He realised that mere conquest of territories would not safeguard the empire, unless it was broad based on the love and goodwill of all his subjects, both Hindus and Muhammadans. He, therefore, first turned his attention to win the confidence of the Hindus. He married a Hindu lay, the daughter of Raja Bihari Mal of Ambar or Jaipur (1562), and later in life, he made similar alliance with other Rajput states. He abolished the hated *Jiziya*, poll-tax on all non-Muslims as well as another hated tax which was imposed on all Hindu pilgrims. These reforms were merely the fruits of a generous policy towards Hindus, and they form the most distinguishing feature of Akbar's administration. He employed Hindu officers in high posts and fully trusted them. The result was that the Hindu subjects were loyally attached to the Mughal empire and peace and prosperity prevailed everywhere.

### Akbar's Character

A foreign observer has described Akbar as "affable and majestic, merciful and severe; loved and feared of his own, terrible to his enemies." Akbar had many charming personal qualities which endeared him to his officers and the people at large. He was sympathetic even towards the common people, and scrupulously just to all. But the most distinguishing trait of his character was his intellectual curiosity. He was illiterate and yet possessed an insatiable thirst for knowledge of all kinds.

He loved to have books of history, theology, poetry and others read to him, and his prodigious memory enabled him to learn through the ear more than an ordinary man could learn through the eye. He was fond of arranging discussions on literary, philosophical and religious questions, and he himself took an active part in them.

## Akbar's Religious Life

His wonderful intellectual curiosity serves as a key to his religious life. He was brought up as a *sunni* Mussalman, but his acquaintance with the mystic Sufi doctrines relaxed his orthodoxy. His profound and versatile knowledge made him liberal in his religious views, and he was eager to know the doctrines of all religions. Nothing is more interesting than the accounts of midnight meetings at *Ibadat Khana,* in which the emperor patiently listened to the exposition of different religious creeds, such as Hinduism, Jainism, Zoroastrianism and Christianity. Akbar had great veneration for these four religions and himself practised many of their rituals. Thus he prostrated himself in public both before the sun and fire, and even celebrated the Persian festivals. At one time he was greatly under the influence of Jaina teachers and adopted their doctrine of non-injury to animals. He gave up his favourite hunting excursion and restricted the practice of fishing. He abstained from eating meat and even issued written orders prohibiting slaughter of animals on certain days. He acted in the same way with regard to Hinduism and Christianity. His liberal and rational mind could not tolerate some of the abominable practices of the Hindus, like the forcible burning of widows on the funeral pyre of husbands, and he took steps to prevent them. Akbar preached and practised complete toleration in religious matters—a remarkable thing in that age.

But he soon carried the matter to an excess, and in A.D. 1579, issued the famous Infallibility Decree according to which the emperor was to be accepted as the supreme arbiter in all causes, whether ecclesiastical or civil. Ultimately, in A.D. 1582, Akbar formulated a new creed composed of various elements, taken, partly from the *Quran* and partly from Hindu and Christian scriptures. The essential features of this new religion were faith in one God, and recognition of the Emperor as His Viceregent on earth. This doctrine was, however, confined to a select group of his followers.

Akbar was a man of untiring industry, and personally supervised every branch of the administration. He rarely slept more than three hours at a time, and seemed to be almost incapable of fatigue. He was a loving friend and a generous foe and must be regarded as one of the most remarkable characters of the age.

## Aurangzeb

The personality of Aurangzeb was a mixture of opposites. He seized the throne by revolting against his father and kept him confined in the Fort of Agra till his death in A.D. 1696. He killed his brother Dara after a mock trial for heresy, forced another brother to leave India and die in exile, while a third brother was kept confined for life.

Another grave defect in his character was that he was suspicious by nature and did not trust anybody, not even his own sons. When great generals like Mir Jumla, Jai Singh and Jaswant Singh died, the emperor felt relieved. It is even supposed by some that he caused the death of the last named general by administering poison. Cruelty and craftiness were the distinguishing traits in his character. His treatment of Shivaji and of his own brothers is an illustration of the point. Thus, whereas Akbar tried to reconcile the Hindus and the Muhammadans and wanted to rule over an empire broadbased on the love and goodwill of all his subjects, Aurangzeb deliberately followed the policy of regarding India as an Islamic State.

The result of the policy was disastrous. Discontent and disorder prevailed throughout the country. The Jats broke out into open rebellion and the trouble continued throughout his reign. The Bundela chief Chhatrasal revolted, twice defeated the imperial forces, and carved out an independent kingdom for himself. There was also an insurrection of a Hindu sect called *Satnami*. But the gravest calamity of all was the disaffection of the Rajputs who were the pillars of the Mughal empire since the days of Akbar, and whom Aurangzeb's policy converted into bitter foes at a time when they might have rendered invaluable services in the Maratha wars.

In spite of all these defects we should not ignore some bright traits in his character. He lived and died as a pious orthodox Mussalman, scrupulously performing all the rites and ceremonials prescribed in religious books. He led a very simple and plain life, never drank wine, and was comparatively free from other vices which degraded most of the Mughal emperors. He also possessed energy and ability of a very high order. But all these were marred by his cruel and suspicious nature, and the narrow-minded bigotry.

Aurangzeb's simplicity was carried to extremes. He left instructions that only four rupees and two annas which he had earned by making caps were to be spent on his shroud, and that 305 rupees which he had earned by copying the *Quran*, were to be distributed in charity on the occasion of his funeral ceremony. He discouraged art and literature. He stopped the compilation of official annals and even forbade the writing of history by private persons.

## Art

The Mughal emperors were great builders with the exception of Aurangzeb. The mightly empire built by the Mughals quickly vanished but their splendid monuments—mosques, tombs, palaces, forts and gateways—and the paintings have kept their memory alive and are mute witnesses to their glory, splendour and wealth.

The dome, built on true principles which form a characteristic feature of their buildings but were probably unknown to or at least very little used by the Hindus, became a familiar feature of architecture in subsequent times. On the other hand, Hindu ideas and architectural styles have exercised great influence upon the development of various local styles of the Mughal Empire. The Hindu influence is also evident in the narrow columns, plasters, corbel brackets and other ornamental features of buildings. Speaking generally, the buildings of Akbar's reign combined both Hindu and Muslim features. Fatehpur-Sikri which Akbar built has been described as a more complete creation than Versailles, and its great portal, the Buland Darwaza, built of marble and sandstone, has been described as one of the most perfect architectural achievements in the whole of India. Humayun's tomb at Delhi is also a fine monument of the period. Though the number of edifices constructed during

Jahangir's reign is much less than of his father's, it can boast of some grand buildings like the tomb of Itimad-ud-daula and the great mausoleum of Akbar at Sikandara.

The beauty of the buildings of Shah Jahan's reign has become proverbial and "it was in his reign that the Indo-Persian style of architecture reached the highwater mark of excellence." The Taj Mahal and the Moti Masjid at Agra are the two best known monuments of Shah Jahan where the Mughal style may be said to have reached the zenith of purity and elegance, some even giving the latter a higher place in this respect. There are many other splendid monuments of Shah Jahan—forts, mosques and palaces—at Delhi, Lahore, Kashmir, Ajmer, Ahmedabad, Kabul and Kandahar, which are usually cast into shade by the Taj and Moti Masjid, though great in themselves. The palaces at Delhi and Agra, particularly the Diwan-i-Khas in the former, have evoked universal admiration. Special reference should also be made to the famous Peacock Throne which is regarded as "the crowning example of the union of the jeweller's art with the Mughal love of display."

By way of conveying some idea of the wealth and other resources of the Mughal emperors, it is perhaps worthwhile to give some idea of the cost of some of the above monuments. The Taj Mahal commenced in 1631, was completed in 1653; and twenty thousand men were daily employed for its construction. The Peacock Throne which was made of pure gold, studded with gems, was valued by a contemporary French jeweller at 150 million francs and its materials alone cost a crore of rupees.

As in the case of the Mughal empire, so in the case of Mughal architecture, both, like waves in the sea, rose to the highest point only to break down. Mughal art rapidly declined after Shah Jahan as the Mughal empire did after Aurangzeb. Only a few buildings of passable merit were erected during Aurangzeb's reign and there was a visible and rapid degeneration in style.

The development of Mughal painting was somewhat akin to that of architecture. The original Persian style was influenced by Hindu ideas and gradually transformed into Indo-Persian or Mughal style. Many Hindu artists were attracted by the Persian style introduced by the Mughals and adapted it to their own particular ideas. The new school which was thus evolved struck a somewhat different note "in its motives, in sentiment, and in temper generally." The following remarks of Percy Brown, an acknowledged authority on the subject, bring out the difference very clearly. The Mughal school "confined itself to portraying the somewhat materialistic life of the Court, with its State functions, processions, hunting expeditions, and all the picturesque although barbaric peasantry of an affluent oriental dynasty," while Hindu artists, "living mentally and bodily in another and more abstract environment, and working for Hindu patrons, pictured scenes from the Indian classics, domestic subjects and illustrations of the life and thought of their motherland and its creed."

The paintings of the Mughal period gave rise to different regional schools which continued to flourish during the succeeding centuries.

# 5

# The Fall of the Mughal Empire

The death of Aurangzeb was followed by the inevitable war of succession among his three sons and the eldest ascended the throne under the title Bahadur Shah. He was succeeded in 1712, after the usual war of succession, by his son Jahandar Shah, a worthless profligate who was deposed and killed by Farrukhsiyar with the help of two brothers, Sayyid Hussain Ali Khan and Sayyid Abdulla Khan. They were made respectively the Commander-in-Chief and Prime Minister and really ruled the empire in the name of their master who was a worthless debauch like his predecessor. Disorder and confusion followed and there were wars with the Sikhs, the Rajputs and the Jats. The Sayyid brothers put a number of phantom emperors on the throne, one after another, the last of them, Muhammad Shah got rid of them and ruled for a long time (A.D. 1719-48). During his reign, different provinces became independent kingdoms for all practical purposes, and thus arose the dynasty of Nizam-ul-Mulk in Hyderabad and the kingdoms of Avadh and Bengal.

The Marathas gradually rose to power and though the dynasty of Shivaji was nominally acknowledged as the royal authority, the real power passed into the hands of the Peshwa, one of the ministers whose descendants wielded real power. Baji Rao, the second Peshwa, formed the bold plan of wresting India from the Mughals. He overran Malwa, Gujarat, Rajputana and Budelkhand. Unable to resist him, the emperor of Delhi had to recognise his sovereignty over Malwa and the whole territory between the Narmada and the Chambal. The vast Maratha dominions were gradually divided between four subordinate chiefs of the Peshwa, namely the Sindhia of Gwalior, the Holkar of Indore, Gaekwad of Baroda and the Bhonsles of Nagpur, which together with the dominions of the Peshwa at Poona formed the five great Maratha principalities and for the time being all of them acknowledged the authority of the Peshwa.

The final death-blow to the Mughal empire was given by the invasions of Nadir Shah, the ruler of Persia, in A.D. 1739. The Imperial army was easily defeated and Nadir Shah occupied Delhi. The citizens of Delhi, on a false report of the death of Nadir, killed a few thousands of Nadir's soldiers. Vengeance was swift and terrible. A general massacre of the inhabitants of certain quarters of Delhi was ordered and carried out with brutal ferocity for five hours.

After the death of Nadir Shah, an Afghan chief named Ahmad Shah Durrani (also known as Ahmad Shah Abdali) occupied the eastern part of his dominions and founded a kingdom in Afghanistan in A.D. 1747. He had accompanied Nadir Shah on his Indian expeditions and, having personally witnessed the weakness of the Mughal Empire, resolved to re-establish Afghan suzerainty in India. With this object he invaded India several times between A.D. 1748 and 1767. In A.D. 1750 he occupied the Punjab. Next year, he conquered Kashmir, and the Mughal emperor ceded to him all the territories up to Sirhind in the east.

### The Marathas

The Maratha power was now the only one that could save India from these disasters. Peshwa Baji Rao died in A.D. 1740, and was succeeded by his son, Balaji Baji Rao. The new Peshwa consolidated Maratha authority and made Poona his official capital. Immediately after the departure of Ahmad Shah Durrani in A.D. 1757, the Maratha forces, led by the Peshwa's brother Raghunath, occupied Lahore after driving away the Afghans (1758).

The Maratha power was now at its zenith. Their dominions extended up to the Himalayas and the Indus on the north-west, and almost to the extremity of the Indian peninsula in the south. These extensive territories owned the authority of the Peshwa's government. The wildest dreams of Shivaji were thus fully realised. Never since the days of Asoka Maurya had there been such a vast Hindu empire in India.

But evil days were soon to come. Ahmad Shah Durrani
reoccupied the Punjab in A.D. 1759, and in A.D. 1760, the
Maratha government sent a vast army to re-establish Maratha
supremacy in northern India.

The Maratha forces easily occupied Delhi (1760) and met
the army of Ahmad Shah Durrani at Panipat. Both parties
entrenched themselves in that historic battlefield. Ahmad Shah
was helped by the Ruhellas and the Vizir Suja-ud-daula of
Avadh, for they were uneasy at the growth of Maratha power.
As the Ruhella leader put it: "The Marathas are the thorn of
Hindusthan—let us by one effort get this thorn out of our sides
for ever." On the other hand, the Marathas had alienated the
Rajputs, who remained neutral, and failed to secure the cooperation
of the Sikhs who formed a strong military power in the Punjab.
Even the Jat chief Surajmal, who had joined the Marathas,
deserted them.

The Maratha commander was advised to follow the old
traditional method of warfare, viz., to get rid of the heavy
luggage, to avoid a pitched battle, and to harass the enemy by
means of light horse. But the Marathas army encamped at
Panipat with a huge army and an enormous number of camp-
followers, and soon want of provisions forced them to risk
everything on a single pitched battle.

On the morning of January, 14, 1761, the Maratha leader
offered battle with his whole army. Maratha soldiers gave a
good account of themselves in their fight with the mountaineers
of Afghanistan, and after six hours of terrible fighting, they
seemed to carry the day. But the superior generalship of Ahmad
Shah Durrani turned the scales. Shortly after half past one, he
charged with a fresh army held in reserve. This decided the fate
of the battle. "In a twinkle of the eye, the Maratha army
vanished from the field like camphor." The Afghans pursued
them for nearly 20 miles and gave no quarter, and nearly
200,000 Marathas were slaughtered. Both Visvas Rao and
Sadasheo Bhao, who commanded the army, and almost all the
notable Maratha leaders lay dead on the field.

The defeat of the Marathas was complete, and their ambition
to establish an empire in northern India was checked. Besides,
the prestige of the Peshwas was weakened and the solidarity of
Maratha power was endangered. Gradually, the authority of

the Peshwa over other Maratha chiefs became more nominal. Although different Maratha leaders achieved great power in succeeding ages, the glory of the united Maratha nation did not long survive the Third Battle of Panipat.

The Mughal Empire had already been shattered, and the Marathas failed to rebuild one. It was now time for a third power to attempt the same task. This was to be the British who came to trade, but founded an empire in India.

## Causes of the Downfall of the Mughal Empire

The downfall of the Mughal empire, within such an incredibly short time after it had reached its zenith, is to be attributed to several causes. Principal among these are, first, the exhaustion of the resources, in men and money, of the empire in the devastating wars of the Deccan; secondly the disorganisation of the administration during the prolonged absence of the old emperor Aurangzeb in the the Deccan; thirdly, the alienation of the Hindus, particularly the Rajputs, by the bigoted policy of Aurangzeb, and fourthly, a startling decline in the character of the nobility and in the efficiency of the army. This is due, at least to a great extent, to the worthless character of the successors of Aurangzeb, who waged seven bloody battles of succession within thirteen years of the death of Aurangzeb, and the factions at court leading to armed contest between rival nobles. The death-blow was given to the empire by the Marathas, but their success was largely due to the sympathy of the large majority of the Hindus and even Shia Muslims. The invasion of Nadir Shah and his easy success merely revealed to an astonished world that the fabric of the empire had utterly collapsed. It was a clear symptom of the decline rather than a cause of it.

# III
# Modern Period

# 1

# The European Trading Companies in India

Since the beginning of the 15th century, European nations sought a sea-route to India. The first attempts, beginning in 1418 were naturally to proceed along the western shore of Africa. The failure of these presumably induced Christopher Columbus, a Genoese, to make an attempt to reach India by a western route, and this led to the discovery of the West Indies and South America in 1492. In 1487 Pedro de Covilham reached India by the overland route and, exploring the Indian Ocean from an eastern base, proved the feasibility of reaching India by sea by the south-eastern route, along the west coast of Africa. Vasco da Gama made a successful voyage to India by this route and arrived at Calicut in May 1491.

The opening of a direct sea-route from the western coast of Europe to India was an epoch-making event and it is difficult to make an estimate of the revolutionary changes it made in the history, not only of India but of the whole world.

In the first place it opened the floodgates of European trade with India. In the beginning the Portuguese had practically the monopoly of this trade, and they made full use of it by establishing bases of trade on the Indian coasts, converting Indians to Christianity, and acquiring wealth and political power by their superior military skill and the knowledge of firearms whose use was till then not known to the Indians. They had settled in Hooghly in Bengal, about 1579 and oppressed the people in

various ways. In particular, they carried on slave trade and
seized by force and fraud both Hindu and Muslim orphan
children to bring them up as Christians. But when they seized
two slave girls of Mumtaz Mahal, the famous Begum of Shah
Jahan in whose memory the Taj Mahal was built, Shah Jahan
took terrible vengeance. The town of Hooghly was captured
(1632), the Portuguese settlement was destroyed and 4,000
prisoners were brought to Agra.

But already, since the beginning of the seventeenth century
other European nations had begun to trade with India. The
British East India Company was formed in 1599 and similar
companies were formed by the Dutch, the Danes and the
French, respectively in 1602, 1616, and 1664.

In 1612 the British Company established a factory at Surat.
Three years later the British ambassador, Sir Thomas Roe,
visited the court of Jahangir and obtained some concessions for
the British Company. Of the other European companies the
Portuguese declined rapidly in the 17th century, and their last
three settlements in India, Goa, Daman and Diu were seized by
the Government of India in 1961. Neither the Dutch nor the
Danes ever became important and the only two rivals in the field
were the British and the French. The French began late but
soon rose to a position of great importance. Their principal
settlement of Pondicherry was founded in 1674 and fortified a
few years later. In 1690-92 they opened a factory at Chandernagore
on a site which was given to them by Nawab *Seatsta* Khan in A.D.
1674. In A.D. 1725 they founded another fortified post at Mahe
on the Malabar Coast. The French soon gained prestige as a
great military power by affording protection to the family of the
Nawab of the Carnatic against the Bhonsles of Nagpur.

The task of raising the French power to the height of
greatness was reserved for Dupleix, the Governor of Pondicherry
(1742). Dupleix was a keen statesman and easily grasped the
real political situation in India. He noted the utter inefficiency
of the Indian armies and boldly conceived the idea that a
handful of Indian soldiers, disciplined in the European fashion,
would be more than a match for the vast undisciplined hordes
of Indian rulers. He observed further the instability of political
dynasties in India and the constant struggles between the
Indian rulers. He arrived at the conclusion that if he helped one

of the contending parties with his small but disciplined force, he could easily gain success and thereby lay the foundation of a great military power in India for the French.

The two discoveries of Dupleix were perhaps more important from the point of view of India than even the discovery of Columbus or Vasco da Gama, for they ultimately led to the conquest of India by the British. The first theory was put to the test when the Nawab of the Carnatic, being afraid of the growing power of the French who had defeated the English and captured Madras from them, sent a force 10,000 strong to recapture Madras as it was situated in his territory, and Dupleix with only 500 men completely routed them.

When the war broke out between France and England in Europe there was also war between the English and the French Companies in India, and there were thus two wars in the Carnatic. Dupleix tested his second policy with equal success in the second war. When the great Nizam Asaf Jah of Hyderabad died, there was a struggle for succession and Dupleix helped one of the rival candidates, who, after ascending the throne, appointed Dupleix Governor of all the Mughal territories south of the Krishna river, and ceded Masulipatnam with its dependencies to the French. A French force under Bussy remained at Hyderabad as adviser to the Nizam and the revenue of northern Sarkars was assigned for the payment of his troops.

Soon the English pursued the same policy and the defeat inflicted by a small British force under Robert Clive upon Chanda Sahib, the Nawab of the Carnatic, in support of a rival claimant raised the power and prestige of the British in the Deccan where the French had hitherto wielded great power.

**British Supremacy**

Clive now pursued the same policy in Bengal as Dupleix had done in Hyderabad, and achieved greater and more permanent success. Nawab Alivardi Khan, Governor of Bengal, who ruled as an independent king, died in 1756 and was succeeded by his daughter's son Siraj-ud-Daula, a young man of 24, who lacked experience, ability and knowledge of men and matters and at the same time was of violent temper and vicious habits, though his character was not perhaps as black as has been painted by the British. He successfully fought against his two rivals for the throne but was highly displeased with the British for their support to one, or both of them. His suspicion was probably not altogether unfounded, but in any case he attacked Calcutta, the chief settlement of the English in Bengal. Calcutta was captured, practically without any fight, and then occurred the notorious Black Hole tragedy—the death by suffocation of 123 out of 146 English prisoners kept in a small room. The truth of this story is doubted by many, but in any case Siraj was not personally guilty of this crime. His conduct after the siege of Calcutta, however, showed irresolution and indiscretion at every step.

As soon as the news of the fall of Calcutta reached Madras, Clive and Watson arrived and reoccupied it without serious opposition. About this time war broke out between the English and the French in Europe and necessarily also in India. The English forces marched against Chandernagore, a French stronghold in Bengal, and captured it in spite of the strongest remonstrances of the Nawab and his instruction to his military officers to oppose the British. There is hardly any doubt that Maharaja Nandakumar, the commander of the Nawab's forces, was bribed. The Nawab concluded a treaty with the English on the most humiliating terms, agreeing to compensate the British for the losses they had suffered in Calcutta, and conceding all their demands, and even agreeing to dismiss the French forces to whom he had promised protection. But even the British could not trust the Nawab whose sympathy for the French was well-known. The English were at war with the French and they were afraid that the French force might join the Nawab and renew in Bengal the policy of expelling the English which Dupleix had so brilliantly initiated in the Carnatic. But it was a game which two could play and so the English sought to get rid of Siraj-ud-daula by conspiring with the party inimical to the Nawab. They hatched a secret conspiracy (the terms of which were embodied in a treaty) with the disaffected chiefs of the Nawab on 10 June 1757. It was stipulated that the Commander-in-Chief, Mir Jafar, and another general, Rai Durlabh, would help the English, as a reward of which the former would be placed on the throne and in turn various rewards and advantages would be given to the English Company and its officers.

The fate of Siraj-ud-daula was decided in the Battle of Palasi (generally written as Plassey) on 23 June 1757. The main forces of the Nawab under Mir Jafar and Rai Durlabh stood still with their large armies and only a small force under Mohanlal and Mir Madan, two trusted generals, backed by a French officer, took part in the battle. But even then the small army of Clive was forced to withdraw when the death of Mir Madan by a stray shot so unnerved the Nawab that he sent for Mir Jafar who saved the English by his treacherous advice to stop the fight for the day by recalling the only troops which were fighting for him. The foolish Nawab, in spite of strong protests from Mohanlal, recalled his troops. As Mohanlal foresaw and told the Nawab, the retreat ended in the dispersal of the Nawab's troops, who fled pell-mell. The Nawab realised the treachery of Mir Jafar, but it was too late. So he too fled but was captured and beheaded. Mir Jafar ascended the throne of Murshidabad, the capital of Bengal.

Fortune favoured the English in the Carnatic also. The Seven Years' War in Europe between the French and the English also involved the two Companies in war in India. After a number of minor engagements, a decisive battle took place near the fort of Wandiwash (22 January 1760). The French army was totally routed and their fate in India was decided once and for all. Of all the foreign trading companies the English alone was left to enjoy the fruits of a superior military skill and organisation and unity of purpose pitted against a disunited India where a large number of independent States fought for supremacy and would not scruple even to fight one another with the help of the British. The English took full advantage of the policy enunciated first by Dupleix. By training Indian troops on the European method and taking full advantage of the struggle for supremacy among the Indian States by joining one against the other, the British who came to trade, remained to rule over the whole of India.

# 2

# Consolidation of British Power

The Battle of Plassey made the British the virtual rulers of Bengal. They enthroned and then removed Mir Jafar, and made Mir Qasim Nawab of Bengal. But the moment he tried to assert his authority he was defeated and fled to the Nawab of Oudh who invaded Bengal but was defeated and was forced to conclude a treaty with the British.

## Bengal

Clive, the victor of Plassey, now the Governor of Calcutta, concluded peace with the Nawab of Oudh, and made a settlement with Shah Alam, the Mughal emperor of Delhi and the nominal suzerain of Bengal. By this new arrangement, known as the system of Dual Government, the English collected the revenues with the help of Indian officials, made necessary expenditure for the government, including payment of 26 lakhs as imperial tribute and a further sum of 50 lakhs as the pension of the Nawab and kept the surplus revenues to themselves. As the military arrangement was also left in their own hands they became virtually the head of both the civil and the military administration.

About this time the system of Government in the Indian territories of the Company was radically changed by a new Act of the English Parliament, known as North's Regulating Act (1773). By this Act the Government of the Indian territories was vested in a Governor-General and a Council of four members. The Governor of Bengal became Governor-General and President of this Council, and the Governors and Councils of Bombay and Madras were made subordinate to it. A Supreme Court was also established in Calcutta with large powers to try the Company's servants. It consisted of a Chief Justice and three puisne Judges.

Warren Hastings, the Governor of Bengal, became the first Governor-General under the new Act.

## Avadh

Reference has been made above in connection with Mir Qasim, to the defeat of the Nawab (Vizier) of Avadh by the English and the conclusion of a peace with him (1764-65). Since then friendly relations existed between these two neighbouring powers.

The Vizier of Avadh was anxious to annex Rohilkhand. He asked for the assistance of English troops to achieve this object, and offered to pay 40 lakhs of rupees in addition to the cost of troops. Hastings closed the offer, and Rohilkhand was conquered with the aid of a British army.

Hastings made a new arrangement with the Nawab of Avadh. By this an army of the Nawab was to be disciplined and controlled by the British, and revenues of several districts were assigned to the latter for meeting the necessary expenditure. This was the thin end of the wedge by which Avadh was gradually converted into a dependent state.

Hastings was soon involved in the war with the two great powers of India, namely Mysore and the Marathas.

## The Marathas

The serious reverse in the Third Battle of Panipat (1761) checked the rising Maratha power for the time being, but in 1769 the Marathas felt powerful enough to resume their raids in north India. They defeated the Jats and the Rajputs, captured Delhi and replaced the legitimate ruler Shah Alam on the throne, occupied the whole of Doab (the land between the Ganges and the Jamuna) and were about to advance against Avadh and Rohilkhand, when the death of the able Peshwa Madhava Rao and the chaos and confusion that almost immediately followed, forced the Marathas to abandon the enterprise. But worse things were in store. Rival claimants for the throne divided the Marathas into two parties, one of which asked for British help. This led to a war with the Marathas.

The British army had arrived within 20 miles of Poona, when they were opposed by a strong Maratha force. The British immediately began to retreat, but were closely invested at Wargaon, and were forced to accept most humiliating terms. They gave up Raghoba and everything that they had hitherto obtained from the Marathas (17 January 1779).

However, as soon as the British troops were safely back in Bombay, the disgraceful Convention of Wargaon was disavowed, and fresh military preparations were undertaken to retrieve the disaster. Hastings took energetic measures and the war was terminated by the Treaty of Salbai (1782) which did bring substantial gain to either side.

## Mysore

A soldier of fortune named Haidar Nayak rose to power in Mysore, and by A.D. 1761 became its virtual ruler. Hyder Ali, as he was now called, soon extended the boundaries of his kingdom, at the expense of the Nizam and the Marathas, and came to be regarded as one of the great powers of the south.

The hopelessly incompetent government of Madras soon involved themselves in a quarrel with Hyder Ali without making adequate preparations for the same. Hyder Ali had a complete triumph, and dictated the terms of the treaty under the walls of Madras (1769). The English had never been so humiliated before by an Indian power.

The British, however, did not observe the terms of the treaty and gave provocation to Hyder by capturing the French possession, Mahe, which he claimed to be under his protection. So in A.D. 1780. Hyder invaded the Carnatic and swept it with fire and sword almost up to the gate of Madras. The British troops were ignominiously defeated. But after the death of Hyder Ali during the war, his son Tipu Sultan concluded a peace with the British (1784).

Within five years another war broke out and the British formed an alliance with the Nizam and the Marathas against Tipu. Tipu was defeated and a treaty was concluded by which Tipu was compelled to pay 330 lakhs of rupees and to cede half his dominions (1792). Lord Wellesley (1798-1805) completed the conquest of Mysore. He was vigorous and active and set out with the deliberate policy of bringing all the Indian States under British power. With this view he formulated a new system known as Subsidiary Alliance. It practically meant an invitation to the native powers to surrender their independence to the British, on condition of protection from foreign invasion and guarantee of existing dominions. Any ruler, who would accept the alliance, was to maintain a British army at his expense, or pay a subsidy for the same and give up all rights of entering into negotiations with any foreign power, without the consent of the British.

Wellesley succeeded in inducing the Nizam to accept Subsidiary Alliance. But Tipu, the son of Hyder Ali, refused to be a bond-slave of the British and sought to strengthen his position by an alliance with the French. War was accordingly declared against him on 22 February 1799. British troops simultaneously advanced against Mysore from Bombay and Madras, and the capital Srirangapatnam was stormed on May 4. Tipu fell fighting bravely in its defence.

The central portion of the kingdom of Mysore was made over to the Hindu ruling family from whom Hyder Ali had secured it. It became virtually a dependent state under the British.

## The Marathas

Since the treaty of Salbai, the Maratha power gained in strength and prestige. The most outstanding figures among the Marathas of the period were those of Mahadji Sindhia and Nana Fadnavis. Mahadji Sindhia not only owned extensive territories in northern India, but gained great advantage by having the titular emperor of Delhi under his control. He appointed Benoit de Boigne to drill his troops in the European style, and was the only native who possessed a regular army sufficiently disciplined to be pitted against British troops. He defeated the Muhammadan and Rajput powers as well as Holkar. His growing power was a cause of anxiety to the British and a conflict seemed inevitable. Mahadji died in 1794, and was succeeded by Daulat Rao Sindhia, his grand-nephew, a boy of thirteen.

A year later died the famous Ahalya Bai of the Holkar dynasty, who had efficiently managed the Indore State for nearly 30 years.

At Poona, the headquarters of the Maratha power, Nana Fadnavis, the astute politician, wielded the real power in the

name of the young Peshwa, Madhav Rao Narain. He guided the
affairs of the state with great ability, and raised the prestige of
the Maratha name. He joined Cornwallis in fighting against
Tipu and obtained a third of the ceded territories, thereby
extending the Maratha frontier to the Tungabhadra river.

But the Maratha State was torn asunder by internal
dissensions ending in a pitched battle between Holkar and the
combined forces of the Sindhia and the Peshwa. The Peshwa,
being defeated, sought the protection of the English and accepted
Subsidiary Alliance (31 December 1802) by the Treaty of Bassein.
The Maratha chiefs chafed at this but could not act jointly.
Wellesley declared war against Sindhia and Bhonsle and war
was simultaneously carried on both in the Deccan and north
India. In the Deccan the chief command was entrusted to Sir
Arthur Wellesley, the brother of the Governor-General and the
future Duke of Wellington. Sindhia's forces were completely
defeated at Assaye, (23 September 1803) and those of Bhonsle at
Argaon (29 November 1803). In north India, General (afterwards
Lord) Lake captured Delhi and Agra, and defeated Sindhia's
army at Laswari (31 October 1830). Daulat Rao Sindhia and the
Bhonsle chief of Berar were thus completely defeated and
accepted the Subsidiary Alliance (1803) by the treaties of Surji
Arjungaon and Deogaon. Both ceded important territories. The
British gained the Doab and other districts north of the Chambal
from Sindhia, and Cuttack from Bhonsle. Berar and Ahmadnagar
were handed over to the Nizam.

The foolish Holkar, who had kept aloof at the critical
moment, now joined the war. He began with brilliant success
against a British detachment under Colonel Monson, but was
soon defeated with heavy losses at the battle of Deeg (November
1805) and fled towards the Punjab. Lake then besieged the fort
of Bharatpur as its king had joined Holkar, but failed to take it,
and suffered serious losses. A treaty was, however, soon arranged
with the King of Bharatpur.

But it was not long before the Peshwa repented his hasty
action. In November 1817, he attacked the British Resident at
Kirkee with 26,000 men, but was defeated by the British army
which did not consist of more than three thousand men. Bhonsle
and Holkar also fought against the British separately, but both
were defeated. The result of the war was practically the liquidation

of the Marathas as a great power. Bhonsle was deposed, and his dominions lying to the north of the Narmada, were annexed by the British. A new Raja ruled over the rest under British control. The Peshwa received more generous treatment. He was allowed to retire to Bithur, near Cawnpore (Kanpur), and a pension of 8 lakhs rupees was settled upon him. But the office of the Peshwa was abolished, and his territories were annexed to the British dominions. A descendant of Shivaji was allowed to rule over the small principality of Satara under British control.

## Nepal and Sind

Shortly before this, war had broken out with the Gurkha ruler of Nepal who was forced to cede some territories and accept a British Resident at his capital city, Kathmandu.

About the same time the British cast longing eyes at Sind and, after a series of unjust aggressions, Sind was finally annexed in 1843.

## The Sikhs

The last great territorial acquisition was the Punjab after two sanguinary wars. The origin of the Sikhs as a religious sect and its conversion to a military power under Guru Gobind Singh has been referred to earlier.

After the overthrow of Mughal power in the Punjab caused by the invasions of Nadir Shah and Ahmad Shah Durrani, the Sikhs became very powerful. They defeated the successor of Ahmad Shah and conquered the whole of the region from Saharanpur on the east to Attock on the west, and Kangra in the north to Multan in the south. But there was no unity among the Sikhs and they were divided into a large number of clans called *Misls*, each ruling over a separate principality. It was Ranjit Singh who united those to the west of the Sutlej under him and established a powerful kingdom. He engaged European officers to train his soldiers, and his army, the celebrated *Khalsa*, became almost unequalled in India for bravery and military skill.

The Sikh *Misls* to the east of the Sutlej, however, sought British protection against Ranjit Singh, and by the Treaty of Amritsar (1809) between Ranjit Singh and the British Government, the former agreed not to interfere with them, and became virtually dependent upon the British.

Being thus checked on the east, Ranjit Singh extended his dominion in the other three directions and occupied Kangra, Attock on the Indus, Multan, Kashmir and Peshawar. At the time of his death (1839), the Sikhs ruled over a vast kingdom and were recognised as a great military power in India.

Ranjit Singh left no able successor and his death was followed by chaos and confusion with the result that the powerful Khalsa army became all-powerful and dictatorial.

In December 1845, the Sikh army crossed the Sutlej and invaded British territories, but due mainly to the treachery of the Sikh generals, they were defeated in four successive engagements (1845-46), though they had shown wonderful skill and bravery and the British losses were very heavy in all these engagements. Hostilities were brought to an end by the Treaty of Lahore (1846), but within less than two years, the British declared war against the Sikhs. The Sikh army gave a good account of themselves at Chilianwala, inflicting heavy losses on the British (13 January 1849), but was totally crushed at Gujarat behind the Chenab (February 1849). The Punjab was annexed to the British dominions by Lord Dalhousie, the Governor-General (1848-56). He also gave the finishing touch to the policy of expansion. Many States were annexed by the Doctrine of Lapse formulated by him. The doctrine laid down that when the ruler of an Indian State, created by and dependent upon the British, died without any issue, his adopted son, if any, had no right to the State, and the paramount power, *i.e.*, the British, might annex it. The doctrine was laid down twenty years before, and approved by the Home authorities, but Dalhousie, for the first time, put it into practice. The kingdoms of Satara, Nagpur and Jhansi and smaller States, like Jaitpur, in Bundelkhand, and Sambalpur in the Central Provinces were annexed to the British territories on this principles.

The Raja of Sikkim had rightly seized two Englishmen, but as a penalty, Dalhousie annexed a portion of his territory situated between Nepal and Bhutan.

By an arrangement made with the Nizam of Hyderabad, Berar and certain districts were assigned to the British for the payment of the British force in Hyderabad. Dalhousie also withheld the pension of eight lakhs of rupees, granted to the ex-Peshwa Baji Rao, from his adopted son Dhondhu Pant, better known as Nana Sahib. The Nawab of the Carnatic having died, the title and rank of Nawab was abolished. The same procedure was adopted with regard to Tanjore.

The British also tried to expand their empire outside India. Their attempt to establish their authority in Afghanistan failed miserably but they conquered Burma. The policy towards Afghanistan was due to the fear of Russian expansion, and that against Burma was to check French influence in South-East Asia.

# 3

# Reforms during the First Century of British Rule

The period of a hundred years after the Battle of Plassey witnessed not only the expansion of British domination practically all over India and a large part of Burma, but also considerable improvement in the system of administration and the social-cum-religious condition of the people, as well as the spread of Western ideas through education heralding what is called the New Age or renaissance in India. Some of these gained momentum only in the next century and would be dealt with later, but reference should be made to others at this stage.

The first reform introduced by Lord Cornwallis (1786-93) was the new system of land revenue, known as the Permanent Settlement, followed by a change in the system of administration. Hastings had introduced the system by which land tax was put on auction, and a settlement was made with the highest bidder for a period of five years. The effect was ruinous. The temporary holder of the land wanted to make as much money as he could during his short tenure: he oppressed the poor tenants and did nothing to effect any permanent improvement in the land. Cornwallis accordingly made the Permanent Settlement with the Zamindars. By this the Zamindars were practically acknowledged as proprietors of the land subject to the payment of an annual revenue, which was fixed forever, and could not be increased. The Permanent Settlement was introduced in Bengal and Bihar in 1793, and in Banaras two years later.

## Administrative Reforms

The whole province was divided into a number of districts, which henceforth served as the unit of administration. Each district had a Civil Court under a British Judge, and four Provincial Courts of Appeal were established intervening between the District Courts and the Sadar Dewani Adalat of Calcutta.

Four Courts of Circuit, each under two British Judges, were appointed for the administration of criminal justice, while the Sadar Nizamat Adalat was placed under the Governor-General-in-Council.

The Collectors were divested of all judicial functions. The Judges of Civil Courts acted as Magistrates and had the control of the Police. Each district was divided into a number of *thanas* (police-stations) with a *Daroga* over each.

Cornwallis, however, followed the principle that the Indians should not be appointed to high posts. For this and other reasons his reforms were almost a complete failure. The whole country was infested with robbers, and life and property were extremely insecure. The courts were heavily in arrears and for many years justice was almost denied.

## Reforms of Bentinck

The Governor-General Lord Willian Bentinck (1828-35) will be ever remembered for his notable reforms. The chief among these was the abolition of Sati. According to a long-standing custom among Hindus, the wife of a man, who had just died, used to burn herself along with her husband. Sometimes she was forced to do so by her relatives. Cases are on record where the unwilling victim jumped out of fire, but her half-burnt body was forcibly thrown back into it. This cruel and inhuman practice was stopped by a legislation.

Bentinck also conferred an everlasting benefit by extirpating the hands of robbers called the Thugs. For years the Thugs had carried on a regular trade in murder. They went out in disguise, mixed with travellers and robbed and strangled them whenever they found an opportunity. Regular bands of Thugs haunted different parts of India, and became a veritable terror to the people. Bentinck, with the help of a very able official, Sir William Sleeman, completely destroyed the organisation of the Thugs.

Bentinck also tried to bring some primitive barbarous tribes, within the pale of civilisation. The Khonds of Madras who used to offer human sacrifices to their goddeses, and the Kols of Bengal, may be mentioned as instances. Both these tribes gradually imbibed elements of civilisation under his benign arrangements.

Prompted by the same noble motive which led to the above reforms, Bentinck laid down the policy of employing Indians in high judicial and executive posts. When the Charter of the East India Company was renewed in 1833, it was emphatically declared that no Indian should be disabled from holding any place, office or employment under the Company.

## Reforms of Dalhousie

Lord Dalhousie (1848-56) also introduced some important reforms. A Lieutenant-Governor was appointed for Bengal and the Public Works Department was created. Big schemes of road and irrigation canals were undertaken. The Railways, the Electric, Telegraph and cheap postage were introduced to improve means of communication. The famous Education Despatch arrived in 1854, and Dalhousie at once adopted measures to give effect to it. A Department of Public Instruction was created and the establishment of schools, colleges and universities was undertaken. The importance of female education was also fully recognised.

## Important Changes

The first half of the 19th century witnessed also the beginning of some far-reaching changes in Indian society which bore fruit in the second half. Among these the most important is the introduction of English education to which reference will be made later. But mention may be made of other changes flowing from this which played a vital part in the national reawakening and may be regarded as the first fruits of English education. These were:

1. The creation of a prose literature in Bengal, with future consequences which affected the whole of India;
2. Publication of newspapers and periodicals both in English and in Bengali;
3. Systematic and organised political agitation demanding removal of abuses and inauguration of salutary reforms in the system of administration introduced by the British, the

most notable being the agitation carried on by Rammohan Roy for the abolition of the Press Act which considerably curtailed the expression of free opinion in books and newspapers and the demand for the introduction of the system of trial by jury. This led to the establishment of political associations for carrying on similar agitations on a large scale and in more regular and effective manner.

The year 1857 completed a century of British rule in India, dating from the Battle of Plassey. It may be regarded as the dividing line between two distinct ages and is marked by two great events which are mainly responsible for bringing out this great change. These are, first, the great outbreak popularly known as the Sepoy Mutiny, or Great Revolt of 1857 and, second, the establishment of three Universities in Calcutta, Bombay and Madras, which is the logical fulfilment of the introduction of English education.

Both require elaborate treatment in some detail, to which we now proceed.

# 4

# The Outbreak of 1857 War

The great outbreak of 1857 war is one of those episodes of Indian history in the modern age which no educated Indian has ever regarded without interest, and a few without prejudice. While some regard it as the mutiny of the sepoys, as the popular name Sepoy Mutiny indicates, others describe it as the first national war of independence in India. The main facts or incidents are, however, fairly well-known and may be briefly stated as follows.

The Indian soldiers, generally known as sepoys (*sipahi*), always outnumbered British soldiers. It was mainly with the help of the sepoys that the British conquered India and maintained order and discipline over their vast dominions. The sepoys certainly welcomed their recruitment in the Indian army and preferred it to enrolment in the army of the Indian Princely States.

But gradually widespread discontent grew against British rule and vague apprehensions prevailed among all classes of people, both civil and military, that the British government intended to convert them wholesale to Christianity. The sepoys had additional grievances in respect of their pay and promotion, and there were mutinies of sepoys on a small scale on several occasions, prior to 1857. At last the introduction at the Enfield Rifle served as the immediate cause of the revolt. The sepoys had to bite off the end of the cartridge which they believed were greased with the fat of cows and pigs, in order to pollute both the Hindus and the Muhammadans, and to convert them to Christianity. Subsequent inquiry showed that these apprehensions were not altogether unfounded and that the fat of cows and pigs had really been used in making these cartridges.

The rebellious spirit was evident at Barrackpur on 29 March 1857, when a sepoy struck a blow at his officer. It soon spread to Meerut and Lucknow. The sepoys at Meerut rose in a body, murdered the Europeans, burnt their houses, and then marched to Delhi. These rebels were soon joined by others at Delhi. There they murdered many Europeans, proclaimed Bahadur Shah, the last of the Mughals, as the rightful emperor of India. The rebellion soon spread to other parts of the United Provinces as well as to Central India, including Bundelkhand. The chief strongholds of the rebels were Delhi, Lucknow, Kanpur, Bareilly and Jhansi.

In these and other places the successful rebellion of the sepoys was followed by popular outbreaks and plunders. The British were taken by surprise and in most places the sepoys had no difficulty in driving away the officers and their families and becoming masters of the localities. But in some places like Kanpur and Lucknow where the British took shelter in forts, improvised entrenchments or some pucca buildings, they defended themselves against the sepoys who far outnumbered them.

The rebellions were merely sporadic outbursts in various isolated towns. Neither the mutinous sepoys nor the local people who revolted or rather took advantage of the absence of authorities to loot and fight among themselves had any common plan of action. The people at large, and most of the landlords, except the ryots and the taluqdars of Avadh, who took this opportunity to retrieve the lands of which they had been deprived did not make common cause against the British. The rulers of many of the Indian States also held aloof. The Sikh soldiers helped the British against the sepoys, who had defeated them only a few years ago and were the chief instruments of the ruin of their region. The Gurkha king of Nepal also helped the British. So the British were able to suppress the revolt, which came to an end in 1858.

The Rani of Jhansi, the most distinguished leader in the Revolt, at first denounced the rebel sepoys, but when she found that the British suspected her of complicity in it and wanted to try her, she joined the sepoys and proved to be the ablest rebel leader against the British. She died fighting bravely, while two other leaders, Nana Sahib and the Begum of Oudh, fled to Nepal. Tantia Tope, the general of Nana, also fought bravely but was captured and hanged. Bahadur Shah was exiled to Rangoon.

The Revolt was marked by terrible cruelties and atrocities on both sides. Reference may be made to the grim tragedy at Kanpur.

At Kanpur the rebels were headed by Nana Sahib, the adopted son of Baji Rao. The English soldiers and residents, nearly a thousand in number, shut themselves up behind a feeble rampart. Nana promised to convey them safely to Allahabad, but as soon as they reached the riverside, the rebels opened fire, and massacred nearly all of them. Nana also murdered nearly two hundred women and children who were kept as prisoners (15th July), and threw their bodies into a neighbouring well.

But while suppressing the Revolt, some of the English officials were equally guilty of barbarities of the worst type.

Lord Canning showed wonderful tact and patience in handling a very dangerous situation. When the rebellion was over, he did not wreak an ignoble vengeance on the deluded people, but showed mercy and moderation.

## Transference to the Crown

One of the most important changes brought about by the Great Revolt was the final abolition of the authority of the East India Company. The shocking news of the revolts and massacres brought home to the people in England the incongruity of the administration of a great empire by a mercantile company. An Act for the "Better Government of India" was finally passed on 2 August 1858, and the responsibility for the Government of India was directly assumed by the Crown. A Secretary of State for India took the place of the President of the Board of Control, and the Council of India, that of the Court of Directors. The Governor-General was henceforth styled as the Viceroy, or representative, of the Crown in India.

This momentous change was announced to the people and princes of India on November 1, 1858, by a solemn proclamation of Her Majesty Queen Victoria. It was translated into the vernacular, and read out in various parts of the country. As the first formal declaration of Indian policy by the Crown, its importance cannot be overestimated. The more important portions of the document may be summarised as follows:

Viscount Canning was appointed the first Viceroy and Governor-General, and all the officers of the Company were confirmed in their posts. The existing treaty obligations were accepted, and any desire for further conquests was expressly repudiated.

## Nature of the Outbreak

Divergent views have been expressed both by contemporary and later writers about the nature of the outbreak of 1857-58. These may be broadly divided into two classes. According to some, the outbreak was really a rebellion of the people against British rule and not merely a mutiny of soldiers. According to others it was primarily and essentially a mutiny of sepoys though in certain areas the civil population took advantage of it to break out into open defiance of authorities. Only a very few might have had any political motive, but not necessarily the achievement of freedom from the British yoke.

We find supporters of both these views among contemporary Englishmen. Eminent Indians, throughout the latter half of the 19th century almost regarded the outbreak as purely a mutiny of soldiers. Thus Kishorichand Mitra, an eminent Bengali, wrote in 1858: "It is essentially a military insurrection. It is the revolt of a lac of sepoys. It has nothing of the popular element in it." The same view was expressed by other eminent Bengali leaders like Sambu Chandra Mukhopadhyaya, Harish Chandra Mukherji, Raj Narain Bose, and Syed Ahmad and three other Bengalis and one Maratha, Godse Bhatji, who were eye-witnesses of the events in different localities.

It was not till the beginning of the present century, when a genuine revolutionary movement of the people began, that the Sepoy outbreak of 1857 began to be looked upon not only as a great revolt of the people but also claimed to be the first Indian War of Independence, and this has now got wide currency. This view, first made popular by the publication, in 1909, of "The Indian War of Independence-1857" by the great patriot Vinayak Damodar Savarkar has now obtained great currency among Indians, but historically it is difficult to accept this view.

In the first place, the actual revolt, both of the sepoys and of the civil population, was confined to the U.P. and a fringe of territory just outside its boundary. There is hardly any justification, therefore, to characterise the movement as Indian or National.

India in the sense of a political or national unit had no meaning or existence in the conception of our ancestors in 1857. They talked of the Sikhs, Rajputs, Marathas, Hindustanis, Bengalis, Oriyas, Tamils, etc., but had no clear conception of an Indian. We learn from Bishop Heber, who travelled widely over north India in 1824, that the people in U.P. regarded the Bengali as much a foreigner as the English. In spite of the slogan of Hindu Pad Padshahi, the Marathas had ravaged without compunction the territories of the Sikhs and Rajputs on the west, the Bengalis in the east, the Tamilians and Kannadigas in the south, and the Hindustanis in the north. The conception of India, as a whole, was to be found only in the literary works of a past age, and still survived in theory, but it had no application to actual politics till the sixties or seventies of the 19th century.

So long as there was no conception of India, there could not have been any idea of freedom of India, far less any struggle for attaining it. But, in reality, the case was perhaps worse. For even among the smaller political units into which India was divided, there was not the same urge for freedom from British yoke. In Bengal, as mentioned above, British rule was regarded by the Hindus as only a change of masters, and for the better.

Nowhere in India did the conception of a national State supersede that of the dynastic State. The allegiance of the people, if any, was due to the ruler and his dynasty, but not to any regional State. There were attempts in 1857 to restore the Mughal dynasty in Delhi, the Peshwa's supremacy in Central Provinces and, the rule of the Nawab family of Oudh. But there was no question of establishing a national State in any of these regions. As such there ccould be no national war of independence before the Indians were conscious of forming a nation and imbued with a sense of patriotism or yearning for independence.

# 5

# English Education

English education may be regarded as the chief contributing factor to the great regeneration of India in the 19th century, generally referred to as the Renaissance. It is, therefore, necessary to trace the history of this education in some detail.

Exigencies of administration and commercial intercourse urged the Indians, specially the residents of Calcutta, Bombay and Madras, to cultivate the knowledge of English in the 18th century, or perhaps even earlier. But it was not till the beginning of the 19th century that Indians appreciated the value of English as a medium of culture also and a number of private institutions for teaching English were established in Calcutta and its neighbourhood. In 1816, a large number of Hindus in Calcutta resolved to establish an institution for the education of their children in a liberal manner as practised by Europeans. A public meeting was held at the house of Sir Hyde East on 14 May 1816, which was attended by fifty or more of the most respectable Hindu inhabitants of rank or wealth including orthodox Pandits. Half a lakh of rupees was subscribed. It was decided to establish a college, "to teach among others, the Bengali and English languages, grammar, arithmetic, history, geography, astronomy, mathematics and in time as the fund increases" (for large subscriptions were promised on the meeting). By its Foundation Charter the college could not admit any student who was not an orthodox Hindu and so it was named Hindoo College and formally established on 20 January 1817.

The Hindoo College became the premier institution for English education and is now represented by the Presidency College, Calcutta.

It is difficult to overestimate the part played by the Hindoo College in spreading liberal Western ideas, particularly those of nationality, patriotism, love of liberty, etc., first in Bengal and then all over India. The establishment of the Hindoo College was followed by that of a large number of institutions both in and outside Calcutta, partly by the ex-students of the Hindoo College and partly by others including Christian missionaries.

There is a general impression that English education was introduced by the British rulers for administrative convenience, and the course was deliberately designed to make the Indians only fit to be clerks. There appears to be little justification for this for English education was not introduced by the British rulers, and they did not even encourage it till the new policy was inaugurated in 1835.

While English education was thus making great headway in Bengal through institutions established by private efforts, and revolutionalising the ideas of young Bengalis, the Government of India set up in 1823 the General Committee of Public Instruction for promoting education with the help of the annual grant of the sum of one lakh of rupees, provided for the purpose in the Charter of 1813, but of which not a pie was spent during the following ten years. The Committee decided to spend the whole amount for the promotion of Sanskrit and Arabic learning.

It was not long before a strong difference of opinion arose among the members of the General Committee of Public Instruction. Half of the Committee called the "Orientalists" were for the continuation of the old system of stipends, tenable for twelve or fifteen years, to students of Arabic and Sanskrit, and for liberal expenditure on the publication of works in these languages. The other half, called the "Anglicists" desired to reduce the expenditure on stipends held by "lazy and stupid schoolboys of 30 and 35 years of age" and to cut down the sums lavished on Sanskrit and Arabic printing.

Macaulay, on arriving in India in 1834, was appointed President of the Committee and threw his whole weight in favour of the Anglicists who ultimately won the day. The chief credit for this is usually given to Macaulay. But official documents make it almost certain that Bentinck would have arrived at the same decision even if Macaulay would not have lent his strong support to it.

The final decision of the Government of India, which put an end to the long and bitter controversy between the Orientalists and the Anglicists, was announced on 7 March 1835, in a brief resolution of which the substance was that the great object of the Government ought to be the promotion of European literature and science among the natives of India; that the medium to be used was the English language; and the Education Fund should be employed on English education alone. It has been regretted by many on the ground that it gave an undue favour to English against vernacular as the medium of instruction. As a matter of fact the decision merely meant that English, and not Sanskrit or Arabic, should be used as the medium of higher education. It had no reference to vernacular which would remain the medium of a system of national education embracing every village in the country.

As a result of the policy adopted in 1835 and the foundation of three universities in Bombay, Madras and Calcutta 22 years later, English education made phenomenal progress in Bengal and elsewhere. The people had no liking for education in vernacular schools and these did not flourish in spite of the efforts of the Government to maintain and extend them.

The spread of English education led to an agitation by the Indians themselves for introducing English as the language of the Court. We find a powerful plea to this effect in a Bengali weekly dated 26 January 1828, "Persian is now the language of the Court all over Bengal. It is not the language of the Judges, pleaders, plaintiffs, defendants or witnesses. We think that if any foreign language is to be retained as court-language, it should be English." Lord Hardinge, the Governor-General (1844-48), issued a Regulation which virtually made English education the only passport to higher appointments then available in India.

This policy of the Government had undoubtedly the effect of popularising English education, but had the evil consequence of gradually emphasizing its material and economics, in place of the liberal and cultural value.

The Muslims, however, generally speaking, held aloof from English education. This difference in the progress of English education among the two great communities was to have important consequences in the future. In the first place, the Hindus made for greater cultural advance on modern lines than the Muslims. Secondly, the share of Muslims in government appointments— which required a knowledge of English—was less than that of the Hindus even on the basis of population of the two communities.

# 6

# Social and Religious Reforms

We may now briefly review the broad features which marked the regeneration of India largely due to the impact of Western ideas through English education.

India came into contact with Western ideas at a very opportune moment, when they were dominated by the French Revolution and the Age of Illumination. India awoke from the slumber of ages as a result of the impact. Rationalism took the place of blind faith, individualism supplanted the tyranny of dogma and traditional belief and authority, and ideas of social justice and political rights took shape and cast off the fatalism or obscurantism of ages. The achievements of the Europeans in arts and science and the phenomenal progress in their society and politics during the preceding two centuries when India had sat still, infused new ideas and generated fresh vigour among men who had been hitherto content to leave everything to fate, look back upon the hoary past rather than the future, and turn their searchlight inwards rather than outwards over the wide world.

It is not possible to describe in detail the result of the impact of the West and the various manifestations of the New Age in different spheres of life and society in the 19th and 20th centuries, but a few illustrative facts can be briefly stated.

Raja Rammohan Roy was the first and the best representative of this new spirit of rational inquiry into the basis of religion and society. He challenged the current religious beliefs and social practices of the Hindus as not being in consonance with their own scriptures. He tried to show that the belief in multiplicity of gods and worship of images, which formed the essence of current and popular Hindu religion, were opposed to the teachings of the *Vedas*. How far his views are historically correct, or morally sound, is of secondary importance. What really matters is his open and public protest against the blind acceptance of whatever passed current on the authority of priesthood or its interpretation of scriptures. The standard of revolt he thus raised against the medieval tyranny of dogma unleashed forces which created what may be called Modern India and makes him worthy to rank by the side of Bacon and Luther.

## Religion

The first fruits of Rammohun's efforts are best seen in the growth of the Brahmo Movement in religion of which he only sowed the seed but which grew into a mighty plant under the care of Debendranath Tagore and Keshub Chandra Sen. Rammohun lived and died a Hindu and believed in the *Vedas* though interpretation of them differed from the current one. But it is a well-known fact that revolution, whether political or religious, gathers momentum as it proceeds, and what was radicalism in one stage becomes moderation in the next. So under Debendranath and Keshub Chandra the Brahmos moved further and further ahead. The *Vedas* were no longer regarded as infallible authority, many departures from social rules and practices like caste system, restrictions in food, marriage and other fields prescribed by Hindu society were given up. Keshub later seceded from the parent body and founded a new church. But a younger group proceeded further and formed what is now known as the Sadharan Brahmo Samaj, which formally declared itself non-Hindu. But the Prarthana Samaj of Bombay which was really an offshoot of the Brahmo Movement in Bengal followed a different line under the inspiration of M.G. Ranade and never detached itself from Hindu society.

The Brahmo religion became an all-India sect under the inspiring leadership of Keshub Chandra Sen. The Prarthana Samaj had not spread widely outside Bombay, and some sects bearing that name changed it to Brahmo Samaj. On the other hand, the moderate views of the Prarthana Samaj made it popular in the Telugu country and 18 out of 29 Brahmo Samajis in the Madras Presidency bear the name Prarthana Samaj.

The purely religious aspect of Brahmo Samaj has not found many followers and it may be said to be a spent force today. But its ideas of social reform, such as the abandonment of caste, introduction of widow remarriage, female education, and the abolition of *purdah* and child marriage have been adopted by orthodox Hindu society. Further the first all-India religious movement, launched by the Brahmo leader Keshub Chandra, undoubtedly had some effect upon the latter all-India political or national movement.

Like the Brahmo Samaj, the Arya Samaj, founded by Dayananda Sarasvati in 1875, was a reformist movement. Like Rammohun Roy, Dayanand believed in the *Veda* (*Samhita* of the *Rigveda,* more specifically), as interpreted by him, as the only authority and discarded and waged incessant warfare against the falsehoods of the prevailing Puranic faith or orthodox Hinduism. He denounced the worship of gods and goddesses, encouraged intercaste marriage, and decried child marriage. On the other hand, he insisted upon veneration of cows and the offer of daily sacrifice of butter in the hearthfire. Unlike Brahmo Samaj, Arya Samaj was not based on the rationalist movement of the West and condemned monotheism as preached by Christianity and Islam. One of the characteristic features of Arya Samaj is the *Suddhi-Sangathan,* which means the reconversion of Hindus, who were once converted to Islam or Christianity but were now willing to come back to the fold of Hinduism.

There is hardly any doubt that the Arya Samaj has made very significant contribution to the development of a new national consciousness among the modern Hindus, particularly of the Punjab.

The Brahmo Samaj and Arya Samaj both made vigorous protest against what they called the evil accretions to Hinduism at a later date due to the influence of the *Puranas* and other sectarian religious literature. This provoked a reaction, particularly in Bengal, in the latter half of the 19th century, and is known as New-Hinduism. Its general characteristic was the glorification of Hindu religion and society in its present form and a spirited defence of the same by many arguments against hostile criticism both by Indian reformers and Christian missionaries. There was an endeavour "to reconcile ancient and medieval Hinduism with all its rituals and ceremonies and faiths with modern science." The best and most rational exposition of neo-Hinduism is to be found in the writings of Bankim Chandra Chattopadhyaya, perhaps the greatest Bengali litterature of the 19th century. He made a critical re-examination, a reinterpretation that had been so powerfully influencing current religious life and thought in Christendom itself. His attempt to prove by strictly historical method that Krishna, the great God of the millions of the Hindus, was an ideal man, has left a profound impression upon Hindu society. It strengthened Hindu revivalist movement and helped the growth of the nascent national movement in Bengal.

The three great religious movements of the 19th century mentioned, were all founded by intellectuals. Towards the end of the century emerged a powerful religious movement founded by a great spiritual leader and promulgated by his spiritual disciple who was also a great intellectual. Ramakrishna Paramahamsa, a poor Brahman worshipper of the Goddess Kali in a temple of Dakshinesvar, a few miles to the north of Calcutta, lived a retired life, but his saintly life and pithy sayings and parables enunciating the highest truths gradually attracted a large number of people including Keshub Chandra Sen, the Brahmo leader. But the greatest of his devoted disciples was a young graduate of the Calcutta University, later known as Swami Vivekananda, who attained worldwide fame by his discourses in the Paliament of Religions held at Chicago in 1893 attended by the representatives of religions from almost all over the world. The reputation won by Vivekananda by his series of lectures on Hindu religion at different places in USA made him a world figure and raised the prestige of India and Hinduism very high. Several centres for the study of *Vendanta* were established in the USA on a permanent basis. He also visited London and Paris and preached the gospel of Sri Ramakrishna which made a deep impression upon scholars like Max Mueller and Romain Rolland, the French savant who wrote biographies of Ramakrishna and Vivekananda respectively.

Early in 1897 Swami Vivekananda returned to India and established monasteries for religious meditation as well as missions for social service. He toured all over India and delivered lectures from Himalaya to Cape Comorin preaching the religious doctrine of his great Master Ramakrishna.

The most striking thing about Ramakrishna was his spiritual life and God-consciousness. Many people had witnessed his ecstatic trances on merely hearing of God or thinking of Him. By his own practice and experience of different modes of salvation prescribed in different religions-different forms of Hinduism like Saiva, Sakta, Vaishnava, Tantrik, as well as Christianity, and Islam—he realised the great truth that all religions lead to salvation, a doctrine which he pithily described as *Yata mat tata path* (different creeds are different roads to God). This harmony of religion is his greatest contribution. As a corollary to this he also preached that different forms of religion are suitable to different persons and, therefore, it is wrong to insist that the one form of religion prescribed by a sect is the only true form, the rest being false. As Vivekananda put it, "As one coat does not fit different persons, so it is wrong to think that there is only one true religion, and the rest are all untrue." So he supported those who worshipped images as well as those who did not. God, he said, may have form or no form as water may also assume the form of ice or vapour.

Though Vivekananda had unflinching faith in Hindu religion, he denounced untouchability and insisted on raising the status of women and the masses. He stressed the pithy saying of Ramakrishna that the highest worship of God is to serve men and look upon them as God. "Where," said Vivekananda, "should one go to seek for God? Are not all the poor, the miserable, the weak, God?" So, social work was a part of religion in the Ramakrishna order, and that is why a monastery was associated with a mission for social service.

The evolution of Hinduism in the 19th century which began with Raja Rammohun Roy completed its cycle with the doctrine of Ramakrishna as propounded by Vivekananda. To use Hegelian phraseology, Brahmo Samaj represented the thesis, the neo-Hinduism was the antithesis, and Ramakrishna the synthesis. To Raja Rammohun the belief in one God and rejection of other gods and the worship of their images was the *sine qua non* of Hindu religion—refuse it and you have no place in true Hinduism. The contrary view was maintained by Vivekananda: "From the high spiritual flights of the Vedanta Philosophy...to the low ideas of idolatry with its multifarious mythology, the agnosticism of the Buddhists, and the atheism of the Jains, all have a place in the Hindu's religion.

"Unity in variety is the plan of nature, and the Hindu has recognised it. Every other religion lays down certain fixed dogmas, and tries to force society to adopt them. It places before society only one coat which must fit Jack and John and Henry all alike. If it does not fit John or Henry, he must go without a coat to cover his body. The Hindus have discovered that the absolute can only be realised, or thought of, or stated through the relative and the images, the crosses, and crescents are simply so many symbols, so many pegs to hang the spiritual ideas on. It is not that this help is necessary for everyone; but those that do not need it have no right to say that it is wrong. Nor is it compulsory in Hinduism."

The denunciations of the cruelties or oddities displayed by certain sections of the Hindus may be regarded as the greatest contribution of Swami Vivekananda to the development of Hinduism in the modern age. The catholicity and tolerant spirit of Hinduism propounded by Ramakrishna and preached by Vivekananda may be regarded as a significant contribution of India to the modern world. "I challenge", says he, "the world to find, throughout the whole system of Sanskrit philosophy, any such expression as that the Hindu alone will be saved and not others." Again, "Do I wish that the Hindu or Buddhist would become Christian? God forbid. But each must assimilate the spirit of others and yet preserve his individuality and grow according to his own law of growth."

## Society

The rational spirit of the 19th century was also displayed in reforms or removal of various abuses in Hindu society. In Bombay the agitation for social reform began early and not only were there a large number of selfless workers like Jotiba Phule, Karsondas Mulji, Pandita Ramabai and last but not least, Mahadev Govind Ranade, but an All-India Movement of social reforms was started by the last-named. Next we find English-educated youths of Bengal carrying on crusades for social reform of all kinds. Most of the social reforms centred round the condition of women and of the lower classes.

Among the major reforms reference has already been made to the abolition of the practice of *Sati*. Another such cruel rite was the killing of infant girls, prevalent among certain Rajput tribes, because their social customs and conventions entailed heavy expenditure and trouble for marriage of daughters. It was estimated that nearly twenty thousand female infants were killed every year by the 125,000 Jharija families of Gujarat. Maharaja Dalip Singh, the son of Ranjit Singh, said that "he had actually seen when he was a child at Lahore, his sisters put into a sack and thrown into the river." Generally the infant was killed almost immediately after birth in two ways: either the mother deliberately neglected to suckle the child or administered poisonous drug (mostly opium) to the nipple of her breast. But other more direct methods were also employed. This inhuman practice was ultimately stopped partly by persuasion, partly by legislation, in the second half of the nineteenth century.

Another important reform was the legalisation of the remarriage of widows by an Act passed in 1856, the result mainly of the untiring efforts of a Sanskrit Pandit of Bengal named Ishwar Chandra Vidyasagar, the Principal of Sanskrit College, Calcutta.

The abolition of the slave trade and slavery by legislation is also a remarkable humanitarian act when we remember the inhuman cruelty suffered by many slaves in Calcutta at the hands of their European masters and especially mistresses, the gruesome accounts of which are now available.

A vigorous agitation against child marriage, carried on by a Parsi gentleman, B.M. Malabari, resulted in the passing of the Age of Consent Act in 1891 forbidding the consummation of marriage before the wife had reached the age of twelve. There was a storm of protest against that Bill, as in the latter case of the *Sati*, and it is of great significance that as in the latter case Rammohun Roy opposed the legislation, so in the present case did Bal Gangadhar Tilak, one of the greatest political leaders of India. Tilak made it quite clear that he objected not to the provisions of the Bill, but to the right of a foreign Government to interfere in the social reform of the Hindus. In the other case Rammohun fought valiantly against the *Sati* rite, but still he thought that persuasion and not legislation should be the proper method to be followed. Both these standpoints are very debatable ones, though they have been adopted in similar cases by others of less renown. But the change in the Indian view points as regards social reform may be judged from the fact that not only the lower limits of marriageable age for both boys and girls have been laid down, but even divorce has been permitted by legislation in the present century.

One of the most important social reforms of the 19th century is the provision of higher education for women, and its inevitable result was the abolition of the purdah system and the employment of women in high public offices. When the first women's college, named after its founder, Bethune College was founded in 1849, with only school classes, the number of pupils did not exceed sixty, but today even in the post-graduate classes of the University of Calcutta women in some departments form the majority of pupils. Though women's education in India has not yet reached a stage comparable with advanced countries in Europe, the change already accomplished may be said to be of a revolutionary character. The same thing may be said of the purdah system and the marriageable age of girls. Not only in the academic sphere, but even in politics, administration, and professions like the legal and the medical, the position of women of the present age was beyond the wildest dreams of their mothers and grandmothers.

# 7

# Political Regeneration

The political regeneration of India formed the most conspicuous feature of the Indian renaissance in the 19th century. As the Hindus, particularly in the urban areas in some parts of the country, had gone through a long period of subjection and persecution under the Muslim rule, they had gradually lost all sense of nationalism and patriotism. The best evidence thereof is the fact that when the British imposed their rule in Bengal, even the most eminent leaders welcomed it and considered it as an act of providence. On the other hand, far different was the reaction in Maharashtra which enjoyed independence up to 1818. This is best shown by the writings of Bhaskar Pandurang Tarkhadkar in 1841. Addressing the British he said: "We cannot look upon your Government in any other light than of the most bitter curse India has ever been visited with."

Again nationalism was a distinctive feature of Arya Samaj, and this difference from Brahmo Samaj, with which it had many points in common, is perhaps due to the fact that the Punjab enjoyed independence until the middle of 19th century, whereas the Hindus of Bengal did not taste it for more than six hundred years.

There is, however, hardly any doubt that a great change was brought about in India as a whole by the introduction of Western ideas of nationalism and patriotism—a great force in 19th century Europe—through the study of English literature of that period.

Among other factors may be mentioned the introduction of the printing press and periodicals which facilitated, through vernacular language, the political education of the people, and the growing volume of discontent and disaffection against British rule. The old attitude towards the English as benefactors changed, as many glaring evils of the British people and the system of administration now cause great dissatisfaction. Among the prominent evils may be mentioned, the exclusion of Indians from all high offices, the undisguised contempt with which, as a general rule, the British officials treated Indians, the growing poverty of the people caused by the huge drain of wealth to England in various direct and indirect ways, the deliberate destruction of Indian industry, the heavy increase in land revenue, etc. The Indians felt, not without reason, that the British deliberately crippled Indian trade and manufacture by erecting a high tariff wall in Britain against Indian goods, and encouraging by all means available the import of British goods to India. The ruin of trade and industry forced millions of men who lost their means of livelihood to crowd into agriculture. India which was a flourishing country of combined agriculture and manufacture "was forcibly transformed into an agricultural colony of British manufacturing colonialism." Among other causes may be mentioned the indiscriminate assault, resulting in serious bodily injury, even death in some cases of Indians by Englishmen for which the offenders were lightly punished or sometimes not punished at all. These incidents were very common and were felt all the more keenly than even the political subjection or the economic exploitation. Another cause of discontent, particularly felt by the higher classes of Indians, was the social exclusiveness of the Europeans as illustrated by non-admission of even the most respectable and highly placed Indians to the European clubs. This, perhaps, more than anything else, alienated the English educated, especially England-returned Indians, from Englishmen and English rule in India. Another grave cause of discontent was the propaganda of the Christian missionaries, with the connivance and sometimes open support of officials, causing a vague dread that the Government was determined to convert Indians to Christianity. Such dread got an impetus by legislation permitting remarriage of widows or removal of disability of Hindus converted to Christianity in regard to inheritance of ancestral property. The introduction of railways, telegraphs, etc., produced a similar effect upon the illiterate masses. The revolt of the sepoys caused by greased cartridges should be judged in the light of these things.

While all these and many.other factors favoured the growth of a strong nationalist spirit in India, one of the most important factors that led to the growth of patriotic and national feeling among the Hindus of India was the revelation of their past glory and greatness. It was really a revelation, for the Hindus till then had no knowledge of their past history, and the curious fables that passed as history, are well illustrated by a book on the *History of India* written by a learned Hindu teacher of the Fort William College in 1803. The only historical work that held the field was the history written by the English historian James Mill in 1818 which was a prescribed text in Indian universities even in the 20th century. The Indians read in this book that the Hindus had ever been in the same abject condition in which the British found them in the 18th century, and the Muslims were far more civilised than the Hindus who fully deserved to be subdued by them. But all these were changed in the course of the next half century by the works of oriental scholars in Europe and the systematic archaeological excavations which commenced in 1861. What must have been the feelings of the Hindus, suffering from an inferiority complex, when they learnt about the great Emperor Asoka whose writ ran practically throughout India and Afghanistan which formed his dominions? The Hindus also learnt that their ancestors were as great as the Greeks and the Romans and belonged to the same family of mankind from which were descended all the famous nations of Europe, and that Buddhism which originated in India was even today the religion of one-fifth of the entire human race. Could there be any Hindu who was not overpowered with emotion when he read the following passage addressed to the I.C.S. probationers in England by Max Mueller, one of the greatest scholars of the time?

"If I were asked under sky the human mind has most fully developed some of its choicest gifts, has most deeply pondered on the greatest problems life, and has found solutions of some of them which well deserve the attention even of those who have studied Plato and Kant, I should point to India. And if I were to ask myself from what literature we, here in Europe, we who have been nurtured almost exclusively on the thoughts of Greeks and Romans, and of one semitic race, the Jewish, may draw that corrective which is most wanted in order to make our inner life more perfect, more comprehensive, more universal, in fact more truly human, a life not for this life only, but a transfigured and eternal life again I should point to India."

This common heritage of a great culture and rich historical tradition imbued the Hindus with an idea of common nationality. The revelation of India's past, supplemented by the bond of a common religion, served to bring them together, and mutual intercourse was facilitated by the use of English as a *lingua franca* and easy means of communication through railways, steamers, cheap postage and telegraphs. Nationalism was thus founded on the bedrock of common religion, culture and historical tradition. But this gave it a Hindu character consciously or unconsciously. Raj Narain Bose, the maternal grandfather of Aurobindo Ghose may be regarded as the father of nationalism in Bengal. He started a society for the promotion of national feeling among the educated natives of Bengal and issued a pamphlet in 1866 outlining its objects. It was a clarion call to the Bengalis to give up everything foreign and use Bengali language, food, dress, manners, customs, etc. A practical demonstration was given by one of his followers, Naba Gopal Mitra, who started the annual Hindu Mela with a view to awaken national feelings by means of patriotic songs, poems and lectures. Bal Gangadhar Tilak preached nationalism in Maharashta. He started the Shivaji *Utsav* and *Ganpati* festivals, making a profound appeal through the twin base of Hindu nationalism, namely religion-cum-culture, and historical tradition. Shivaji was also held out as a hero for inspiration. Similarly, the Sikhs derived their national inspiration through the memory of Banda and Guru Gobind Singh who sacrificed themselves for the honour of their religion. The Muslims imbibed national feeling even earlier than the Hindus. The great movement Wahabism started in 1820 by Sayyid Ahmad with the object of purifying Islam soon developed into a definite plan to restore the rule of Muslims. The underlying religious theory was that the Muslims must not live in *Dar-ul-harb, i.e.,* a country under a non-Muslim ruler. They must declare *jihad* or holy war against such a ruler, and either establish *Dar-ul-Islam, i.e.,* Muslim rule, or migrate to another country ruled by Muslims.

Numerous Muslims joined the standard of Sayyid Ahmad who declared holy war against the Sikhs and later on the British. He had some success at first against the Sikhs and captured Peshawar. But the Sikh soldiers defeated and killed Sayyid Ahmad at the battle of Balakot in 1831. Though the leader died, the movement survived him for more than thirty years. When the British conquered the Punjab, the Wahabis turned against them and kept up a steady opposition. During the period between 1850 and 1857 the British sent as many as sixteen expeditions against them without much success.

In 1858 again a British force of 5,000 was sent against them. Several more expeditions had to be sent during the next five years. The Wahabis gave a good account of themselves; in 1863 they repulsed a British force with heavy casualties and even captured a British picket. In this desperate situation a fresh British expedition of 9,000 troops was sent. The Wahabis were defeated in several engagements and the confederacy of Pathan tribes organised by them was broken. A series of State trials awarded heavy penalties upon them and thus the movement was finally stamped out of India.

As in the case of the Hindus, so also with the Muslims the basis of nationalism, at least in the early stages as stated above, was a common religion and common historical tradition of past glory and greatness. However, in the context of Indian nationalism it was unfortunate and proved to be suicidal.

## Political Organisation

Nationalism and patriotism are valuable sentiments as they generate a passion for political regeneration leading to the achievement of freedom. But something more is necessary to secure these ends. Having robust faith in the goodwill of the British, it was at first thought that prayers and petitions to the authorities, both in India and England, stating the grievances and suggesting measures of reform were all that was necessary. Petitions signed by prominent citizens were, therefore, sent up for the abolition of the Press Ordinance and the introduction of the Jury system as mentioned above. Somewhat later, such agitation was carried on through articles in newspapers and speeches at public meetings. But gradually the need was felt for establishing political associations for carrying on regular and systematic agitation on a more or less permanent basis. This idea received a great impetus from an event which is of importance from many points of view.

Four Bills were introduced by the Government of India in 1849 with a view to extend the jurisdiction of the East India Company's criminal courts over the British-born subjects who were then subject only to the Supreme Court of Calcutta. The violent agitation of the European community against these 'Black Acts' forced the Government to withdraw them. It gave a great shock to the educated community of Bengal who felt the need of a strong political association, not only to safeguard the interests of India against the organised attacks of the European community, but also to represent Indian views to the Parliament on the eve of the renewal of the Charter of the East India Company in 1853. The result was the amalgamation of two political associations in Bengal into one new association named the British Indian Association.

The British Indian Association was founded on 29 October 1851. From the very beginning it had an all-India outlook. We learn from its first Annual Report that the committee of the Association corresponded with the leading political figures of other provinces. It also noted with satisfaction the establishment of associations of a similar character at Poona, Madras and Bombay. According to the second Annual Report, the Committee of the British Indian Association kept up a friendly correspondence with the Associations of the sister Presidencies.

The Association had great faith in British goodwill and sense of justice, and its Secretary, Debendranath Tagore wrote in the report that "there can be no doubt that, when the real state of things is understood, the British Parliament will not long delay justice to India." Accordingly, in 1852, when the new Charter Act was under consideration, a petition was sent to the Parliament in the name of the British Indian Association and other native inhabitants of the Bengal Presidency, complaining against grievances and praying for relief. It dwelt at great length upon the evils of the union of political or executive power with the legislative, and prayed for the establishment of a legistature, which should "be a body not only distinct from the persons in whom the political and executive powers are vested, but also possessing a popular character so as in some respects to represent the sentiments of the people and to be so looked upon by them." Hence the petitioners desired that "the legislature of British India be placed on the footing of those enjoyed by most of the colonies of Her Majesty." They accordingly proposed the constitution of a Legislative Council, composed of 17 members, including three representatives of the people and one nominated official from each of the Presidencies. It was added that until "the people are considered qualified to exercise their right of electing their own delegates to the Legislative Council, the native members may be nominated by the Governor-General."

Among other prayers in the petition may be mentioned the reduction of the salaries of the higher officers, such as the Governor-General, the members of the Council, the local Governors, Residents, and the principal Covenanted Officers; separation of the functions of Magistrates and Judges, abolition of salt-tax, *abkari* and stamp duties, and the discontinuance of the payment for ecclesiastical establishments.

The British Indian Association, in spite of its advanced views as compared with those of the preceding generation, soon failed to keep pace with the growth of nationalism and the advanced political ideas that followed in its wake, and so the Indian Association was started in 1875 of which the heart and soul was Surendranath Banerjea. It was intended to be the centre of an all-India movement.

Soon after the British Indian Association was founded in Calcutta, Bombay followed suit and the first political association in the Bombay Presidency, named the "The Bombay Association", was inaugurated on 26 August 1852.

A branch of the British Indian Association was established in Madras, but it soon became an independent society under the name Madras Native Association.

All the three Associations had sent petitions to the British Parliament in 1853 criticising the system of administration in India and suggesting remedial measures more or less on the same lines.

This line of policy adopted by the above bodies has been known as that of the Moderate School of politicians whose best representative was Dadabhai Naoroji. His principles may be summed up as follows:

"If the British people were true to themselves, true to their inbred sense and traditions of equality, justice and fair play, they would help India to obtain freedom. The Government of India may be unsympathetic or even hostile, but the real masters are the people of England.... We, Indian people, believe that although John Bull is a little thick-headed, once we can penetrate through his head into his brain that a certain thing is right and proper to be done, you may be quite sure that it will be done."

It seems to us very strange that eminent Moderate leaders in India—men distinguished for their learning and discernment— should have forgotten that history does not show any example of people who have sacrificed their own material interests for the sake of another people. Churchill who understood human character more than our Moderate leaders, never ceased to remind the British people, whenever some kind-hearted or idealistic British statesman pleaded for the case of India, that one-fifth of the British people live in India. The same truth was uttered by an English manufacturer as far back as 1840 when giving evidence before the Parliamentary Committee of Inquiry into the sad plight of the Indian labourers due to unfair treatment by the British. "I certainly pity", said he, "the Indian labourer, but at the same time I have a greater feeling for my own family than for the Indian labourer's family." "This has been the attitude of John Bull from the first and it is not his fault if our Moderate leaders gave them unsolicited testimonials for virtues which they never claimed and then felt surprised that they proved unworthy of them." This fanatic belief in the innate spirit of self-denial of the British public has been the foundation of the constitutional agitation which formed the only politics of the Indians until the rise of the Extremist party in the first decade of the 20th century.

"The great contribution of the Indian Association of Calcutta was to bring the various Indian provinces upon the same common platform (a thing that had not been attempted before), and to unite them through a sense of a common grievance and the inspiration of a common resolve," as Surendranath Banerjea put it. The opportunity was afforded by the Regulation of 1876 which reduced the age-limit of the competitors for the Indian Civil Service Examination from 21 to 19 which was bound to prove a great handicap to many Indian candidates. Surendranath Banerjea was deputed to visit different parts of India to carry on an agitation against this Regulation. But, as he himself put it, "The underlying conception and the true aim and purpose of the Civil Service agitation was the awakening of a spirit of unity and solidarity among the people of India." In 1877 he made a prolonged tour of Upper India as far as Lahore, and next year he made a similar tour in the Presidencies of Madras and Bombay. At all these places he addressed public meetings which endorsed the original resolution passed in Calcutta. The existing political organisation in many places agreed to make a common cause, and in some places he organised new political associations to act in concert with the Indian Association of Calcutta. The foundation for concerted political action in India was thus well and truly laid by Surendranath, whose grateful countrymen recognised his services by giving him the epithet of the "Father of Indian Nationalism." The discerning eye of Henry Cotton, a member of the I.C.S., destined one day to achieve high distinctions, remarked: "The Bengali Babus now rule public opinion from Peshawar to Chittagong...during the past year the tour of a Bangalee lecturer... assumed the character of a triumphal progress and at the present moment the name of Surendranath Banerjea excites as much enthusiasm among the rising generation of Multan as in Dacca." The Indian Association took similar advantage of two other obnoxious measures of the Government, namely, the Vernacular Press Act, intended to muzzle the newspapers in Indian languages which spread the message of nationalism and the newly awakened sense of political consciousness, and the Arms Act restricting the possession of arms by Indians passed in 1876.

Two events in 1883 gave fresh stimulus to the political consciousness of the people. The first of these was a Bill introduced by Mr. Ilbert, Law Member of the Viceroy's Council, and generally known as the Ilbert Bill. The European British subjects could not be tried in criminal cases by any Indian Judge and the Bill sought to remove this galling and glaring instance of racial inequality. As mentioned above a similar attempt in 1849 failed owing to the opposition of the Britishers in India to what they called the "Black Acts". Similar violent agitation, but far more intense and rowdy in character, was carried on in 1883 against the Ilbert Bill by the Englishmen in India who organised a Defence Association with branches all over India for this purpose. The Government yielded and the Bill was so mutilated as to serve no useful purpose.

The Indian politicians learnt from the success of the Englishmen the value of organisation in political struggle. They also became conscious, more than ever before, of the ignoble status of Indians in their own country.

Immediately after the Ilbert Bill agitation occurred another sensational event, the imprisonment of Surendranath Banerjea for contempt of court. It evoked sympathy and protest throughout India and even a Kashmiri Pandit, ignorant of English, burst into tears when he heard the news.

The proverb that good cometh out of evil was fully illustrated when these events of 1883 brought to the forefront the desirability of a political organisation of an all-India character. The Indian Association, Calcutta, took the lead and a National Conference was held in Calcutta on 28, 29, and 30 December 1883.

The Conference, which met in the Albert Hall on 28 December 1883, was attended by more than a hundred delegates, both Hindu and Muslim, and the places they represented, outside Bengal, included Bombay, Madras, Lahore, Allahabad, Delhi, Cuttack, Jabalpur, Nagpur, Ahmedabad, Bankipur, Muzaffarpur, Darbhanga, Deoghar, Sagor, Bhagalpur, Meerut, Tejpur, Hossainpur, etc.

The proceedings began with a national hymn. The questions that were taken up for discussion included industrial and technical education, the wider employment of Indians in the Civil Service, separation of the judicial from the executive functions, representative government, National Fund and Arms Act.

The second session of the National Conference was held in Calcutta in 1885 on 25, 26, and 27 December. It was more representative than the first, being joined by the British Indian Association, representing the landed aristocracy which had kept aloof from the first session. More than thirty political Associations, mostly of northern India, sent their representatives to the Conference.

Surendranath moved the first resolution on the reconstitution of Legislative Councils in such a way that popular opinion might be reflected in it. Among other subjects which were discussed may be mentioned the Arms Act, the Civil Service question, the separation of the judicial and executive functions, and the curtailment of expenditure, mainly under three heads, viz., annual military expenditure, the 'home charges', and the enormous cost of civil administration. In short, almost all the questions that formed the chief planks in the Congress platform during the first twenty years of its existence were discussed in the two sessions of the National Conference.

The Indian Association wanted to give a permanent character to the Conference. Accordingly, Surendranath moved "that a conference of delegates from different parts of the country should be held next year." The delegates from Allahabad and Meerut lent their support to the resolution. The latter suggested that the venue of the Conference should be changed every year and it should meet in places like Bombay, Madras, Allahabad and other great capitals of India. This resolution was carried with acclamation.

At the conclusion of the proceedings of the National Conference, a telegram to the following effect was sent to the political conference about to be held at Bombay. "The delegates in conference assembled in Calcutta desire to express their deep sympathy with the approaching conference in Bombay."

This Conference was the Indian National Congress with which the National Conference merged and thenceforth the Indian National Congress became the true representative of Indian political views. The National Conference deserves the credit for giving the first concrete example of an all-India political movement and marks the culmination of the political evolution in Bengal for half a century.

A mystery hangs over the genesis of the Indian National Congress, particularly, if we remember that news of this organisation was not communicated to the National Conference until at the very last moment when Surendranath Banerjea was invited to attend it. He however, expressed his inability to do so in view of the impending session of the National Conference.

Allan Octavian Hume, a member of the I.C.S., is generally credited with the foundation of the Congress. His biographer, Wedderburn, another I.C.S. officer, states that the reactionary measure of Lord Lytton "brought India within measurable distance of a revolutionary outbreak, and it was only in time that Mr Hume and his Indian advisers were inspired to intervene." So Hume organised the Indian National Congress, as he observed, as a "safety-valve for the escape of great and growing forces, generated by our own action, was urgently needed, and no more efficacious safety-valve than our Congress movement could possibly be devised."

The first session of the Indian National Congress was held in Bombay on 28 December, 1885, attended by 72 delegates, representative of the different regions. W.C. Bonnerjee, a leading Barrister of Calcutta, presided and nine resolutions were passed demanding, among other things, a larger number of elected members of the Supreme Local Legislative Councils, reduction of military expenditure and its equitable apportionment between England and India, introduction of Simultaneous Public Service Examinations in England and India and the raising of the age of candidates.

The second session of the Congress was held in Calcutta and Hume secured in advance the full support of Surendranath Banerjea which led to the suspension of the National Conference as mentioned above. This session marked a distinct advance over the first as the delegates were elected of whom 434 actually registered their names and presented credentials. Another innovation was the admission of the public. A distinct change in the tone and spirit of the Congress was noted in the Calcutta session and the general feeling was that the Congress only echoed the voice of Bengal. This was highly irritable to both Englishmen and the Indian Muslim leader, Syed Ahmad Khan of Aligarh. The latter actually dissuaded the Muslims from joining the third session of the Congress on the ground that the satisfaction of its demands would lead to Bengali rule. Unfortunately this left a permanent effect. If we leave aside the Lucknow session of 1899 where a large number of Muslim delegates attended their attendance during the first ten years was 10 per cent, in the second ten years, 4.8 per cent, and the next ten years, ending in 1915 with only 2.4 per cent.

Year after year, the Congress met for three days in different cities by rotation, and passed a number of resolutions, protesting against the abuses and reforms in the various branches of administration. These included the separation of the executive and judicial functions (passed ten times between 1886 and 1906), trial by jury, reduction of sale-tax and income-tax, extension of the Permanent Settlement, etc.

The only tangible success of the agitation carried on by the Congress during the first twenty years was the Indian Councils

Act of 1892 which provided for the nomination of non-official members to the Governor-General's Council as well as in the Provincial Councils, with very limited powers, and it fell far short of popular demands. But the principle of separate representation for the Muslims was adopted in the Act. This was indicative of the policy of divide-and-rule thenceforth systematically adopted by the British Government in Indian administration. The Viceroy, Lord Dufferin, went out of his way to remind the Muslims that "fifty millions of men are themselves a nation and a very powerful nation." The Secretary of State for India, Lord Salisbury, said in a public speech that "it would be impossible for England to hand over the Indian Muslims to the tender mercies of hostile numerical majority." The seeds of Pakistan were thus sown more than half a century before it was actually born.

Before the Indian National Congress completed twenty years of its existence, a new party arose with a different ideology and method of work. This party was led by Tilak, Aurobindo Ghose, Bipin Chandra Pal, Lajpat Rai and others. They disapproved of the mendicant policy for securing reforms and decided upon a bold assertion of the rights with the strength of the mass of people. Before any exact plan or programme could be devised by the new party, the whole political atmosphere was changed by the Partition of Bengal in 1905, followed by the *Swadeshi* and Boycott Movement. The nationalists at last found the opportunity for which they had been waiting so long—an immediate and concrete cause to fight for.

It is not possible here to describe in detail the twin movements generally known as *Swadeshi* and Boycott. In 1905 Lord Curzon partitioned the Province of Bengal into two parts. The Bengalis felt that their future was at stake and that it was a deliberate blow aimed at the growing solidarity and self-consciousness of the Bengali people. They tried to avert this vivisection by all lawful means. Never before in the history of British India, was any measure of the Government opposed so vehemently or persistently or with such unanimity.

Between December 1903 and October 1905, more than 3,000 public meetings were held, the attendance in each varying from 500 to 50,000. The political associations and newspapers launched a campaign raging against the measure, and a representation signed by about 70,000 people was submitted to the Secretary of

State for India. Even the *Statesman,* the English daily of
Calcutta, observed that there never was a time in the history of
British India when public feeling and public opinion were so
little regarded by the supreme Government as they were by the
present administration.

Indeed, it may be said that Curzon's obstinate refusal to pay
any heed to the popular view in this matter sounded the death-
knell to the method of constitutional agitation. For the first
time, the leaders of Bengal, of all classes and creeds, and all
shades of public opinion, including Rajas and Zamindars, decided
to stand firmly by the side of the nationalist section of the
political leaders. What prayers and petitions failed to achieve,
they decided to force the Government to concede by boycotting
British goods, specially Manchester cloth, until the partition
order was withdrawn. Hundreds of public meetings were held
all over Bengal to pass the resolution for boycotting British
goods. At last there was a mammoth gathering on 7 August
1905, in which, amid unprecedented scenes of enthusiasm, the
resolution of boycotting British manufactures was formally
moved and passed with deafening shouts of *vande mataram*
which had now become the war-cry against British imperialists.

This meeting emphasised the need for promoting the
manufacture of *swadeshi* or indigenous goods. It was pointed
out that 'boycott' and '*swadeshi*' were supplementary. The
boycott of foreign goods required that their place should be
taken by goods produced in India. But this was not possible
unless people deliberately eschewed foreign goods and purchased
indigenous products, even at a sacrifice of money and comfort.

But these economic calculations soon ceased to have any
meaning. Both boycott and *swadeshi* shortly outgrew their
original meaning and object. The idea of economic boycott as a
weapon to coerce the British to undo the partition of Bengal
gradually receded into the background. It developed into an
idea of non-cooperation with the British in every field with the
object of securing freedom for India.

The first issue of the *Vande Mataram,* a daily edited by
Aurobindo Ghose, appeared on 6 August 1906, with his famous
call for "Absolute autonomy, free from British control" and a
detailed programme of what he called 'non-cooperation' and
'passive resistance', to which reference will be made later.

Henceforth, this formed the chief plank on the platform of the nationalists. A local grievance merged itself into the common grievance of India's bondage, and the temporary weapon devised to remedy the former became a potent instrument of fighting freedom battle.

Due to the growing strength of nationalist sentiments, the *swadeshi* movement had spread from Bengal to other parts of India. According to confidential reports of the Intelligence Branch of the Government, the "Boycott-Swadeshi movement assumed an all-India character even towards the end of 1905. The progress of the movement was reported from 23 districts in U.P., 15 towns in C.P., 24 towns in the Bombay Presidency, 20 districts in the Punjab and 13 districts in the Madras Presidency."

As in Bengal, so in this extended area, the purely economic aspect of the movement was superseded by the new meaning and significance attached to it by Aurobindo. It attained a much more comprehensive character and became a concrete symbol of nationalism. Surendranath hoped that "the *swadeshi* would bring the masses and the classes together in our political agitation which would thereby acquire a formidable force." Gokhale observed in 1907: "I have said more than once, but I think the idea bears repetition, that Swadeshism at its highest is not merely an industrial movement, but that it affects the whole life of the nation, that Swadeshism at its highest is a deep, passionate, fervent, all embracing love of the motherland, and that this love seeks to show itself, not in one sphere of activity only, but in all; it involves the whole man and it will not rest until it has raised the whole man. My own personal conviction is that in this movement we shall ultimately find the true salvation of India."

Mohandas Karamchand Gandhi, then a little known figure, observed in 1908, that "the real awakening (of India) took place after partition of Bengal;" he was also shrewd enough to prophesy that "that day may be considered to be the day of the partition of British Empire." He also realised the wider significance of the agitation in securing the repeal of the Partition. "The demand for the abrogation of the Partition is tantamount to a demand for Home Rule," he said. "As time passes, the nation is being forged.... . Hitherto we have considered that for redress of grievances we must approach the throne and if we get no redress, we must sit still, except that we may still petition. After the Partition, people saw that they must be capable of suffering. This new spirit must be considered to be the chief result of the Partition." He explained the characteristics of the new spirit as the shedding of the fear of the British or of imprisonment, and the inauguration of the Swadeshi Movement.

But the Moderates as a party fought shy of the idea of boycott though they welcomed *swadeshi*. Even Gokhale argued that 'boycott' had a sinister meaning—it implied a vindictive desire to injure another. He, therefore, recommended that we would do well to use only the word *swadeshi* to describe our present movement. But this typical attitude of the Moderate Party ignored the historical fact that the boycott was deliberately adopted by the Bengalis to injure British interests, and that the twin ideas of *swadeshi* and boycott, as explained above, were supplementary to each other, as one could not succeed without the other. It was the difference on this point that led to the final clash between the two wings of the Congress known at the time as the Moderate and the Extremist. The two, however, differed on fundamental points. The Extremists were really the product of the new spirit of nationalism that swept the country, but it was by the impact of the *swadeshi* movement that they emerged as a major political party in the country with a distinct ideology and programme.

The fundamental differences in ideology led to differences in the essential features of the political programme of the two parties. These differences centred round two main points, namely, the political goal and the method to achieve it. As regards the goal, Tilak summed up his idea in one sentence: "Swaraj is my birthright and I will have it". The Extremists interpreted *swaraj* to mean complete autonomy without any dependence on the British rule. Aurobindo said, "There are some who fear to use the word freedom, but I always used the word because it has been the *mantra* of my life to aspire towards the freedom of my nation." But Gokhale, the most gifted and eminent member of the Moderate Party said, "Only mad men outside lunatic asylums could think or talk of independence.... We owe it to the best interests of the country to resist the propaganda with all our energy and all our resources...there is no alternative to British rule, nor only now, but for a long time to come, and any attempts to disturb it, directly or indirectly, are bound to recoil on our own heads." That an astute politician like Gokhale, whose patriotism nobody can possibly doubt, should entertain such views, merely proves how deep-rooted they were in the philosophy of the Moderate Party.

As regards the method, the Extremists rejected petitioning as mad and fantastic, and prescribed organised passive resistance as the only effective means by which the control of national life could be wrested from the grip of an alien bureaucracy. A draft resolution on passive resistance was published in the *Vande Mataram*, the great organ of the Extremist Party, edited by Aurobindo. It recommended boycott of British goods, British courts of justice, and schools aided and controlled by the government and refusal to go to the executive authorities for help, advice or protection. The programme was further explained, by Aurobindo in "An open Letter to My Countrymen", dated 31 July 1909: "Our methods are those self-help and passive resistance. Just as 'No representation, no taxation' was the watchword of American constitutional agitation in the eighteenth century, so 'No control, no co-operation' should be the watchword of our lawful agitation—for constitution we have none—in the twentieth century. We sum up this refusal of co-operation in the convenient word 'Boycott', refusal of co-operation in the industrial exploitation of our country, in education, in government, in judicial administration, in the details of official intercourse."

Throughout the year 1906 there were angry discussions and mutual recriminations between the Moderates and the Extremists over their respective policies and programmes. The Congress met in Calcutta in December 1906, in a tense atmosphere. Bengal being the strong citadel of the Extremist Party, they scored at least a partial victory in 1906. The Congress passed three resolutions, supporting boycott, *swadeshi* and national education. By adopting them the Indian National Congress identified itself with the boycott and *swadeshi* movement of Bengal and incorporated the Extremist Party's programme within its own. This was not liked by many Moderates, and heated controversies between the two parties continued throughout the year 1907. The controversy gave rise to the fear in the minds of the Extremists that the three resolutions passed in Calcutta would be omitted or whittled down by the Moderates at the next session of the Congress. This fear was enhanced

when the venue of the Congress was shifted from Nagpur, a
stronghold of the Extremists, to Surat where Pherozeshah
Mehta, the Moderate leader, had a large following. It is not
necessary to describe at length the fracas that broke up the
Congress meeting at Surat. It is certain, however, that Tilak, on
behalf of the Extremist Party, repeatedly declared in private
conversation as well as in public, that if assurances were given
that the three resolutions passed in Calcutta in 1906 would
again be accepted at Surat, he would not create any trouble. It
is a fact that no such assurances were forthcoming, and the
excuse offered for this serious lapse was unconvincing. The
result was that a free fight took place in the Congress *pandal,*
the police were called in, and the Moderate leaders, by adopting
a new Constitution, excluded the Extremists from the Congress.

# 8

# The Era of Administrative Reforms

The split in the Congress at Surat was followed by a series of important events. The first was the grant of reforms in Indian administration by the Indian Councils Act of 1909. It increased the number of non-official members to the Imperial and Provincial Legislative Councils and provided for the appointment of an Indian as member of the Viceroy's Executive Council as well as in the Indian Council, advisory body to the Secretary of State for India in England. The Reforms of 1909 for sometime dazzled the Moderates. But their joy was shortlived. As soon as the Regulations with provision for separate communal electorate were published, the Moderates were disillusioned. For nine years after the Surat fracas, the Moderates ruled over the Congress in splendid isolation with their old ideals and programme. But the country had lost faith in them, and the Congress had very little following. The Congress held its annual session as usual but the spring had gone out of the year.

The second great event was the birth of a secret revolutionary party which sought to terrorise the government as well as rouse the sleeping masses from political stupor by murdering officials, committing dacoities for money to get arms and making bombs for an ultimate armed revolt against the British. It was first revealed by the finding of arms in a garden near Calcutta in 1908 and the case instituted by the government against Aurobindo and a number of young men. Aurobindo was acquitted, but many were transported to the Andamans and sentenced to various terms of imprisonment. Since then this secret revolutionary conspiracy became a regular feature of Indian politics. It gradually spread all over India, the important centres being Bengal, Maharashtra and the Punjab.

The third was the Home Rule Movement. Tilak was sent to jail in 1908 and, Aurobindo having retired from politics took to a spiritual life in Pondicherry. The Extremist Party, therefore, ceased to play an important part in politics. Tilak after his release in 1914 became the uncrowned king of Indian politics, and though the Moderates and the Extremists were once more united in 1916, it proved to be unsuitable for realising national aspirations. Hence Tilak and Mrs Annie Besant started the Home Rule Movement. *Swaraj* or independence became the war-cry of the Movement carried on separately by the two leaders on the basis of a plan jointly settled by them. Tilak made a direct appeal to the people in a language easily understood by them, and ushered in a mass movement of incalculable potentiality. A nationalist India had grown out of the ashes of the old policy of mendicancy, and the dream of the Nationalists or socalled Extremists was realised. Fear seized not merely the Moderates but also the British Government.

The fourth great event was the outbreak of the First World War in 1914 in which Indian soldiers rendered valuable services in various theatres of war in Europe, Africa and Asia and the British Government at Home promised a substantial measure of self-government to India.

In pursuance of this promise the following historic declaration was made in the House of Commons by E.S. Montagu, the Secretary of State for India on 20 August 1917, that "the policy of the British Government is that of the increasing association of Indians in every branch of administration and the gradual development of self-governing institutions with a view to the progressive realisation of Responsible Government in India as the integral part of the British Empire."

This was given effect to by the Government of India Act, 1919, the main provisions of which are noted as follow:

**Central Government**: The Government of India was composed of the Viceroy and Governor-General, his Executive Council, and two legislative bodies, known as the Legislative

Assembly and the Council of States. The Executive Council contained two or three Indian members. The non-official members were in a majority in both the Legislative Chambers, and the majority of members in the Legislative Assembly were elected by the people.

**Provincial Government**: Each province was placed under a Governor and had a Legislative Council, 70 per cent of whose members were elected by the people. The Governor had an Executive Council consisting of 2 to 4 members, half of whom were Indians, and 2 to 3 ministers chosen from amongst the elected members of the Legislative Council. The different departments of Government were divided into two classes— 'Reserved' and 'Transferred'. The Reserved departments such as the Police, Judicature, Irrigation and General Administration were administered by the members of the Executive Council while the Transferred Departments, such as Education, Sanitation, Local Self-government, Excise, Public Works Departments, etc., were in the hands of the ministers.

**Rawlatt Act:** Unfortunately the Government of India Act did not produce the result which was expected from it by way of pacifying the country. This was mainly due to the enactment of a repressive legislative measure by Lord Chelmsford's Government, popularly known as the Rowlatt Act in March, 1919. It gave rise to a serious agitation led by Mahatma Gandhi. Serious popular outbreaks followed, especially in the Punjab, and in one case deplorable loss of lives occurred, when a meeting, at Jallianwala Bagh in Amritsar, held in defiance of the Government order was forcibly dispersed by soldiers. General Dyer fired many rounds on the unarmed people assembled in a small compound with only a single narrow exit, as a result of which 379 were killed and 1,200 injured. As a consequence, a large section of the people became alienated from the government and poet Rabindranath gave up his knighthood in protest.

# 9

# Mahatma Gandhi

The Extremist party in the Congress opposed the proposed reforms on the ground that they would not vest any real power and responsibility in the Indians. A special session of the Congress was held in Bombay on 29 August 1918, to consider the question, but the veteran leaders headed by Surendranath Banerjea, refused to attend the session. They boycotted the Congress and sometime later started a new political organisation named Indian Liberal Federation. When the reforms were discussed by the Congress in its annual session in December, 1919, a party headed by Deshbandhu Chittaranjan Das proposed to boycott the reforms. Mahatma Gandhi suggested that although the reforms were very unsatisfactory and fell far short of the Congress demands, they should be given a trial. This proposal was ultimately accepted.

But Mahatma Gandhi soon changed his mind. About this time, the Muslims in India were disaffected against the British on account of the defeat of the Khalifa, i.e., Sultan of Turkey, in World War I. The Turkish Empire was destroyed, and it was suspected that this was mainly the work of the British. The Muslims, under the leadership of Maulana Muhammad Ali and Shaukat Ali, started an agitation against the British, and Mahatma Gandhi also joined them. This is known as the Khilafat agitation. The Hindus were also greatly irritated by the Rowlatt Act, the Jallianwala Bagh massacre and various other respective measures. There was general excitement and a strong national feeling was roused among the masses. Within the first six months of 1920, there were about 200 strikes involving about one and a half million labourers. Perhaps all these conditions combined to bring about the change in the attitude of Mahatma Gandhi.

In September 1920, a special session of the Congress was held in Calcutta when Mahatma Gandhi enunciated his famous doctrine of "Non-violent Non-cooperation'. According to this policy the Indians would boycott the British Government in all possible ways, in particular by surrendering government titles, boycotting the new legislative assemblies, giving up the legal profession of lawyer, refusing to take their suits to law courts, boycotting government schools and college, and ultimately refusing to pay taxes. On the other hand, everyone should use the spinning wheel and weave *khaddar*. By another resolution the Congress declared that its aim and object was *swaraj* or self-rule, to be attained by peaceful and legitimate means within the British Empire, if possible, and without, if necessary.

This new policy, accepted by the Congress, was received with enthusiasm by the whole country and a mass movement on a large scale was started in 1920-21. So long the national feeling evoked by the Congress was confined to the middle class educated community, but now it spread among the masses. When the Legislative Assemblies were elected according to the new rules, only a few Moderates offered themselves as candidates for membership, and two-thirds of the voters did not register their votes. Many students left Government institutions and several lawyers, including C.R. Das and Motilal Nehru, gave up their practice. Each of these leaders earned about fifteen to twenty thousand rupees a month, but they gave up this princely income and cheerfully accepted not only poverty but also prison life. Their example inspired the country with patriotism and a spirit of sacrifice.

This countrywide agitation was sought to be repressed by the government by severe measures. Most of the eminent leaders were imprisoned, processions were broken up by police by means of *lathi* charge, and batch of volunteers were arrested. About 30,000 were imprisoned, but even this did not diminish in any way the enthusiasm of the people. Both the prison and the *lathi* charge lost their terror and the people were determined to achieve independence at any cost.

In the annual session of the Congress held in December, 1921, it was decided to start "Civil Disobedience Movement" under Mahatma Gandhi. It meant that either individuals or groups of persons would deliberately violate the law and court imprisonment.

There was great enthusiasm all over the country, and the proposal came from various quarters to stop the payment of taxes. But Mahatma Gandhi decided to start the movement at first only in Bardoli, a small taluk in Gujarat. Gandhiji wrote to the Governor-General that he would begin this movement if the government refused to release political prisoners and revoke the repressive ordinances. But a few days later came the news that an excited mob at Chauri Chaura in the Gorakhpur district in U.P. clashed with the police, with the result that 22 members of the police were killed. Immediately on receipt of this news Gandhiji stopped the Civil Disobedience Movement. Many important leaders strongly protested against this and there was great disappointment all over the country. Thus ended the first mass movement.

Gandhiji then decided that the people should devote themselves to constructive work. Emphasis was laid on spinning and weaving, establishment of national institutions, improvement of the Harijans, introduction of *panchayats* in villages and towns, and the prohibition of drinking.

Soon a section of the Congress proposed to enter the assembly with a view to wrecking the reforms from within by uniform, consistent and continuous obstruction. Gandhiji was at first against the idea, but C. R. Das and Motilal Nehru supported it and formed the Swarajya Party. It was ultimately decided by the Congress that the Swarajya Party would work in the legislative assemblies, whereas the other members of the Congress would devote themselves to constructive work. When the new election was held, a number of Congress members were returned to the legislative assemblies. They created great difficulties in the way of government and also humiliated them in many ways. But, as this did not produce the desired result, it was decided in 1926 to boycott the legislature again.

In 1927 a Parliamentary Commission was appointed under the chairmanship of Sir John Simon, to report on the working of Constitutional Reforms granted in 1919, and to suggest further lines of advance towards the goal of Responsible

Government promised to India. The fact that no Indian member was included in the Commission made it very unpopular in India, and it was boycotted by a large section of Indians, including the Indian National Congress.

At the beginning of 1928 the different political parties in India made a joint effort to frame a Constitution for India. On this occasion, Mr Jinnah, the leader of the Muslims, presented a number of demands on behalf of his community. But these were not accepted by the Congress and this increased the bitterness between the two communities.

The new Constitution framed by the Congress proposed Dominion Status for India, i.e., the form of government which prevails in the British Dominions like Canada and Australia. As this was opposed by many members, it was decided that India would accept the Dominion Status only if it were conceded before 31 December, 1929; otherwise, she would stick to her demand for complete independence, and organise non-violent non-cooperation, non-payment of taxes, etc.

The Simon Commission visited India twice in 1928 and 1929, took evidence and submitted its report in 1930. After the publication of the Simon Commission's report, a Round Table Conference was held in London to devise a suitable constitution for India. The members of the Conference included representatives of the various interests concerned, namely, the British Government of India, the rulers of Indian States, and the different communities and political groups of British India. But the Indian National Congress refused to join it.

As the government did not accept the demands of the Congress for Dominion Status, the Lahore session of the Congress, held in December 1929, reaffirmed complete independence as the object of the Congress. Accordingly, at midnight of December 31, 1929, Pandit Jawaharlal Nehru, the President of the Congress, raised the National Flag of India in Lahore, "Independence" Day was celebrated on 26 January, 1930 and it was decided to hold similar celebrations every year on that day. According to the directions of the Congress, Civil Disobedience campaign was started again under the leadership of Gandhiji on 6 April 1930. Gandhiji started with 78 trusted followers to violate the law by preparing salt at Dandi on the seashore. As in 1921-22, excitement ran high all over India and led to violence. The government took strong measures, but as this did not produce the desired effect,

Lord Irwin, the Viceroy, concluded a written agreement with Gandhiji on 4 March, 1931. By this, Congress agreed to withdraw the Civil Disobedience Movement and join the Round Table Conference. On the other hand, the British Government agreed to release the political prisoners and to revoke the repressive ordinances. Mahatma Gandhi attended the Round Table Conference as the sole representative of the Congress.

As the Round Table Conference did not accept its demands, the Congress decided to resume the Civil Disobedience Movement and the boycott of British goods. Three days later, i.e., on 4 January, 1932, Gandhiji was sent to prison and the government launched a campaign of repression. Before any concrete steps were taken in support of the new movement most of the important leaders and about one lakh of Congress workers were sent to prison. As a result the movement could not be properly organised and was ultimately abandoned by the Congress in 1934.

Shortly after this, a new Act was passed in 1935 by the British Parliament introducing important changes in the system of Indian administration. The more important of these are noted below:

1.  The Executive authority in a Province was to be exercised by the Governor normally with the aid and advice of a Council of Ministers, but if necessary, without it.

2.  The Provincial Legislature consisted of two Chambers, namely the Legislative Council and the Legislative Assembly in some Provinces and only the latter in others. With the exception of a few nominations in the case of the Legislative Council, the members of the two Legislatures were to be elected by the different communities and a few special interests.

3-4. Federal Court for India and a Public Service Commission both for India and each Province were established.

5.  Two new Provinces, viz., Sind and Orissa were created.

# 10

# The Last Decade of British Rule

As a result of the elections held in 1937, on the basis of the Act of 1935, most of the Hindu members elected to the legislature either belonged to the Congress party or were sympathetic to its ideals and programme. But there were not many Muslim members belonging to the Congress party.

When the Congress formed ministers in eight provinces, and refused to take in the Cabinet anyone outside the Congress rank, not only Jinnah but many other Muslim leaders turned against the Congress. This gradually increased the power and prestige of the Muslim League and its leader Jinnah. Jinnah openly declared that Muslims could not expect any justice or fair play from the Congress. Thenceforth, the Congress and the League moved farther and farther apart from each other. The difference that thus arose over the constitution of the Cabinet in 1937 further accentuated the differences between the two communities. The Muslim League openly advocated the idea that Muslim formed a separate nation from the Hindus and that it was impossible for the two to live in the same country.

## Cripps' Mission

The Second World War began in September 1939. When Germany overran nearly the whole of Western Europe including France, the Congress offered more than once to cooperate in war efforts, if the British Government accepted the demand for independence and immediately established a Provisional National Government

at the Centre. The Muslim League, however, refused to join the
Congress in this demand and the Viceroy did not accept it. But,
when the Japanese occupied the Malay Peninsula and Singapore
and rapidly advanced in Burma, the British Government became
anxious for a settlement with the Congress. On March 8, 1942,
the Japanese occupied Rangoon. Three days later, the British
Prime Minister announced in the Parliament that Sir Stafford
Cripps would visit India with a proposal for compromise.

Sir Stafford Cripps promised Dominion Status and Constituent
Assembly after the war. But, as he refused to introduce
immediately any substantial change in the Indian administration,
the Congress refused his proposals. The Muslim League supported
Cripps in this respect, but opposed the proposal of the Constituent
Assembly and the granting of Dominion Status to India. For,
two years before this the Muslim League had endorsed the
demand for Pakistan, i.e. the constitution of an independent
state consisting of those regions where the Muslims formed the
majority of the population. The name Pakistan was formed by
the initial letters of Punjab, Afghan (N.W.F.P.). Kashmir and
Sind and the last part of the world Baluchistan. The idea was
first propounded by Iqbal in his Presidential Address in the
Allahabad session of the Muslim League in December, 1930 and
a young Muslim first made a concrete proposal at the time of the
Round Table Conference, but the Muslim leaders unanimously
rejected the idea of Pakistan and characterised it as 'a student's
scheme', 'chimerical and impracticable.' But when, in 1940, the
proposal of Pakistan was adopted by the League, its leaders
declared they could not accept any settlement which did not
concede Pakistan.

Sir Stafford Cripps proposed that at the beginning the whole
of India will constitute the dominion, but later, any province, if
it so willed, could opt out of it. This undoubtedly held out the
possibility of Pakistan. But as it did not immediately concede
Pakistan, the Muslim League opposed the proposals of Cripps.
The Cripps' Mission ended in failure as the proposals were
rejected both by the Congress and the Muslim League on
different grounds.

**August Movement of 1942**
The Congress then decided to start a mass struggle on the
widest possible scale. A proposal to this effect was accepted on

August 8, 1942, and during the night that followed, the government arrested Gandhi and the other leaders and declared the Congress an illegal organisation. There were, however, violent outbreaks in different parts of the country; in some places the excited populace damaged the railway lines and stations and cut off telegraph and telephone wires. The government put down the revolt with strong hands. About 80,000 persons were sent to prison, 940 were killed and 1,630 wounded through police, or military firings.

As a result of these strong measures, peace was established in 1943, but in the meanwhile a great famine was stalking Bengal.

### Azad Hind Fauj

The formation of Indian National Army in Burma and Singapore was another memorable event in 1943. At the beginning of 1941, the popular leader Subhas Chandra Bose, who was detained in his own house under government surveillance, managed to escape and reached Berlin through Afghanistan and Russia. Hitler received him with honour and cordiality, and agreed to help him in driving away the British from India. At great personal risk he crossed the Atlantic and the Indian Ocean in a submarine and reached Japan in 1943. After formulating plans with the Japanese Government, he went to Singapore. All the Indian soldiers who were prisoners in the hands of Japan were handed over to Bose who came to be styled as Netaji (The Leader). He built up with their help the Indian National Army or the Azad Hind Fauj. At the same time, he inaugurated at Singapore the Government of Free India which was acknowledged by both Germany and Japan. The Indian National Army showed unparalleled bravery in the fight which brought it within the frontier of India. But when Japan was defeated, it was forced to retreat, and ultimately surrendered to the British.

### New British Policy

The Second World War ended in a complete victory of the Allies with the surrender of Japan in September 1945. Shortly before this, as a result of the new elections to the British Parliament, held in July 1945, the Labour Party came to power and Attlee became the Prime Minister in place of Churchill. The new ministry made an earnest effort to solve the Indian problem and as a first step, ordered the reelection of both the Central and Provincial legislatures in India. The new elections were held at the beginning of 1946 with the result that most of the elected Hindu members belonged to the Congress and Muslim members to the Muslim League.

On February 19, the British Government announced that three members of the British Cabinet would visit India to promote the early realisation of full self-government in India. The Cabinet Mission arrived in March and made an attempt to devise a constitution acceptable to both the Congress and the League. But as the two bodies could not come to any agreement, the Mission published its own recommendations on May 16, 1946. According to its proposals, the whole of India would form one Federal Union. The Central Government would deal with Defence, Communication and Foreign Policy, while the other subjects would remain under the jurisdiction of the Provincial Governments. A Constituent Assembly would be formed to draw up the detailed constitution.

**Direct Action of the Muslim League**
The Muslim League at first accepted these proposals but rejected them on account of differences with the Congress regarding the composition of the Viceroy's Executive Council as well as the interpretation of some clauses in the Cabinet Mission Plan. As the Congress accepted the plan, the Viceroy decided to reconstitute his Executive Council with the members of the Congress alone. The Muslim League strongly protested against it and declared that they should resort to 'Direct Action'. On August 16, a number of Muslims in Calcutta suddenly began to loot Hindu shops, burn Hindu houses and kill their inmates. Soon the Hindus retaliated, and for several days Calcutta witnessed loot, murder and arson on a large scale. Some time later, the Muslims attacked some Hindu villages in the district of Noakhali. A number of people were killed and a large number of women received most humiliating treatment. As a reaction action against this, riots broke out in Bihar and U.P. where the Hindus treated the Muslims in a similar manner.

**Constituent Assembly**
In the midst of all these troubles, Jawaharlal Nehru and his colleagues joined the Viceroy's Executive Council on September

2. The Viceroy realised that the real power of administration was gradually passing into the hands of the Congress. A number of representatives of the Muslim League were, therefore, nominated to his Executive Council. Further, the British Government declared that if the Muslim League did not join the Constituent Assembly, its decision would not be binding on those Provinces where the Muslims constituted the majority of the population.

In spite of this, the Constituent Assembly began its session on December 9,1946, and Rajendra Prasad was elected its President. The Muslims, with the exception of two members from the North-West Frontier Province, abstained from the Assembly in a body, and it was, therefore, doubtful how far the decisions of the Assembly would be accepted by the British Government.

At last on February 20, 1947, the British Government publicly declared that the British would quit India not later than June, 1948. Lord Mountbatten was appointed Viceroy to succeed Lord Wavell in order to make arrangements for the peaceful transfer of power from the British to the Indians. The declaration was highly resented by the Muslim League and communal riots broke out in the Punjab and the North-West Frontier Province. The recurrence of these serious communal riots convinced the Hindus of Bengal and the Hindus and Sikhs of the Punjab that it was no longer possible to live with Muslims. They, therefore proposed that these two Provinces should be partitioned.

## Lord Mountbatten

*Announcement of June 3.* Lord Mountbatten took over as the Viceroy on March 24, 1947. After consulting the different political leaders and the British Cabinet, he made his famous announcement on June 3. The main results of this announcement may be summarised as follows:

1. By an act passed in the British Parliament, the administration of India was to be handed over to the Indians with effect from August 15, 1947.
2. Two separate States, with Dominion Status, were established in India, namely, (1) Pakistan, consisting of West Punjab, NWFP, Sind, Baluchistan, and Eastern Bengal including

Sylhet; and (2) the Indian Dominion comprising the rest of the British India.

3. The Indian States were given option to accede to any one of those dominions, and all of them joined one or the other.

4. The Constituent Assemblies were set up to devise the future constitution of these dominions. Pending their decision the administration was to be carried on under the Act of 1935 with suitable readjustments.

5. Both Pakistan and India were given the right to secede from the British Commonwealth, if the Constituent Assembly so decides.

Lord Mountbatten and Quaid-e-Azam Jinnah were appointed Governors-General, respectively of Indian Dominion and Pakistan. Nehru was appointed the Prime Minister of the former and Liaquat Ali Khan of the latter. Neither the British Government nor the British Cabinet were to have any authority over Indian administration, and both the Governors-General and the Provincial Governors were to act according to the advice of their ministers. The new system was brought into operation at midnight on August 14-15, 1947.

# 11

# Retrospect and Review

The momentous events of the 30 years from the historic declaration of Montagu on 20 August 1917, to the inauguration of Indian Independence on 15 August 1947, have been covered briefly. It is, however, necessary to make a few general observations on the current of history flowing so rapidly during this period.

In the first place, the politics of this period was dominated by Mahatma Gandhi, and so naturally, all the credit for the final achievement of Independence is usually given to him. But an unbiased review of historical events does not fully support this view.

Gandhi leapt into fame and became the acknowledge leader of the rejuvenated Congress Party by starting the Non-cooperation Movement in 1921. But it is difficult to maintain that it advanced the cause of Indian independence to a material extent though promises were held out that it would bring independence within a year.

As regards the results of the Non-cooperation Movement, we have the benefit of an exhaustive enquiry by a Committee appointed by the Congress. It admitted that there was only partial success. But one of the most interesting observations of this Committee deserves special notice. It is to the effect that critics who blame Gandhi for the failure of the Movement should remember that such a course was also recommended by Tilak. The Committee might have easily added the name of Aurobindo who published a detailed plan of what he called no-cooperation in almost exactly the lines later followed by Gandhi. The point to be noticed, however, is this: So long as popular opinion was not satisfied with the results of Non-cooperation Movement, the name of Tilak was invoked, as one who was also equally responsible for such a course of action. But in later days, Gandhi's Non-cooperation Movement was given the sole credit for the attainment of independence, and no reference was made to Tilak or Aurobindo, who initiated it.

Pandit Nehru has put in a nutshell the best and most reasonable explanation of the secret of Gandhi's unique leadership. It was not his philosophy or ideals, statemanship or political wisdom and acumen, but his magnetic personality that attracted the individual and the masses alike.

However, there is no denying the fact that it was the saintliness and personality of Gandhi that made him dominate Indian politics.

The Non-cooperation Movement was formally started in 1921. There is no doubt that it evoked a very wide response all over the country, betokening a gereral mass-awakening, the extent and intensity of which was a revelation both to the people and to the government. But the credit for this cannot go to Gandhi alone. Not even two years had passed since he had seriously entered into Indian politics and emerged as a leader. It is impossible to imagine that during this short period he could convert an inert mass into an active body all over this vast subcontinent. It would be more realistic to say that the ground was prepared by the great national movement including its militant aspect, during the preceding sixteen years. The Swadeshi Movement, which started in Bengal but gradually spread to distant regions, and the Home Rule Movement of Tilak and Besant, based upon mass contact, leavened the common people with a political consciousness unknown before. Gandhi admitted that the Home Rule League workers had prepared the ground in Gujarat, and the same thing was true of other places. Militant nationalism kept alive before the people the ideals of extreme sufferings and supreme self-sacrifice for the cause of the country, which political movements alone could not impart. The cumulative effect of these, and other causes such as the miseries of the people and growing discontent against the government, prepared the ground for a vast mass upsurge such as India never saw before, at least after the outbreak of the 1857 war. No balanced historian would perhaps deny the influence of these predisposing causes, and hold that Gandhi alone, by his precepts and exertions, created this mass awakening all over this great subcontinent in less than two years' time during which he was preoccupied with many political affairs.

On the other hand, it is impossible to minimise the importance of the role played by Gandhi. No one without his personality and saintly character could have inspired the confidence and created the will and enthusiasm which alone could galvanize the masses into action. The saints have always had a profound appeal to the Indian mind. It is to the great credit of Gandhi—perhaps unique in the world's history—that he could exploit the spirit of devotion and complete self-surender—usually reserved for a spiritual *guru*—for political purposes.

The next great movement of Gandhi was the Civil Disobedience Movement which began with great fanfare in 1930 but had a miserable end. Here again, however, Gandhi's march to Dandi must be admired as a grand conception, superbly executed with consummate skill. The Movement called forth unique example of patient suffering on the part of a number of men who followed the instructions of Gandhi to the letter. The memorable salt-raid at Dharasna, of which a vivid picture has been given by an American eye-witness, has an epic grandeur of its own, and shows at its very best what the reverence for Gandhi, the saint, could accomplish. But Gandhi the politician proved a failure in this second campaign, as in the first. It is hard to defend his pact with Irwin on any rational ground. It is harder still to understand why the great Movement, which was declared by Gandhi himself to be a fight to the finish, was suddenly abandoned for the sake of the comparatively minor issue of separate electorate for depressed classes. Nehru echoed the voice of the country when he said: "I felt annoyed with him (Gandhi) for choosing a side-issue for the final sacrifice... . After so much sacrifice and brave endeavour, was our movement to tail off into something insignificant? I felt angry with him at his religious and sentimental approach to a political question and his frequent references to God in connection with it."

The Quit India Movement of 1942 was the last and undoubtedly the bitterest fight for freedom waged by Gandhi against the British in India. It surpassed all the earlier movements in dimensions and intensity. It is true that Gandhi disclaimed all responsibility for the violent outbreak in 1942 but there is no denying the fact that he was the leader of this last struggle for India's freedom. This movement marks the end of Gandhian era. It was clear to discerning eyes that Gandhi's policy of non-violence, non-cooperation had outlived its utility for the achievement of independence and was no longer popular with the Indian nationalists who were convinced that more radical and revolutionary methods were needed in the changed circumstances to achieve their goal. Even Sardar Patel, a firm believer in non-violence and a devoted disciple of Gandhi, approved of the revolutionary methods adopted by the people after the arrest of their leaders. In this context, it will be interesting to assess the result of the earlier two non-violent campaigns launched by Gandhi and the contribution they made to India's struggle for freedom.

What was the net result of these campaigns? It is impossible to describe them here in detail, but reference should be made to two great contributions that they made to India's struggle for freedom. In the first place, the Congress Movement had become a real mass movement, and national awakening had extended to the people at large. Secondly, the Congress was turned into a genuine revolutionary organisation.

During the First World War the Indian revolutionaries sought to take advantage of German help in the shape of arms and ammunition to free the country by armed revolt. During the Second World War Subhas Chandra Bose followed the same method and created the INA. The battle for India's freedom was also being fought against British, though indirectly, by Hitler in Europe and Japan in Asia. None of the three scored any direct success, but few would deny that it was the cumulative effect of all the three that brought freedom to India.

To sum up: the credit for Indian independence must be apportioned between three important factors, namely the saintly personality of Gandhi, which created a great mass movement, the revolutionary movement inside India which culminated in the constitution of the Azad Hind Fauj of Subhas Chandra Bose, and the holocaust in Europe created by Hitler which left England, though victorious, exhausted in resources of men and money. She rightly felt it was no longer possible for her to maintain political control over India in revolt.

# IV
# India Since Independence

# India since Independence

On July 18, 1947, the British Parliament passed the "Indian Independence Bill" and placed it on the Statute Book as "The Indian Independence Act 1947". India, by this Act, was partitioned into two independent Dominions known as 'India' and 'Pakistan'. Both were given the power to frame and adopt any constitution. This Act also brought about certain changes in the status of the executive heads at the Union Government level.

On August 15, 1947, India became an independent Dominion. Lord Mountbatten, the last Viceroy of India, assumed the status of the first Governor-General of the Dominion of India. He was succeeded by C. Rajagopalachari in June 1948. Rajagopalachari remained in office till the first President of the Republic of India was elected on January 26, 1950, when the new Constitution of India was adopted and India became a Republic.

Dr. Rejendra Prasad (1884-1963) became the first President of India. He laid down his office in 1962. The distinguished scholar and philosopher Dr. Sarvepalli Radhakrishnan (1888-1975) succeeded him as the second President of India. In 1967, the well-known educationist, Dr. Zakir Hussain, became the third President. He could not complete his full term. He died in May 1969. V.V. Giri (1894-1980) followed him as the fourth President. After the expiry of Giri's term of office, Fakhruddin Ali Ahmed (1905-1977) assumed the office of the President of India. Due to his untimely death on February 11, 1977, B.D. Jatti, (1912) the Vice-President of India, became the acting President, till N. Sanjiva Reddy (1913) was elected as President. On expiry of his term, Giani Zail Singh (1916) assumed the office of the President of India in 1982 for a term of five years. He retired after completing his tenure on July 24, 1987, and was succeeded by Ramaswamy Venkataraman, who was elected in a three-cornered contest. S.D. Sharma, Governor of Maharashtra, was declared elected Vice-President unopposed on August 21, 1987. A consensus had been reached between Congress (I) and the Opposition about his nomination. President R.Venkataraman retired on July 25, 1992 and was succeeded by Dr. Shankar Dayal Sharma, then Vice-President of India.

In a parliamentary democracy, it is customary that although the President is the executive head, the real executive power rests with the Council of Ministers with the Prime Minister as its head.

Jawaharlal Nehru was elected as the first Prime Minister of India and remained in office till his death in May 1964. Nehru was not only the builder of modern India and architect of India's foreign policy, but he was also the author of the doctrine of "Panchsheel" or philosophy of co-existence of countries with different socio-economic order and the concept of non-alignment. He was succeeded by Lal Bahadur Shastri (1904-1966) for a brief period which was overshadowed by the Indo-Pakistan war of 1965 and its aftermath. He suddenly died of a heart attack in Tashkent (USSR) in January 1966, immediately after signing the Indo-Pakistan agreement for peace in the Indian sub-continent.

After a brief interim arrangement, Indira Gandhi was elected as the Prime Minister of India and continued till the beginning of 1977. During this period, the country was faced with problems, both internal and external, including the 1971 Indo-Pakistan war which eventually led to the creation of Bangladesh. She dealt with all the problems with determination and fortitude and declared emergency in 1975 which made her temporarily unpopular. She lost the elections in 1977. In 1977, when the Janata Party came to power, Morarji Desai (b. 1896) became the Prime Minister of India. He was in office till the middle of 1979 when he was replaced by Charan Singh (1902-1985) as Prime Minister for a brief period till the 1980 elections. In 1980 with the overwhelming victory of the Congress (I), Indira Gandhi came back as the Prime Minister of India. She was assassinated on the lawns of her residence by two of her security guards on October 31, 1984. Her forty-year old surviving son Rajiv Gandhi was sworn in as Prime Minister. He was the youngest Prime Minister of the country. After the completion of his tenure in 1989, he was succeeded by V.P. Singh of the Janata

Dal which came into power on December 2, 1989 with the outside support of Bharatiya Janata Party (BJP) and Leftist Parties. V.P. Singh resigned on November 8, 1990 after having lost a vote of confidence and was succeeded by Chandra Shekhar. This minority Government also resigned on March 13, 1991 and fresh elections were ordered by the President.

Rajiv Gandhi, Congress (I) leader was assassinated by a woman wearing a 'Belt Bomb' at Sriperumbudur in Tamil Nadu on May 21, 1991 during, election campaign. P.V. Narasimha Rao, being the leader of the largest Congress Party was sworn in as Prime Minister by the President R. Venkataraman after elections on June 21, 1992.

## Unification of India

Immediately after her independence in August 1947, India was faced with many difficult problems—unprecedented influx of refugees accompanied by large-scale killings on both sides of the frontier between the two Dominions. By November 1947, about 8 million refugees had crossed the frontior. However, with dedication and determination the Government of India was able to bring the situation under control by December 1947, and could divert its attention to other pressing problems, the most important being the unification of the country.

The Indian Independence Act 1947 ended all treaties made by the British government with the Princely States numbering about 562, covering half of the total area of the country and one-quarter of its population. The integration of these princely states with the Indian Union presented the greatest challenge to the new Government. The task was achieved by the unique combination of the political sagacity and firmness of Sardar Vallabhbhai Patel, and great tenacity of purpose and the power of persuasion of the eminent civil servant V.P. Menon. Lord Mountbatten also played a crucial role in the process. All the states but three, joined the Indian Dominion within seven weeks when the Princes signed the instrument of accession to India.

The Nizam of Hyderabad and the ruler of Travancore entertained the dream of becoming independent rulers after the British had left. The ruler of Kashmir was also harbouring the same thought. The Muslim Nawab of Junagadh, a predominantly Hindu state in Saurashtra, also posed a problem. He announced his intention to join Pakistan, though the State did not accept the position of the ruler which was contrary to the wishes of the people, and was obliged to send its forces. The Nawab fled to Pakistan and the State was merged with India after referendum.

The Prince of Travancore soon realised that his dream of independent Travancore could not be achieved and he acceded to India on the advice of his Dewan, Sir C.P. Ramaswamy Iyer.

The Nizam of Hyderabad which was a predominantly Hindu state, surrounded by India, was determined to stay independent. He tried to suppress the agitation within the state for merger with India, with the help of Razakars, a militant Muslim group. Having failed to persuade him, the Government of India took recourse to police action which resulted in the accession of the state.

The most difficult and complex problem was that of Jammu & Kashmir. Its Hindu ruler with an overwhelming Muslim population signed a standstill agreement with both the dominions but did not decide to which dominion it would accede. His indecisiveness encouraged Pakistan to apply economic and military pressure while India remained indifferent. Meanwhile, tribesmen in the north-west of Pakistan with the support of Pakistan authorities invaded Kashmir and began to march towards its capital Srinagar. The ruler of Kashmir fled to Jammu and approached India after signing the Instrument of Accession of 26 October 1947. The Union Government accepted it as suggested by Lord Mountbatten, the then Governor-General of India, that on a suitable subsequent date the people of the state would be given an opportunity to decide for themselves. The Government of India now tried to liberate the state from the invaders. Pakistan expressed its inability to order the raiders back, which also included regular Pakistani troops in the guise of volunteers. India insisted on total withdrawal of Pakistan troops as a pre-condition for a fair plebiscite. The Government of India now approached the United Nations to vindicate its legitimate claim. Pakistan also complained to the United Nations that Kashmir's accession to India has been achieved by fraud. The U.N. brought about a cease-fire on 1 January 1948 and its observers were posted on the cease-fire line which in effect became an international frontier. Jammu & Kashmir was classified as Part B State in view of its special status. However, it became an integral part of the Indian Union after a duly elected representative government of Jammu & Kashmir voted in its favour on 20 June 1957.

The complete unification of the country was achieved when the French and the Portuguese settlements within the geographical boundaries of India were eventually merged in the Indian Union. The French Government held a referendum in its possessions of Chandernagore and Pondicherry which voted for merger with the Indian Union. The *de facto* transfer of the territories took place on 1 November 1954. The Portuguese Government did not agree to hand over Goa, Daman and Diu in spite of the agitation of the local people who suffered untold miseries. The Government of India could not remain a silent spectator for long and moved its forces into Goa on 18 December 1961. By an amendment of the Constitution, Goa, Daman, and Diu became Union Territories. However, the socio-cultural milieu has been preserved both in the old French and Portuguese territories.

**Reorganisation of States**
Although the Linguistic Provinces Committee, set up in 1948, reported against the creation of provinces on linguistic lines, the position in respect of the State of the Union has, however, been changing ever since under linguistic and other pressures. As a result of the death of Sriramulu, Andhra was recognised as a separate state on linguistic grounds in 1953. An example having been set, the Union Government appointed the States Reorganisation Commission to examine the question of reorganisation of States. On the basis of its report, it was decided, in 1956, that the distinction between Part A and Part B states (with a Rajpramukh as their leader) should be abolished.

The Indian Union then had 14 States in addition to six Centrally administered territories. One State was added in 1960, by splitting Bombay State into two States (Maharashtra and Gujarat). Nagaland was made into a State in 1961 and Haryana in 1966. The year 1971 followed with the recognition of four States, Meghalaya, Manipur, Tripura and Himachal Pradesh. The merger of the Himalayan kingdom of Sikkim in 1975 added another State to the Indian Union. After an accord with Laldenga, the rebel leader, Mizoram was given the status of a state in 1987. That year two more states, Arunachal Pradesh and Goa, were created, raising the total number of states of 25 and of Centrally Administered Territories to 7.

## Conclusion

The story of the accession, integration and reorganisation of the state of the Indian union narrated above makes an important chapter in the history of India. The Union Government was of the opinion that, as people living in compact areas became fit for responsible government, their aspirations should be satisfied by the grant of statehood. The flexible attitude towards the political aspirations of all people living in any part of the country has been responsible for the creation of a well-knit political entity. India's policy to develop the backward regions and uplift the people of those areas was rightly calculated to give them a sense of belonging. Only in that way would she fulfil her destiny to become a great and living democracy.

## Political Parties

Before independence, the Indian National Congress, which fought for the independence of the country, served more as a common platform of various shades of political views than as a homogeneous political party. The other major party, the Muslim League, which was responsible for the division of the country, was established in 1906, exclusively for safeguarding the interests of the Muslim community. To counteract it, the Hindu Mahasabha was founded in 1910. The Communist Party, which took its shape in 1924 did not make much headway till 1938. In fact, during World War II it sided with the British Government after Russia had joined the Allies and alienated the sympathies of the people of India. In late 1937, there arose a group of socialists inside the Congress. This group ultimately formed a separate party, the Socialist Party of India.

At the time of independence, the Indian National Congress being the single largest party, the British government handed over the power to it. The Congress had, by and large, a good record of democratic traditions. After the partition, the Muslim League remained a party only in name with hardly any influence. Similarly, the Hindu Mahasabha gradually lost its importance, particularly after the emergence of the Bharatiya Jana Sangh. However, many other political parties came into existence mainly at the regional level. There was a split in the Communist Party after the hostility between China and the USSR came to the surface. The group which supported China came to be known as the Communist Party of India (Marxist) or CPI(M). In the 1977 elections it won the majority of the seats in West Bengal and Tripura and increased its seats in the Parliament.

The First General Elections held in 1952 were contested by the four recognised "All-India Parties". Out of the total seats of 489, as many as 364 were won by the Congress. The Communists secured 16 seats; however 11 candidates also came into the Parliament with their support. The socialists won 12 seats. The rest of the seats were shared by other parties like the Hindu Mahasabha, the Jana Sangh, the Kisan-Mazdoor Praja Party. After the elections, there was an attempt to forge a common party of all those who believed in the principle of democratic socialism, thus the Praja Socialist Party was formed by merging the Socialist Party, the Kisan-Mazdoor Praja Party and the Krishak Party of Andhra. In the Second General Elections, only four parties which had secured at least 3 per cent of the total valid votes were recognised as the National Parties by the Election Commission. These parties were the Indian National Congress, the All-India Bharatiya Jana Sangh, the Communist Party of India and the Praja Socialist Party. There were, however, 19 state parties including the Akali Dal, the Forward Block, etc., which contested the elections. In the Third General Elections in 1962, 16 state parties were recognised which included the newly formed Swatantra Party and the revamped Muslim League. In the Fourth General Elections in 1967, the recognised all-India parties were the Indian National Congress, the Swatantra Party, the Communist Party of India (CPI), the Communist Party of India (Marxist) or CPI (M), the Bharatiya Jana Sangh, the Praja Socialist Party (PSU), and the Republican Party of India.

The Indian National Congress, which served as a common platform in the pre-independence days for all those fighting for the freedom of the country irrespective of their ideologies, became a major national party. There was, therefore constant stress and strain built up in the organisation from the beginning. However, due to the skilful handling of the situation by Jawaharlal Nehru and by his towering personality, the Indian National Congress remained a single party after the attainment of independence. With the death of Nehru, the power struggle came to the surface in 1969, when the Congress Party split into two: (a) Congress (O) and Congress (R). The Republican Party was dropped from the list of all-India parties in the Fifth General Elections.

In 1975, seven national parties emerged, viz., the Indian National Congress, the Congress (O), the Bharatiya Jana Sangh, the Communist Party of India, the Communist Party of India (Marxist), the Socialist Party and the Bharatiya Lok Dal.

When the General Election was announced, the Bharatiya Lok Dal, the Congress (O), the Socialist Party and the Jana Sangh formed an alliance and fought the elections under the name of the Janata Party. The Janata Party won the 1977 elections with an overwhelming majority of seats in the Lok Sabha. After the elections, there was further split in the Congress, which led to the formation of the Congress (Indira) or Congress (I). The Janata Government lasted about two and a half years. The Congress (I) came back to power with a big majority in the mid-term poll in 1980, after the Janata Party splintered into several parties such as the Lok Dal, the Bharatiya Janata Party and the Janata Party. The splitting of the major all-India parties led to the rise of regional parties, some of which captured power at the state level, such as the Telugu Desam in Andhra Pradesh, All-India Anna Dravida Munnetra Kazhagam (AIADMK) in Tamil Nadu, while the National Conference remained in power in Jammu and Kashmir. The Communist Party of India (Marxist) came into power in West Bengal and Tripura, the Janata Party in Karnataka and a Congress (I)-led coalition government was formed in Kerala. In the rest of the states, Congress (I) Governments were formed.

After the death of Sheikh Abdullah, the Chief Minister of Jammu and Kashmir in 1982, his son Farooq Abdullah was sworn in as the Chief Minister of the State. Soon after there was a split in the National Conference leading to the formation of a party known as National Conference (K) known after the name of the President of the Party Begum Khalida Shah, daugher of Sheikh Abdullah. Her husband G.M Shah, who had masterminded the revolt, was also to muster the support of majority of M.L.A.s including those of the Congress (I) members in the Assembly and was sworn in as Chief Minister in July 1983. In 1984, there was also a split in Telugu Desam Party in Andhra Pradesh which led the governor to dismiss the Ministry of N.T. Rama Rao and swear in Bhaskar Rao, leader of the splinter group who was backed by Congress (I) M.L.A.s. But as he was unable to prove his majority on the floor of the House during the stipulated period and there were countrywide demonstrations against the installation of a minority ministry, N.T. Rama Rao was called upon to form the ministry by the new governor, Dr. S.D. Sharma. The Akali agitation created a law-and-order problem in Punjab which led to the promulgation of the President's rule in October 1983. Sikkim too was brought under President's rule after the dismissal of the ministry led by N.B. Bhandari in May 1984. Bhandari has now formed a new party known as Sikkim Sanghram Parishad.

The dissolution of the Sikkim Assembly resulted in fresh elections which again returned to victory Sikkim Sanghram Parishad led by N.B. Bhandari who was sworn in as Chief Minister.

Rajiv Gandhi was able to arrive at an accord with Sant H.S. Longowal, the leader of the dominant moderate Sikh Akali Party. The signing of the accord on June 26, 1985, cleared the decks for elections to the Punjab Assembly in which the Akali Dal won an overwhelming majority of seats and formed a Ministry with Surjit Singh Barnala as Chief Minister. However, due to the inability of the Ministry to meet the terrorists' challenge and deterioration in the law-and-order situation, President's Rule was imposed on the State and the Assembly kept in suspended animation.

In the same strain, Rajiv Gandhi struck a deal with the Assam agitators and hammered a solution which brought peace to the eastern region. The Assam State Assembly elections resulted in an overwhelming majority for the Assam Gana Parishad which formed a government with P.K. Mohanta as Chief Minister.

Rajiv Gandhi as Congress (I) President reached a compromise with Farooq Abdullah, President of the National Conference, J & K State, to fight the State Assembly elections jointly after the dissolution of the Assembly in which the Alliance came out victorious and Farooq Abdullah was sworn in as Chief Minister.

Elections in Andhra Pradesh and Karnataka were held in 1986. The Telugu Desam came to power in the former State with N.T. Rama Rao as Chief Minister and the Janata in the latter with R.K. Hedge as Chief Minister. Subsequently, elections were held in West Bengal, Tripura and Kerala. The C.P.I.(M) came to power in all these states. However, in Kerala it formed a coalition government with certain splinter groups.

Rajiv Gandhi reached an accord with the rebel leader, Laldenga, and elections were held to the Assembly in Mizoram where he formed a ministry in collaboration with the Congress.

In the Haryana State Assembly elections held in June 1987, the Congress (I) was routed and the Lok Dal (B) came out victorious and formed a Government in collaboration with the B.J.P. with Devi Lal as Chief Minister.

On the eve of the Eighth Lok Sabha elections (December 1984), Lok Dal headed by Charan Singh first joined hands with *Bharatiya Janata Party* to first form the National Democratic Alliance (NDA) but later on formed a united front with various other parties and the new party was known as Dalit Kisan Mazdoor Party.

Lok Sabha elections as scheduled were held from December 24 to December 27, 1984. Elections, however, were not held in the 14 Parliamentary constituencies in Assam where the electoral rolls were being revised and 13 in Punjab due to law-and-order situation. Elections to Manipur, Arunachal Pradesh, Goa, Daman and Diu, and Tamil Nadu Assemblies were held along with the Lok Sabha poll. On the advice of the State Cabinets, the Andhra Pradesh Assembly and the Karnataka Assembly were also dissolved but elections to the State Assemblies were held later.

The elections to the Lok Sabha resulted in landslide victory for the Congress (I) Party which won 401 seats out of a total of 508 seats for which the elections were held. General Elections were held in 1989 in which V.P. Singh's Janata Dal with the support of BJP and the National Front comprising CPM, CPI, RSP, Forward Bloc, DMK, TDP, and other splinter groups formed the Government. The Lok Sabha was dissolved in 1991 and fresh elections were ordered by the President. Congress (I) emerged as largest party with 231 members. The strength of the other parties: BJP 119, CPI: 14, CPI(M): 35, AIADMK: 11, Congress (S): 1, TDP: 13 members.

BJP wrested power in the State Assemblies of Uttar Pradesh, Madhya Pradesh, Himachal Pradesh, and Rajasthan where it formed the Ministries, while the Janata Dal secured its majority in Bihar and Orissa, AIADMK in Tamil Nadu and the Congress retained its majority in the rest of the States (excepting Kashmir and Punjab where elections could not be held due to law and order problem), where it formed the Ministries. However, elections were held (1992) in Punjab where Congress came into power.

In December 1992, four BJP-ruled states, viz., M.P., U.P., H.P. and Rajasthan were dismissed by the President in the wake of Ayodhya happenings where fresh elections were held in October-November 1993. Congress came to power in M.P. and H.P. while BJP formed the ministeries in Rajasthan and New Delhi. In U.P. the alliance of Samajvadi Janata Party (SJP) (SP) and Bahujan Samaj Party (BSP) with the help of Congress and other splinter groups formed the ministry.

**Newspaper**

Newspapers play a vital role in moulding public opinion. *The Bengal Gazette, Calcutta Gazette* and *The Calcutta Chronicle* were started in the 1780s. However, it was only in the later part of the nineteenth contury that regular newspapers were started in India. *The Times of India* was founded in 1838 by Robert Knight who also started the *The Statesman*. Some of the leading newspapers such as *The Pioneer* of Allahabad, *The Madras Mail, The Hindu* and *The Amrita Bazar Patrika* were started in the next decade. Among the vernacular papers, B.G. Tilak's *The Kesari* and *The Marahatta* deserve special mention. World War I and the clamour for *swaraj* in India led to the start of several newspapers such as *New India* by Annie Besant, *Young India* by Gandhiji and *Independent* by Motilal Nehru. *The Hindustan Times, The Bombay Chronicle, The Indian Express* and *The National Herald* were also started during this period. The Indian newspapers greatly helped in the struggle for freedom. They awakened the people to their rights and brought to light the evils of foreign rule. They greatly helped in moulding public opinion. Some of them forfeited their securities, their presses were closed down and censorshp imposed during the non-cooperation movements launched by Gandhiji but they bore the brunt of the government repression in their determination to help India achieve her freedom. Their number also rose and on the eve of Independence there were 481 dailies and 2,213 weeklies.

In 1988 there were 2,281 dailies and 78,134 weeklies, 134 tri/bi-weeklies and 15,308 other periodicals. The newspapers in Hindi had the largest circulation of 139.84 lakh copies followed by English with 110.39 lack copies. 179 newspapers had a circulation of more than 50,000 copies.

The four main news agencies, *viz.*, Press Trust of India (PTI), United News of India (UNI), Samachar Bharati and Hindustan Samachar which merged in 1976 to form 'Samachar' started functioning as independent news agencies from 14 April 1978.

The Press Council of India was set up on 1 March 1979 for safeguarding the freedom of the press and for maintaining and improving the standard of newspapers and new agencies in India.

## Constitution

The Indian Constitution which came into force on 26 January 1950 is the most comprehensive document containing 395 articles, 222 parts and 8 schedules. The number of schedules have now risen to ten. There are separate chapters on Fundamental Rights, Directive Principles of State Policy, provisions regarding the welfare of scheduled castes and scheduled tribes and other backward classes, citizenship, relations between Parliament and State Legislatures, Union Judiciary and High Courts and between the Union and States. The Constitution declares India to be a Sovereign Democratic Republic, envisages a parliamentary form of government and confers on all its adult citizens, irrespective of caste, creed or sex, not only the right to vote or choose representatives, but also the right to hold public office.

The structure of the Union Government is shaped on the model of the Canadian Constitution and the Government of India Act of 1935. The principle of Cabinet Government, on the other hand, is borrowed from the British Constitution with such changes as were necessary to suit Indian conditions. The Parliament is bicameral in structure—Rajya Sabha (Upper House) and Lok Sabha (House of People). Executive authority is vested in the President and the Council of Ministers. The President is in fact a constitutional head and the real executive is the Council of Ministers headed by the Prime Minister. The Constitution of India provides for an independent judiciary which is largely free from the interference and influence of the executive. The administration in States which are at present 25, is based on the pattern of the Centre. The executive is headed by the Governor. The real power lies with the Council of Ministers with the Chief Minister as the head. Every state has a legislature which, in some states, is bicameral. In every state there is a High Court with the Chief Justice and a number of judges. The appeals from the High Court can be heard by the Supreme Court.

With the inclusion of Konkani, Manipuri and Nepali in the Eighth Schedule of the Constitution in 1992 the number of recognised languages has risen to 17.

## International Relations

After World War II, two power blocs started emerging in the international sphere, one with the ideology of the free economy under the leadership of the USA and the other with Marxist and Socialist ideology under the leadership of the USSR. The USA and the USSR started growing into the stature of superpowers. Along with this, there started an arms race between the two blocs. India's international relations and foreign policy is to be viewed in the context of global political and social environments.

After attaining independence, India became the largest democracy in the world. As such it has its own responsibility and obligation to fight for a just international order. Therefore, the Constitution of India gave expression to its broad international aims and interests. While defining the "Fundamental Rights", it stated that some of these rights are subject to the security of the state, friendly relations with foreign countries. The Directive Principle of State Policy calls for "just and honourable relations among nations" and the promotion of international peace and security, respect for international law and treaty obligations and settlement of international disputes by arbitration.

On 15 August 1947, when India emerged as an independent nation to fulfil its "tryst with destiny" Nehru, the author of India's foreign policy, explained its objectives which were "the pursuit of peace, not through alignment with any major group or power, but through an independent approach to each controversial or disputed issue, the liberation of subject peoples, the maintenance of freedom, both national and individual, the elimination of racial discrimination and the elimination of want, disease and ignorance, which afflict the greater part of the world's populations." This spirit has always been the guiding principle of India's foreign policy and international relations.

Keeping this principle in view, Nehru gave the new concept of the Commonwealth—a free association of sovereign commonwealth nations—and accepted the British King/Queen as the symbolic head of this free association. From the very beginning he kept India out of the power blocs and started evolving the new policy of "non-alignment" and the philosophy of "Panchsheel"—peaceful co-existence of nations with different ideologies and social orders. This gave birth to the third force in the international politics. Under Indira Gandhi's leadership India was elected as the Chairperson of the Non-Aligned countries. In fact, India's foremost task was to act as an intermediary between the two blocs with two superpowers as leaders to prevent a major war and to ensure peace in the world. India played a major role for preserving international peace, in spite of the localised conflicts and tensions building up from time to time.

India has always desired close relations with her neighbours. Within a few years after independence, she signed friendship treaties with Bhutan, Nepal, Afghanistan, Iran, Iraq and arrived at an agreement within Sri Lanka for solving the problem of Indians settled there. The ethnic conflict in Sri Lanka between the Sinhalese and the Tamilians had added to the strains in India's relations with its island neighbour. Failing to find a military solution to the problems, Sri Lanka's President Jayewardene, agreed to defuse the situation by arriving at a political agreement to which India is also a party. The accord, signed in July 1987, was expected to meet some of the aspirations of the Tamilian militants and, at the same time, ensure the integrity of Sri Lanka. Under the agreement, Indian forces were sent to Sri Lanka at the latter's request to maintain law and order and help in the surrender of arms by the militants. However, the Indian Peace Keeping Force (IPKF) had to be withdrawn after suffering heavy casualties due to the insistence of the late President R. Premadasa.

India helped Indonesia to regain her independence from Dutch rule, and made a distinct contribution towards the freedom of a large number of countries in Asia and Africa including Morocco, Algeria and the Congo. She set up Joint Commissions for Co-operation in economic, scientific and cultural fields with USA, USSR and East European countries. India did not hesitate to send her forces to the Maldives at the request of the legally established Government when a military Coup was attempted.

India has always been eager to have friendly relations with Pakistan in spite of the legacy of the Partition, influx of a large number of refugees and the invasion of Kashmir by Pakistan. She strictly adhered to the terms of the Tashkent Declaration after the war of 1965 and handed over 2,000 sq. kms. of Pakistani territory captured by her forces. But a few years later military dictator Yahya Khan, unable to control the internal discontent due to economic difficulties and the revolt of the people of East Bengal (now Bangladesh), tried to divert their attention by making prolonged attacks. Pakistan raided the Indian airfields in December 1971 without provocation. Within a remarkably short period, the Pakistani army was routed both in the east and western front, and its 93,000 officers and soldiers surrendered to the Indian army in the eastern sector. That also heralded the birth of Bangladesh.

The military victory over Pakistan did not in any way detract India from its commitment to peace in the subcontinent. By signing the Shimla Agreement between Indira Gandhi and Z.A. Bhutto in July 1972, India and Pakistan pledged to restore normal relations and cooperate in cultural, economic and scientific fields. After the Shimla Agreement, India released all the 93,000 Pakistani prisoners of war. Relations with Pakistan showed little improvement. In his election campaign speeches in December 1984, Rajiv Gandhi had observed that while the longstanding Kashmir problem remained, there were serious reservations on three other issues: Pakistani's quest for a nuclear bomb, its acquisition of sophisticated weapons ostensibly to meet the situation caused by the Soviet presence in Afghanistan, and India's complaint that Pakistan was training and aiding secessionists and terrorists in Punjab and Kashmir. With the restoration of democracy in Pakistan and coming into power of Benazir Bhutto as the leader of Pakistan People's Party (PPP) it was hoped that the relation between the two countries would improve and Pakistan would stop aiding the terrorists in Punjab and Kashmir. With this objective in view, India's Prime Minister,

Rajiv Gandhi discussed the matter with Benazir Bhutto during her visit to Islamabad in connection with the SAARC meeting. However, her tenure was short-lived and she was dismissed by the powerful military Junta and in the new elections, Nawaz Sharif became the Prime Minister of Pakistan and the PPP was routed. Nawaz Sharif followed aggresively Zia's policy of giving arms and ammunition and also financial support to secessionists in Jammu and Kashmir and Punjab. Training camps were opened where new recruits were trained in the use of sophisticated weapons and sent across the border. India's new Prime Minister P.V. Narasimha Rao held talks with his counterpart, Nawaz Sharif of Pakistan, on five occasions to normalise relations between the two countries and settle the outstanding issues according to the Shimla Agreement but nothing concrete has come out so far.

India has always tried to maintain friendly relations with China. In fact, since the emergence of the People's Republic of China in 1949, India not only recognised it but also strongly advocated new China's admission to the United Nations as the sole representative of the Chinese people. In spite of India's extending the hand of friendship and close personal relationship between Nehru and Chow Enlai, without any provocation, China occupied Indian territories on 20 October 1962. India was caught unawares and lost a substantial area of its territory to China. Since then, the relations between the two countries remained strained. Only recently are there signs of some reconciliation, and India and China have restored their diplomatic relations at the ambassadorial level. Although Sino-Indian contacts have multiplied since 1976, the border dispute continues to be an obstacle to full normalisation of relations. A new complication that has emerged in the uneasy relationship is the reported Chinese assistance for Pakistan's nuclear programme and Beijing's attempts to increase its influence in Nepal. India's relations with China were further strained in 1987 when the latter occupied a small trip of Indian territory near the north-east border as a protest against India's grant of statehood to Arunachal Pradesh, an internal affair of this country. However, India took the initiative in restoring normal ties by deputing its Foreign Minister to China and accepting the Chinese offer to settle the border dispute by peaceful means. Equally significant is the marked qualitative improvement in ties with China, especially after the visit of the Chinese Premier, Li Peng, to New Delhi as a return visit of Rajiv Gandhi and that of President R. Venkataraman, to Beijing. The degree of mutual confidence attained by the two countries has already enabled them to withdraw one and a half divisions of their armies from the border.

Prime Minister P.V. Narasimha Rao undertook visits to several countries including Germany, China, South Korea, Iran, Oman and United Kingdom during 1993-94. His visit to China was quite fruitful. It was helpful in ensuring peace and tranquillity along the border by reducing the number of the troops on each side, keeping each other informed about military exercises and not to transgress each other's airspace. To give impetus to trade an additional pass Shipla on the border was opened which would become operative in the summer of 1994. Extradition treaties were signed with several countries including U.K. to curb the activities of the militants. Reciprocal visits to India were paid by several Presidents and Prime Ministers including those of Russia, Uzbekistan, United Kingdom, Poland, Bhutan, China, Germany, Israel and several other countries. Diplomatic relations were established with Israel and South Africa for the first time.

Narasimha Rao also visited Germany and Japan to impress the Government and industrialists to come forward to invest in India in view of liberalisation of economic policy but results have not been very encouraging. Narasimha Rao also attended the NAM Conference at Jakarta and suggested the enlargement of the Security Council and setting up of a Planet Protection Environmental Fund. He also undertook a trip of France in October 1992 for mutual cooperation in the fields of science and technology and invited French industrialists to invest in India. Another important development was the signing of the first-ever Extradition Treaty by India's Home Minister S.B. Chavan with his counterpart in United Kingdom in October 1992.

As regards superpowers, India has always had very cordial and friendly relations with the USSR which has always stood by India in its time of crisis. In 1971, President Nixon's partisan attitude during the Indo-Pakistan war and the sending of a task force of the US Seventh Fleet into the Indian Ocean to assist Pakistan in boosting its morale, brought India closer to Russia with whom she signed the Treaty of Friendship in 1971. Both the countries have signed a number of long-term agreements on economic and technical collaboration.

Soon after taking over as Prime Minister, Rajiv Gandhi paid a visit to the Soviet Union in March 1985 to attend the funeral of the Soviet leader, Konstin Cherenko, and followed it up with an official visit in May 1985. He endorsed the USSR worldview and signed an agreement for Soviet participation in various Indian projects during the next 15 years which involved an amount equivalent to 1.3 billion dollars. His visits to Moscow and Gorbachev's return visit to India further strengthened Indo-Soviet relations. Long-term treaties of friendship and cooperation in various fields were signed. Russia reiterated its wholehearted support to India during Rajiv Gandhi's visit to the USSR in 1987 and the opening of the Cultural Festival of India. India maintained her close relations with its traditionally, the USSR, and the treaty of peace, friendship and cooperation was extended for 20 years. However, the disintegration of USSR into several independent states has completely changed the political map of the world.

Like many other countries, India too was caught off-guard by the sudden and dramatic developments in the Soviet Union. The fast-changing scenario seemed to have caused much confusion in South Block initially. But soon efforts were initiated to ensure continuance of close economic and other links with Russia, which accounted for about 80 per cent of the former USSR, and other independent republics.

India which had been dependent on USSR for supply of defence equipment was in a difficult predicament. The visit of the then Defence Minister Sharad Pawar to Russia, most important of the newly-formed Commonwealth of Independent States (CIS) of erstwhile USSR, and signing of some agreements, have eased the situation.

India's relations with the other superpower, the USA, has followed a very uneven course. India had cordial relations with the USA during the years 1947 to 1951. These started deteriorating sharply during Eisenhower-Dulles period, i.e., 1952 to 1960, when USA become a close friend of Pakistan. However, during the period of President Kennedy, the relations between the two countries not only improved, but may be said to have reached the peak of Indo-US friendship. After Kennedy, these started deteriorating very fast and touched the lowest ebb during the days of Nixon-Kissinger. The situation has not changed much since then.

Rajiv Gandhi visited USA next and showed eagerness for import of its advanced technology but, at the same time, conveyed his government's apprehension about US military aid to Pakistan, despite Islamabad's widely known clandestine nuclear weapons programme.

India continued to play a leading role in the Non-Alignment Movement (NAM). After completing his tenure as Chairman of NAM, Rajiv Gandhi was elected Chairman of the Africa Fund set up by it. His visit to the United States in 1986 and the inauguration of the year-long Cultural Festival of India there revived hopes of an improvement in Indo-US relations. However, the Reagan administration continued military aid to Pakistan with the avowed object of tilting the balance of power in its favour.

The Government's approach to US, which emerged as the sole superpower following the disintegration of the Soviet Union, has been marked by a degree of realism and maturity. Though issues like trade restrictions under Special 301, nuclear non-proliferation and missile curbs have tended to strain bilateral relations, India has been careful not to allow these to mar the overall relationship.

For instance, while refusing to sign the NPT, and the decision to go ahead with the satellite vehicle and missile programme which it considers discriminatory India readily agreed to have bilateral talks on this subject as well as other contentious issues. The best testimony to the balanced and mature approach was provided by the first ever joint exercises by Indian and US navy vessels in Indian waters.

However, USA too changed its stance, particularly after the fall of the Najibullah Government in Afghanistan, which was helped by USSR. USA is no longer interested in giving latest sophisticated weapons to Pakistan who was arming the rebels against Afghanistan. It has helped to improve relations with India and is pressurizing Pakistan to stop giving aid and encouraging terrorists in Punjab and Jammu and Kashmir, and has supported India's stand to settle the Kashmir issue according to the Shimla Agreement.

However, Indo-US relations suffered a setback after Bill Clinton took over as President and gave top priority to human rights. Pakistan's propaganda led astray the new US administration which not only did not press the previous Bush Administration's threat to declare Pakistan as a terrorist state because of the clinching evidence they had gathered about Pakistan's support to terrorists in Jammu and Kashmir and Punjab besides some other countries, but also tried to have the Pressler Amendment waived to resume supply of arms, particularly F-16 aircraft, to Pakistan. Some US officials even tried to question the accession of J & K to India which further estranged relations between India and USA. However, India's protests and stress on Pakistan's interference in India's internal affairs by sending trained militants which also included Pakistanis and foreigners, and the report of ambassadors of various countries who visited Jammu and Kashmir, somewhat convinced USA who refrained alongwith overwhelming majority of the nations in the United Nations Human Rights Commission meeting in Geneva in March 1994 to press Pakistan to withdraw its resolutions on human rights violations in J & K.

## Economic Development

Throughout the struggle for freedom, the Indian National Movement had been linked up with socio-economic development. Soon after the enactment of the Government of India Act 1935, which introduced provincial autonomy, the Congress Governments were formed in eight provinces.

Meanwhile, Netaji Subhas Chandra Bose became President of the Indian National Congress. He introduced the concept of national planning and constituted a National Planning Committee of the Congress under the chairmanship of Nehru. The Committee consisted of well-known scientists, educationists, economists, industrialists, financiers. It was soon realised that planning for development could only be taken up by a free national government strong enough to be in a position to introduce fundamental changes in the social and economic structure.

In the course of World War II serious shortcomings became apparent in the country's economy. One of the main reasons for the debacle of the Allied Army in the first phase of the War in the eastern theatre, was the failure of the colonial government to build up a technical and industrial infrastructure in India to

support the War effort by maintaining effective logistic support
to the army. A Development Department was created under the
guidance of Sir Ardeshir Dalal, a member of the Viceroy's
Executive Council. Sir Ardeshir's approach to the question of
planning was pragmatic. He was of the view that the rapid
strides taken by science and technology had made it possible to
cure most of the economic ills of the world, particularly in
providing basic necessities of life to all. However, as soon as he
was able to formulate a strategy for planning, Sir Ardeshir had
to resign in view of the transfer of power to the Indian leaders.

Realising the importance of planning for coordinated socio-
economic development in the country, the necessary provision
has been made in the Constitution of India. Three of its features
are: First, economic and social planning is a concurrent subject,
the Constitution vesting power in the Union to ensure coordinated
development in essential fields of activity. Secondly, the
Constitution includes provision for promoting cooperation between
the Union and the States in investigation of matters of common
interest, and thirdly, the Constitution also sets out in broad
outlines the pattern of the welfare state envisaged and
fundamental principles on which it should rest.

The Planning Commission set up in 1950 consists of the
Prime Minister as Chairman, the Finance Minister, the Minister
of Planning and other cabinet ministers as members, while
there are also full-time members. There is also a Deputy
Chairman whose main function is to coordinate the work of the
Commission.

The Planning Commission in India is an advisory body and
the plans have to be accepted by the Parliament before
they become effective. Planning in India is a great cooperative
effort.

In the First Plan (1951-1956) the major thrust was on
agriculture and social services, with about 58 per cent of the
plan allocation. Industrial development got the lowest priority.
However, from the Second Plan onwards more and more emphasis
was on industrial development, transport and communications
with the avowed objective of building up a sound infrastructure
to support proper agricultural development. The power sector
did not get its share in the past which is now being done. The
major objective of the planning is to build up a socialistic pattern
of society through democratic institutions.

The impact of the planning could be appreciated if the growth in some of the selected areas is considered. In 1951, the beginning of the Plan, the literacy rate was only 16.6 per cent of the population which rose to 36.17 per cent by the end of 1980.

The Planning Commission was busy preparing the draft for the Eighth Plan (1992-1997) when India was faced with a serious economic crisis. In 1991 the Gulf War led to increase in oil prices.

P.V. Narasimha Rao was faced with a serious economic situation when he took over as Prime Minister. Foreign Exchange reserves left by the previous governments (Rs.1,666 crore in January 1991 despite purchase of Rs. 3,334 crore from IMF) could meet only India's urgent imports barely for two weeks. Internally the prices of essential commodities were rising and the inflation was rising at a rapid pace. India needed drastic austerity and liberalisation course not only as a result of pressure from the International Monetary Fund, as the Left would like to make us believe, but also out of objective economic needs. The appointment of former Governor of Reserve Bank of India, Dr. Manmohan Singh, as Finance Minister made it clear that a strong change of policy hitherto being pursued on the Nehruvian pattern was in the offing. The rupee was devalued twice, controls on foreign investments were done away with, there was total liberalisation in investment by foreign industrialists who were encouraged to come forward and invest in India, privatisation of government undertakings, particularly those running into loss, and several other measures were taken to boost the sagging Indian economy. To meet the demand for foreign currency to meet the urgent and necessary imports, billions of dollars were borrowed from the International Monetary Fund (IMF) and other International Agencies. As the *Financial Times* of 16 November 1991 wrote: "The economic reforms introduced by the new Congress administration of Prime Minister P.V. Narasimha Rao go further than any previous deregulation measures towards integrating into the world economy what has been a highly protectionist country." Though the economy has shown an upward trend and the rate of inflations has come down and the foreign reserves have registered a notable increase yet India is still facing perhaps the worst crisis in her economy since independence.

Dr. Manmohan Singh, India's Finance Minister, in his speech in the Parliament on March 17, 1994 assured the House that the rate of inflation will be brought down and the prices of the essential commodities will also be brought to a more moderate level. India's foreign exchange reserves had risen manifold and now stood at US $ 11 billion. Exports too had registered 21 per cent rise during the last year and foreign investments are on the increase.

Energy production and consumption in a country determines the status of its economic development. The requirements of energy in India are met from both non-commercial and commercial sources. The major non-commercial sources of energy come from biomass sources like firewood, vegetable and animal wastes which meets the bulk of the energy requirements in the rural areas. As regards commercial energy sources, the most important are oil, coal and hydel-power. Electricity is perhaps the most convenient and versatile form of energy. The rate of growth of electricty consumption to some extent determines the economic health of a country. Although power development was initiated in India as early as 1900, the progress of electricity generation was not at all impressive till 1947. The installed capacity was as low as only 1.9 million kilowatts, the development being concentrated only in a few urban areas. However, after independence, there has been a phenomenal progress in the power sector. At the end of the First Five-Year Plan the electricity generation rose to 3.42 million kilowatts. By the end of the Second Plan, it rose to 5.7 million kilowatts and in the Fourth Plan, the installed capacity was raised to 18.46 million kilowatts, of which 10.85 million kilowatts was from thermal-power projects, the rest from hydroelectric projects. The installed capacity in the country by the end of 1988-1989 was 221.1 billion units through diversification of energy sources.

On the agricultural front, India used to produce about 50 million tons of goodgrains before independence. In 1989-90, she produced more than 173 million tons and attained a measure of self-sufficiency. With modernisation India is capable of producing twice this quality. However this year (1992) India is obliged to import one million tons of wheat from USA to beef up reserves. The life expectancy has been doubled from around 30 at the time of independence to over 55 now.

In the field of transport, which is the most important infrastructure of economic development, the most important is the railways and shipping industry. Like food production, self-reliance in the transport capability is the key for rapid economic development. The Indian Railways which commenced in April 1853 covering the stretch of only 34 kilometres from Bombay to Thane, is now Asia's largest and the world's fourth largest railway system after USA, CIS (former USSR) and Canada. In March 1989, the Indian Railways had a route length of 61.98 thousand kms with a total track length of 107.804 thousand kms and a running track length of 74.845 thousand kms. The Indian Railways is now being built indigenously and has its production units at Calcutta, Varanasi, Perambur, Bangalore, Patiala and Kapurthala.

The total production of crude oil in 1988-89 has gone up to 3.20 crore tonnes while India's consumption is 35 million tonnes. Natural gas production during 1989-90 was 940 crore cubic metres. India has thus been able to cut 25 per cent in petroleum imports.

In the field of shipping, India has the largest merchant shipping fleet in the developing world and ranks 18th in the world in the shipping tonnage. As compared to 1.92 lakhs G.R.T. at the time of independence, the country's operating tonnage at the end of 1990 was 6.33 millions, G.R.T. gradually reaching the target of self-reliance in the shipbuilding industry.

Another important infrastructure for socio-economic development is the development of human resources in terms of number and quality. In the age of science and technology, the most important human resource for economic and industrial development is the trained technical and scientific personnel. In this field, India's development is phenomenal. Today India produces the largest number of such personnel in the developing world and occupies the third place in the world next only to USA and the CIS (former USSR).

As regards industrial development, India, in the pre-independence days, had to import everything from a pin to all essential machinery.

India's industrial development since independence is spectacular. The general index of industrial production with the base year 1980 (i.e., 100) has gone up to 155.1 in 1986-87; the country is more or less self-sufficient in the production of consumer goods and some basic items such as iron and steel. At the time of independence, India's iron and steel industry comprised mainly the Tata Iron and Steel Company at Jamshedpur, the Iron and Steel Company at Burnpur (West Bengal), and Mysore Iron Works, with a total capacity of only 1.3 million tonnes. Since then several steel plants in the public sector, viz., Bhilai Steel Plant in Madhya Pradesh, Durgapur Steel Plant in West Bengal, Rourkela Steel Plant in Orissa, Bokaro Steel Plant in Bihar, Alloys Steel Plant at Durgapur, Salem Steel Plant in Tamil Nadu, Vishakhapatnam Steel Plant in Andhra Pradesh, have been established. Besides there are 214 mini steel plants with a total capacity of over 83 lakh tonnes per annum. Thus the total capacity of the steel production is about 22 millions of tonnes. The number of cotton textile mills has increased from 378 in 1947 to 1,014 in 1984, the number of sugar mills has gone up to 392 while the cement industry with 90 cement plants in large sector and 184 cement plants in mini sector has the total capacity of about 6 hundred tonnes per annum (1989). Thus India today produces everything from a pin to highly sophisticated jet planes and ranks among the ten most industrialised countries of the world.

India is also among the few countries which has achieved almost self-reliance in the use of space, science and technology. Its main thrust is in the areas of satellite communications, resources, survey and monument, environmental monitoring and meteorology and development of indigenous satellite and launch vehicles to achieve these objectives.

In the overall analysis, India's achievements are commendable. However, due to the high rate of population of growth, India could only progress slowly towards the path of economic emancipation. If India's population could have been contained at the level of economically developed countries, India's per capita income would have gone up threefold from the present 3,284 rupees in 1987-88. The growth rate of national income in 1987-88 was Rs. 2,57,813 crores.

## Fine Arts and Culture

There was all-round stagnation to the artistic field after the downfall of the Mughal empire. The new rulers were not interested in the promotion of Indian culture which decayed, the artists deprived of government patronage dispersed. This continued up to the early years of the 20th century when the national awakening led to the revival of the ancient arts. The credit for reviving music and putting it on a scientific basis goes to Bhatkhande (1860-1936) and Paluskar (1872-1921). Paluskar trained a large number of pupils, the most distinguished of whom were Onkarnath Thakur and Vinayakrao Patwardhan. Carnatic music continued to follow the old classical traditions which flourished in the 18th and 19th centuries in the south. Some of the great masters of the style were Thyagaraja (1767-1847), Muthuswami Dikshitar (1776-1835) and Shyama Shastri (1762-1827). Rabindranath Tagore (1861-1941), the great poet evolved a new style of music known as Rabindra Sangeet which is a mixture of Hindustani music and the folk music of Bengal.

## Music

After independence, the responsibility for the patronage of fine arts devolved on the Government and the public in place of princes and the feudal aristocracy. In January 1958 the Sangeet Natak Akademi was established to promote research in the fields of dance, drama and music and for this purpose to establish a library and a museum, to encourage the exchange of ideas and enrichment of techniques, to promote cultural exchanges in the fields of dance, drama and music with other countries. These objectives have been promoted through music festivals and seminars, grants to training institutions or for research and publication recordings of performance of eminent artists, recording and filming of folk songs and dances, and by presentation of national awards in recognition of eminence in music, dance, drama and film. The Akademi gives liberal grants to institutions engaged in teaching various forms of Indian music, both Hindustani and Carnatic. Besides instituting Annual National Awards, a National Music Festival is organised every year to provide a meeting place for various forms of Indian music. Performances of music are broadcast from the stations of All India Radio and consist of classical, light classical, light folk, tribal and film music. Besides, the Song and Drama Division of the Ministry of Information and Broadcasting of the Government of India, utilises live entertainment media to make the masses aware of various stage forms like puppet shows, plays, dances, dramas, ballads, Harikathas and sound-and-light shows for this purpose. Television has also played an important role in promoting interest in Indian music and encouraging the amateur as well as outstanding artists. Western music has also become quite popular. The orchestration on the Indian music is the direct result of Western impact.

Some of the great music names in Indian music in recent times are S. Balachander (Veena), Hari Prasad Chaurasia (Flute), Ravi Shankar (Sitar), Ustad Alauddin Khan and Ustad Hafiz Ali Khan (Sarod), Ustad Bandu Khan (Sarangi), Ustad Bismillah Khan (Shehnai), Ahmed Jan Thirakaw (Tabla), V.G. Jog (Violin), Sharan Rani Backliwal (Sarod), Malik Arjun Mansur (Hindustani Music), Bhim Sen Joshi (Hindustani Music), Zakir Hussain and Alla Rakha (Tabla), Kumar Gandharv (Hindustani Music), Sidhdheswari Devi (Hindustani Music), Balmurlidhar (Carnatic Music), besides others.

## Museums

Apart from natural history and botanical museums with their flora and fauna, a number of museums depicting India's age-old cultural heritage were established after independence. In 1958 the National Museum was set up in New Delhi. Equally important are Prince of Wales Museum, Bombay; Government Museum, Madras; Bharat Kala Bhavan at Banaras Hindu University and Jaipur Central Museum at Jaipur; Sir Salar Jung Museum, Hyderabad; Asutosh Museum, Calcutta University; Rabindranath Tagore Museum in Calcutta; Gandhi Memorial Museum and Nehru Memorial Museum and Library in New Delhi are some of the other well-known museums. The National Gallery of Modern Art is engaged in organising exhibitions of modern artists. The National Crafts Museum, New Delhi, collects and exhibits fine specimens of traditional art. National Children's Museum, International Dolls Museum at New Delhi and another for children at Amreli, Motilal Nehru Bal Sangrahalaya of Allahabad and the exhibition of tribal arts, crafts and culture in Chhindwara, Ranchi and Shillong deserve mention.

## Theatre

The advent of Europeans gave impetus to this art which had languished during medieval times. The credit for setting up an English theatre for Indians goes to Dwarkanath Tagore, grandfather of the great poet Rabindranath Tagore. The Western impact led to the introduction of "proscenium stage, rolling curtains, change of scenes, less of music and dance." A National Theatre was established by Girishchandra Ghose. Parsis took a lead part in setting up commercial Gujarati and Urdu theatres. Prithviraj Kapoor broke away from the influence of commercial theatre and staged some fine plays. With the advent of independence this art, like others, developed rapidly. Universities such as Baroda, Calcutta, Madras and Punjab started drama departments. Sangeet Natak Akademi (established in 1953) and the Asian Theatre Institute are engaged in the promotion of this art. The Centre for Performing Arts at Bombay and Kala Mandir at Calcutta also deserve mention. Besides, there are several other organisations such as the Indian Peoples Theatre Association and Little Theatre Group. Some of the producers such as Shiela, Begum Zaidi, Habid Tanvir, Ebrahim Alkazi, Satya Dev Dubey and Utpal Dutt deserve mention.

## Painting

The disintegration of the Mughal empire led to the decline of the Indian painting. European oil paintings took the place of fresco and miniature paintings. The government schools established at Calcutta, Bombay, Madras and Lahore promoted the Western style to the complete neglect of Indian art. However, the ancient and medieval paintings were revived through the efforts of such well-known indologists as Cunningham, Fergusson, Cousins, Havell and Percy Brown. Rabindranath Tagore, the pioneer of this school, produced some excellent paintings with Indian themes such as *Krishna Leela, Buddha and Sujata* with indigenous material. The Bengal School, as it came to be known, had a galaxy of artists such as Nandlal Bose, Surendra Nath Gangooly, Sarada Charan Ukil, Ashit Kumar Haldar besides others. Jamini Roy and Amrita Sher-Gill in their own style produced unique paintings on local themes.

The Lalit Kala Akademi was established in 1954, to give official support for the development of fine arts. The Akademi is expected to help improve standards, refine public taste, coordinate activities in the visual sphere of painting, sculpture, architecture and applied arts. The Akademi organises annual national exhibitions not only in Delhi but also in other places. It also sponsors exhibitions abroad. Grants are given to the young artists for specific projects. The Triennale of Contemporary Art is also organised where the works of the participating countries are displayed. Indian artists are given financial support to participate in exhibitions abroad while the works of foreign artists are displayed here.

The modern school of painting came into existence after independence. The object of the modern painting is not to create an object for the delight of the beholder but it should be thought-provoking. Art has now become symbolic and not merely representation of an object. It is not confined to brush and colour but uses different mediums to convey its feelings. The materials which it employs are glass, ceramics, leather, plastic, steel. The distinguished artists are Bhabesh Sanyal, Krishna Hebbar, Sailoz Mukherjee, Madhava Mena, Laxman Pai, besides others.

## Sculpture

The British tried to revive the Indian sculpture to increase exports of handicraft. However, the Art Schools opened in the four big cities—Calcutta, Bombay, Madras and Lahore—laid stress on imported plaster casts of Greek and Roman models which were copied by Indian students. Marble and bronze statues produced during the period did not show any originality. But there were a few sculptors such as D.P. besides Hiranmoy Roychoudhry, F.N. Bose and Pramatha Mullick, who made a distinct contribution by their works. To Ram Kinkar goes the credit of breaking away from the old school. Some of his outstanding works are *Santhal family, Mr. Gangoli.* The other well-known artists are K.C. Arya, Amar Nath Sehgal, Sanyal Prashar, Dharmani, Pradosh Dasgupta, Chintamani, Piloo Pochakanwall, Dhanpal, and Janak Narain.

The younger generation of artists are using different kinds of material such as wood, metal, and stone. Their works show originality and technical ability. Wood sculpture was handled by Sankho Chaudhuri and Dharamraj Bhagat commendably. Stone has been used with distinction by Balbir Singh, Ram Kinkar and Davierwalla. Terracotta was used by Chintamani Kor, Biman Das and others.

## Dance

The art of dancing was revived by Rukmini Arundale and Krishna Iyer. This art took long strides during the last 45 years when all the four main styles of dancing—Bharatanatyam, Kathak, Kathakali and Manipuri—produced some of the greatest

masters in their respective fields. Particular mention may be
made of Bala Saraswati, Shanta Rao, Mrinalini Sarabhai,
Yamini Krishnamurthy and Kamala Laxman in Bharatanatyam,
Sitara Devi, Birju Maharaj and Gopi Krishna in Kathak, Guru
Krishna Kutty and Raghava in Kathakali and Guru Bipin
Sinha and the Jhaveri sisters in Manipuri.

## Architecture

The architectural contribution of the British is evident in the
government houses, churches, bungalows, high courts, railway
stations and police stations. Their earlier architectural style
was Greco-Roman, Scottish, Gothic etc., Some of the well-
known buildings of the period were St. James Church, Kashmere
Gate and Metcalfe House, in Delhi; Belvedere and Writers'
Building in Calcutta; and Government House and the Gateway
of India in Bombay. Later, Edward Lutyens and Herbert Baker
built a new capital in New Delhi. Lutyens borrowed the Islamic
pavilion, the Buddhist railings, and Hindu ornaments and
bracelets in the construction of huge complex of buildings which
included the Viceroy's House, Legislative Council, Secretariat,
etc.

Since independence there has been an unprecedented building
activity throughout the country. Some of the State capitals such
as Chandigarh and Bhubaneswar were constructed while others
were expanded. Every effort is being made to meet the acute
shortages of houses, hotels, hospitals, factories and public
buildings. The architect now does not build for decoration or
ornamentation, but relates himself to the people in a purposive
sense. Effort is made to utilise the maximum space which has
led to the building of skyscrapers. New townships and housing
colonies have come up in almost all the cities. There has also
been change in material and mode of architecture. Ferroconcrete
has revolutionised architectural concepts and has led to the
adoption of a uniform pattern of super constructions, subject, of
course, to variations due to climatic conditions. As the population
has increased tremendously and is touching 80 crores, there is
rush towards metros and urban areas for better prospects and
jobs. Multistoreyed apartments have now come up in all the
major cities designed by well-known architects. Embassies in
Delhi compete with each other, and Satish Gujral has conceived
the Belgium Embassy as a monumental geological formation of

earthbanks and brick vaulting with associations and images recalling domes, lingams and various other tantric artefacts. Ram Sharma's Central Institute of Buddhist Studies in Ladakh is an outstretch of the architectural profession to remote regions, and in its extensive use of solar energy for power generation and heating, a symbol of appropriate technological advance, Stein's International Centre in Delhi and Sher-i-Kashmir International Conference Buildings in Srinagar are unique works of art in stone and mortar while Charles Kurien's Tara Apartments and Kaveri Apartments designed by Kotharis are example of new craze and necessity to meet the growing demand for apartments.

## Broadcasting, Television and Films
Broadcasting has great potentiality in providing a medium for cultural exchange. Starting with 21 primary stations and 4 auxiliary stations in 1950, All India Radio known as Akashvani, has now 100 stations and two relay centres and 180 transmitters. These cover all important cultural and linguistic regions of the country and beam programmes of music and dance, plays and features, poetical recitations and celebrations of fairs and festivals. The external services broadcasts stimulate interest in the rich heritage of our art, culture and traditions.

On September 15, 1959, Doordarshan was born with just one 5-megawatt transmitter. Today it has 533 transmitters beaming programmes to an estimated 22 million households in urban areas and 11 million householders in rural areas. And from being part of All India Radio, it now enjoys 20,000 staff of its own.

From a thrice-a-week, one-hour telecast set-up in 1959, it became a daily one-hour telecast unit on August 15, 1965. Colour transmission and national network came in 1982, morning transmission in 1987 and afternoon telecast in 1989. The second channel in metros were introduced subsequently.

India is one of the major film producing countries of the world. In 1988 the Central Board of Film Certification certified 773 Indian and 118 foreign feature films, 1,662 Indian and 486 foreign short films. Besides, the Films Division produces documentaries and newsreels which are screened on the TV and cinema houses in the country.

India is trying to arrive at an international cultural synthesis by signing cultural exchange programmes with various countries. So far cultural agreements have been signed with 62 countries. Cultural Exchange Programmes have been signed with 35 countries.

## Publishing

Book-publishing in vernacular and English languages has made rapid strides since independence. Ranking eighth among the book-producing countries, India is now one of the leading publishers of books in the world. However, the average print order for an Indian book is about 2,000 while the world average is over 13,000. There are about 15,000 private publishers besides some official agencies such as the Publications Divisions, National Book Trust, Children's Book Trust and National Council of Educational Research and Training.

# Bibliography

Aiyangar, S.K., *South India and Her Muhammadan Invaders,* Madras, 1921.

——, *Ancient India and South Indian History and Culture,* Calcutta, 1941.

Ashraf, M., *Life and Condition of the People of Hindustan (1200-1550),* New Delhi, 1970.

Badauni, Abdul Qadir, *Muntakhab-ut-Tawarikh,* English tranolation by J S A. Ranking, S.H. Lowe and W.H. Haig.

Barni-Zia-ud-din *Tarikh-i-Firoz Shahi,* Persian Text by S.A. Khan B.I. (1860-62), Elliot and Dowson. Vol. III.

Bhattacharya, Bhabani, *Glimpses of Indian History,* New Delhi, 1980.

Chhabra, G.S., *Advanced Study in the History of Modern India,* Vol. I, II, III, New Delhi, 1985.

Chopra, P.N. (Ed.), *Gazetteer of India,* Vol. II; *History and Culture,* New Delhi, 1973.

——, *Life and Letters under Mughals,* New Delhi, 1976.

——, *Quit India Movement of 1942,* New Delhi, 1975.

Dodwell, H.H., *A Sketch of the History of India (1858-1918),* London, 1925.

Elliot and Dowson, *History of India as told by its own Historians,* London, 1866, ff.

Firishta, Muhammad, Qasim, *Tarikh-i-Firishta,* English translation by J. Briggs entitled *History of the Rise of Mohommedan Power in India,* 4 Volumes.

Firuz Shah, *Futuhat-i-Firuz Shahi,* English translation by Sheikh Abdul Rashid and M. Makhdumi.

Gibb, H.A.R., *Ibn Battuta, Travels in Asia and Africa,* Broadway series.

Gokhale, B.G., *Bharatavarsha: A Political & Cultural History of India,* New Delhi, 1982.

Gopal, S., *British Policy in India (1858-1905),* Cambridge, 1905.

Haig, W. (Ed), *The Cambridge History of India,* Volume, III, Cambridge, 1928.

Husain M., *Life and Times of Muhammad-bin-Tughluq,* London, 1938.

Husain, Yusuf, *Glimpses of Medieval Indian Culture,* Bombay, 1962.

Lane-Pool, Stanley, *Medieval India under Muhammedan Rule,* Delhi, 1963.

Macauliffe, M., *Shivaji and his Times,* Calcutta, 1929.

——, *The Sikh Religion: its Gurus, Sacred Writings and Authors,* 6 Vols. Oxford, 1909.

Mahajan, V.D., *The Nationalist Movement in India,* New Delhi, 1981.

Majumdar, R.C. (Ed), *The History and Culture of the Indian People,* Bharatiya Vidya Bhavan, Vols. I-XI, Bombay.

Majumdar, R.C., *Ancient Indian.* Delhi, 1960.

——, *History of the Freedom Movement in India,* Vols. I-III, Calcutta, 1962-63.

——, *The Sepoy Mutiny and Revolt of 1857,* Calcutta, 1957.

—— and others, *An Advanced History of India,* London, 1958.

Mehta, J.L., *Advanced Study of the History of Medieval India,* New Delhi, 1985.

Mukherjee, H., *India's Struggle for Freedom,* Calcutta, 1962.

Panikkar, K.M., *Asia and Western Dominance,* London, 1953.

Thompson, E. & Garratt. G.T., *Rise and Fulfilment of British Rule in India,* Allahabad, 1958.

Tripathi, R.P., *Some Aspects of Muslim Administration in India,* Allahabad, 1963.

Sachau, E.C., *Alberuni's India,* 2 Vols., 1931-1936.

Saletore, B.A., *Social and Political Life in the Vijayanagar Empire,* 2 Vols., Madras, 1934.

Sankalia, H.D., *Prehistory and Protohistory of India and Pakistan,* Bombay, 1962.

Sardesai, S.G., *The Main Currents of Maratha History*, Bombay, 1949.

——, *Shivaji and His Times*, Calcutta, 1929.

Sarkar, J.N., *History of Aurangzeb*, 5 Vols., Calcutta, 1912-24.

——, *Shivaji and His Times*, Calcutta, 1919.

——, *Fall of Mughal Empire*, 4 Vols., Calcutta, 1932-52.

Sastri, Nilakanta, *A History of South India*, Oxford, 1966.

Sen S.N., *Eighteen Fifty-seven*, Calcutta, 1958.

Sharma, Brij Narain, *Social Life in Northern India, 600 A.D.-1000 A.D.*, Delhi, 1966.

Sharma, S.R., *The Religious Policy of Mughal Emperors*, Calcutta, 1940.

Sherwani, H.K., *The Bahamani Kingdom*, Bombay, 1947.

Sinha, N.K., *Rise of the Sikh Power*, Calcutta, 1960.

Sitaramayya, B. Pattabhi, *The History of Indian National Congress*, Vol. I-II, Bombay, 1946-47.

Smith, V.A., *Akbar, the Great Mogul*, 1917.

Smith, V. Revised, by Spear P., *The Oxford History of India*, Oxford, 1967.

Srivastava, A.L., *Akbar, The Great*, 3 Vols., Agra, *The Sultanate of Delhi*, Agra, 1963.

Qanungo, K.R., *Sher Shah and His Times*, Bombay, 1965.

Qureshi, I.H., *The Administration of and Sultanate of Delhi*, 1944.

Ray, H.C., *The Dynastic History of Northern India*, 2 Vols., 1931-36.

Rayachaudhuri, H.G., *Political History of Ancient India*, Calcutta, 1950.

# INDEX

Abdali, Ahmad Shah, 123
Abdulla, Farooq, 208, 209
Abdulla, Sheikh, 208
Achaemenids, 29, 30
Adbhutasagara, 51
Adina Masjid, 101
Aditya I, 64
Afghanistan, 10, 31, 32, 34, 37, 45, 104,
    123, 124, 141, 165, 191, 215, 219
Africa Fund, 219
Agastya, 62
Age of Consent Act (1891), 161
Agra, 38, 85, 103, 106, 109, 114, 115,
    120, 130, 138,
Ahalya Bai, 138
Ahmad, Sayyid, 166, 167
Ahmadnagar, 90, 91, 104, 107, 109,
    112, 115, 138
Ahmad, Fakhruddin Ali, 201
Ahmedabad, 87, 115
Ahom, 86
Ajivikas, 24
Ajmer, 44, 52, 53, 54, 101, 115
Akali Dal, 207, 209
Akbar, 99, 103, 104, 105, 106, 107, 111,
    114,    115-118,    119,    120;
    administration,    115-116;
    character, 117; court of, 116;
    policy towards Hindus, 116-117;
    religious life, 117-118
Alam, Shah, 134, 135
Alaptagin, 45
Alberuni, 94, 95, 96
Alexander, 30, 31, 37, 49, 83
Algeria, 215
Ali, Hyder, 136, 137

Ali, Maulana Muhammad, 184
Ali, Shaukat, 184
Aligarh, 175
Alkazi, Ebrahim, 228,
Al-Hajjaj, 78
All India Anna Dravida Munnetra
    Kazhakam (AIADMK), 208, 210
All India Radio, 231
Alla Rakha, 227
Allahabad, 13, 29, 38, 51, 115, 172, 173,
    190, 211
Alor, 80
Ambar (see Jaipur also), 116
Ambar Rana, 105
Amreli, 227
Amrit Bazar Patrika, 211
Anahilapataka, 52
Anandapal, 46-47, 48
Anangabhima III, 60, 61
Ananthavarman, 60
Andamans, 182
Andhra Pradesh, 59, 205, 208, 209,
    210, 225
Angkor Vat, 73
Anhilawara, 44, 52
Anmakonda, 59
Annals and Antiques of Rajasthan,
    105
Antialcidas, King, 25
Arabia (Arabs), 77, 94, 96
Aranyahas, 12
Argaon, 138
Arjunayanas, 39
Armenia, 25
Arms Act, 171
Athasastra, 35

Arunachal Pradesh, 210, 216
Arundale, Rukmini, 229
Arya, K. C., 229
Arya Samaj, 157, 163
Aryans, 7, 9-17, 27, 69; food, drink and occupations, 15-16; polity, 14; religion and society, 15-17; settlements, 13
Asian Theatre Institute, 228
Asoka, 21, 32, 33-34, 40, 62, 69, 72, 124, 165, 211, an ideal king, 34; empire, 36; greatness of, 34; pillar, 36; stupas, 33
*Asramas*, 15
Assam, 4, 39, 51, 55, 209, 210
Assam Gana Parishad, 209
Assaye, 138
*Aswamedha*, 14, 37, 39
Attlee, 191
Attock, 139, 140
Aurangzeb, 32, 103, 104, 105, 107, 118-119, 122, 125
Australia, 187
Austria, 14
Avadh, 13, 29, 122, 124, 135, 147
Avanti, 29, 42
Ayodhya, 211
Azad Hind Fauj (INA), 191, 198

Babur, 85, 86, 88, 90, 92, 102
Backliwal, Sharan Rani, 227
Bacon, 156
Bactria, 34, 37
Badami, 57
Badaoni, 114
Bahamanabad, 79, 80
Bahmani kingdom, 84, 86, 89-90, 91, 92, 111
Bahujan Samaj Party, (BSP), 211
Baker, Herbert, 230
Bakhtyar, Muhammad, 60
Balachander, S., 227
Balakot, 167
Balban, Ghiyas-ud-din, 81
Ballala Sena, 51
Balmurlidhar, 227
Baluchistan, 8, 31, 34, 104, 193
Bamian, 78
Banabhatta, 41

Banaras (Varanasi), 37, 43, 51, 54, 63, 142, 227
Banerjee, Surendranath, 169, 171, 172, 174, 177, 184
Bangalore, 224
Bangladesh, 215
Bankipur, 172
Bardoli, 186
Bareilly, 147
Barnala, Surjit Singh, 209
Barni, Zia-ud-din, 100
Baroda, 123, 228
Barrackpur, 147
Basti, 19
Basu Maladhar, 99
Battle of Deeg, 138
Battle of Panipat, 92, 95; Third Battle, 103, 114, 125
Battle of Plassey, 133, 134, 135, 142, 145
Battle of Talikota, 91
Battle of Tarain, First, 53-54; Second, 54, 93, 94
Batuta, Ibn, 96, 100
Begarha, Mahmud, 87
Beharam, King, 53
Beijing, 216, 217
Belur, 66
Bengal, 29, 36, 39, 41, 42, 43, 50-51, 55, 58, 60, 61, 65, 84, 86, 99, 101, 102, 104, 107, 113, 114, 115, 122, 130, 131, 132, 133, 134-135, 142, 144, 150, 153, 158, 163, 168, 172, 174, 176, 177, 180, 182, 195, 196; partition of, 176, 178
*Bengal Gazette*, 211
Bentinck, Lord William, 143, 153; Abolition of sati, 143, destruction of thugee, 143; reforms of, 143-144
Berar, 13, 90, 104, 112, 114, 138
Berlin, 191
Besant, Annie, 182, 196, 211
Besnagar, 25
Beta I, 59; II, 59
Bethune College, 162
Bezwada, 57
Bhagalpur, 172
Bhagat, Dharamraj, 229

*Bhagavad Gita,* 25
*Bhagvata* 99
Bhagavatas, Bhagavatism, 24-26, 27
Bhakti Movement, 98
Bhandari, N. B., 209
Bhanudeva II, 61; III, 61
Bhao, Sadasheo, 124
Bharatas, 14
Bharatiya Jana Sangh, 208
Bharatiya Janata Party (BJP), 202, 206, 210
Bharatiya Lok Dal, 208
Bharatpur, 138
Bhatji, Godse 149
Bhatkande, 226
Bhera, 46
Bhillama, King, 58
Bhima, King, 51
Bhoja, King, 43, 52
Bhonsles, 123, 130, 138
Bhubaneswar, 230
Bhutan, 141, 214, 217
Bhutiyas, 10
Bhutto, Z. A., 215
*Bible,* 11
Bidar, 89, 90, 91
Bihar, 13, 19, 29, 32, 86, 87, 99, 102, 115, 142, 192, 210
Bijapur, 90, 91, 101, 107, 108, 109, 110, 111,
Bijayagupta, 99
Bikaner, 105, 106
Bimbisara, 29, 31, 32
Bindusara, 104
Birbal, Raja, 116
Birju Maharaj
Bithur, 139
Bittideva, 66
Bodh Gaya, 39
Bohemia, 10
Bombay, 78, 137, 145, 151, 153, 156, 160, 168, 172, 173, 174, 177, 205, 227, 228, 229
*Bombay Chronicle,* 24
Boigne, de Benoit, 137
Bonnerjee, W. C., 174
Borbudur, 73
Bose, F. N., 229

Bose, Nandlal, 228
Bose, Raj Narain, 149, 166
Bose, Subhas Chandra 191, 198, 220
Boycott Movement, 176
Brahmacharya, 15
*Brahmanas,* 12, 13, 28
Brahmanas, Brahmanism, 16, 17, 20, 26, 35, 71, 79, 98
Brahmo Samaj, 156, 157, 163; Movement, 156
Brahadrath, 34
Brij Raj, 36
British East India Company, 130, 148; Charter of, 144, 168
British Indian Association, 168, 169, 173
Brown, Percy, 121, 228
Buddha, Gautama, 19, 20, 22, 23, 24, 29, 33, 34, 37, 67, 99; Eightfold Path, 19; nirvana, 19; Noble Truths, 19
Buddhists, Buddhism, 18, 19-21, 23, 24, 25, 26, 27, 29, 33, 34, 37, 39, 98, 165; Hinayana, 20; Mahayana, 23; *samgha,* 20; *Tripitikas,* 19; *upasaka,* 20
Bull, John, 170
Bulund Darwaza, 120
Bundelkhand, 13, 43, 57, 122, 140, 147
Bundi, 106
Burma, 72, 141
Burnpur, 205
Bussy, 131

Cabinet Mission Plan, 192
Calcutta, 132, 145, 151, 152, 153, 158, 161, 171, 173, 174, 180, 181, 185, 192, 224, 227, 228; University, 158, 126, 227, 228
*Calcutta Chronicle,* 21
*Calcutta Gazette,* 211
Calicut, 129
Caliphs, 77, 78
Canada, 187, 224
Canning, Lord, 148, 149
Cape Comorin, 61, 159
Carnatic, 130, 131, 136, 141
Central Government, 183
Central Board of Film Certificate, 231

Centre for Performing Arts, 228

Ceylon, 33, 39, 62, 63, 64, 65, 67

Chach, King, 77

*Chachanama,* 79

Chahamana, 46

Chaitanya, 97, 98, 99

Chakrayudha, 42

Chalukyas, 52, 53, 57, 58, 63, 64, 66, 87; Somesvara I, 59

Champa, 73

Chand Bibi, 104

Chand Sultana, 104

Chanda Sahib, 131

Chanakya, 31

Chandavar, 54

Chandernagore, 130, 132, 205

Chandellas, 43-44, 46, 51, 52

Chandidas, 99

Chandigarh, 230

Chandradeva, 50

Chandragiri, 90

Chandragupta, 38, 104; II, 57, 104

Chandra Shekhar, 202

Chattisgarh, 58

Chattopadhyaya, Bankim Chandra, 158

Chauhans, 44, 52, 87

Chaudhuri, Sankho, 229

Chaul, 87

Chaurasi, Hari Prasad, 227

Chauri Chara, 186

Chavan, S. B., 217

Chedi, 52, 58

Chelmsford, Lord, 183

Cheras, 38, 62, 63, 64, 65, 67

Cherenko, Konstin, 218

Chhatrasal, 119

Chhindwara, 227

Chicago, 158

Chidambaram, 67

Chilianwala, 140

Children's Book Trust, 232

China, Chinese, 23, 37, 41, 63, 69, 71, 72, 84, 86, 95, 207, 216, 217

Chintamani, 229

Chitor, 82, 87, 88, 106

Chittagong, 171

Cholas, 38, 51, 57, 58, 59, 62, 63, 64-66; Aditya I, 164; Karekala, 59;

Rajaraja I, 64, 65; Rajendra, 50, 59, 64, 65

Chou En-lai, 216

Christianity, 1171, 129, 146, 147, 157, 159, 164, 165

Churchill, 191

Civil Disobedience Movement, 186, 188, 197

Clinton, Bill, 220

Clive, Robert, 131, 132, 134

Columbus, Christopher, 129, 131

Communist Party of India, (CPI), 206, 207, 208, 210

Communist Party of India (M), 207, 208, 210

Confucius, 23

Congo, 215

Constituent Assembly, 193

Constitution of India, 212-213, 229; Directive Principles, 212, 213; Fundamental Rights, 212, 213

Convention of Wargaon, 136

Cooch Behar, 86, 107

Cornwallis, Lord, 138, 142

Cotton, Henry, 171

Cousins, 228

Covilham, Pedro de, 129

Cripps, Sir Stafford, 190, Mission, 189-191

Cuddapah, 59

Cultural Exchange Programmes, 232

Cultural Festival of India, 218

Cunningham, 228

Cuttack, 138, 172

Curzon, Lord, 176

da Gama, Vasco, 129, 131

Dabhol, 89

Dacca, 171

Dadu, 97

Dahir, 79

Dakhil Darwaza, 101

Dakshineswar, 158

Dalal, Sir Ardeshir, 221

Dalhousie, Lord, 140, 141; creation of Public Works Department, 144; creation of Department of Public Instruction, 144; introduction of

railways, telegraph and postage, 144; reforms of, 144-145
Dalit Kisan Mazdoor Party, 210
Daman & Diu, 130, 205, 210
Damijamardanadeva, 86
Danasagara, 51
Dandi, 187
Danes, 130
Dara Shikoh, 118
Darlus, 29
Das, Biman, 229
Das, Bhagwan, 105, 111
Das, Deshbandhu Chittaranjan, 186
Dusas, 16
Dasgupta, Pradosh, 229
Davierwala, 229
Dabal, 78, 79
Deccan, 35, 37, 38, 56-61, 89, 90, 92, 107, 108, 109, 111, 112, 125, 138
Delhi, 13, 54, 83, 85, 86, 88, 101, 103, 114, 115, 120, 123, 137, 147, 150, 227, Sultanate, 60
Desai, Morarji, 200
Devagiri (Daulatabad), 53, 82, 83, 84
Devapala, 42, 43
Devi Lal, 200
Dhanga, 43
Dhanpal, 229
Dhanyakataka, 57
Dhara, 52
Dharasana, 197
Dharmani, 229
Dharmapala, 42
Dhyoi, 51
Dikibitor, Muthuswami, 226
Divya, 51
Diwan-i-khas, 120
Doab, 135, 138
Doarasamudra, 58, 66
Doctrine of Lapse, 140
Doordarshan, 231
Dravida Munnetra Kazhakam (DMK), 210
Dravidians, 9, 11
Dubey, Satya Dev, 228
Dufferin, Lord, 175
Dulles, Eisenhower, 218
Dupleix, 130, 131, 132, 133
Durgapur, 225

Durgavati Rani, 104
Durlabh, Rai, 132, 133
Durrani, Ahmad Shah, 123, 124, 139
Dutch, 130
Dutt, Utpal, 228
Dyaus, 15
Dyer, General, 183

East, Sir Hyde, 151
Eastern Gangas, 92
Education Despatch, 144
Egypt, 6, 8, 30, 77
England, 131
English Education, 151-154
Extradition Treaty, 217

Fa-hien, 40
Fadnavis, Nana, 137, 138
Faizi, 116
Farghana, 102
Farukhsiyar, 122
Fatehpur Sikri, 88, 120
Faal, Abul, 116
Ferozabad, 84
*Financial Times (The)*, 222
Firuz, Jalal-ud-din, 81
Fort of Agra, 118
Fort William College, 165
Forward Block, 207, 210
France, French, 77, 131, 132, 133, 189
French Revolution, 155

Gaekwad, 123
Gahadavala, 50, 52
Ganapati, 59, 60, 67
Gandhara, 42
Gandharva, Kumar, 227
Gandhi, Indira, 202, 214, 215
Gandhi, M.K, 178, 183, 184-188, 191, 195, 197, 198, 199, 211
Gandhi, Rajiv, 202, 203, 209, 215, 217, 218
Gangas, 58, 60, 67
Gangakondasolapuram, 65
Gangooly, Surendra Nath, 228
Ganjam, 41
Garos, 5
Gaur, 101

Gaya, 19
*Geeta Govinda*, 51
General Committee of Public Instruction , 152
General Elections : First, 207; Second. 207; Third, 207; Fourth, 207; Fifth. 208; Eighth, 210
Germany, 189, 217
Ghazni, 45, 46, 48, 53, 54, 104
Ghiyas-ud-din bin sam, 53
Ghor, 53
Ghori, Muhammad, 53, 54
Ghose, Aurobindo, 166, 175, 177, 179. 181, 182, 195, 196
Ghose, Gurishchandra, 228
Giri, V. V., 201
Goa, 58, 63, 89, 205, 206, 210
Gokhale, 178, 179
Golconda, 90, 91, 92, 107, 110, 111
Gondawana, 104,
Gopala, 42
Gopi Krishna, 230
Gorakhpur, 186
Gorbachev, 218
Government of India Act (1919), 182; (1935), 220
Govinda III, 57
*Grahastya*, 15
Grand Trunk Road, 113
Greece, Greeks, 11, 30, 32, 34, 35, 56, 63, 71, 73, 95, 96, 165, 166
Gulilots, 87
Gujarat, 40, 41, 44, 42, 53, 57, 58, 59, 82, 86, 87, 88, 101, 104, 112, 161, 186, 196, 205
Gujral, Satish, 230
Gulbarga, 89, 91
Gulf war, 222
Guptas, 37, 40, 41, 56, 57, 103
Gwalior, 25, 43, 102

Haig, Sir Wolsley, 115
Haldar, Ashit Kumar, 228
Hammir, Rana, 82, 88
Hammurabi, 69
Harappa, 5, 6, 8
Hardinge, Lord, 153
Harihara, 90
Harshavardhana, 41, 57

Haryana, 205, 210
Hasanabad, 89
Hastings, Warren, 135, 142
Havell, 228
Hebbar, Krishna, 229
Heber, Bishop, 150
Helvodora, 25, 26
Hemadri, 59
Hemchandra (Hemu), 103, 112, 114-115
Herat, 31, 32, 77
Himachal Pradesh, 205, 210
Hindoo College, 151, 152
*Hindu (The)*, 211
Hindu Mahasabha, 206
Hinduism, 23, 117 157, 158, 159
Hindustan Samachar, 212
*Hindustan Times (The)*, 211
*History of India*, 165
Hitler, 197
Hiuen Tsang, 41
Holkar, 123, 137, 138
Home Rule, 178, 182, 196
Hossainpur, 172
Hoysalas, 58, 59, 66, 68, 82
Humayun, 102, 103, 114; Tomb, 120
Hume, Allan Octavian, 174
Huns, 40, 42, 96
Hussain, Zakir, 227
Hyderabad, 57, 58, 59, 122, 131, 141, 203, 227

Ilbert, 172; Bill, 172
Iliyas, Shams-ud-din, 61
Iltutmish, Sultan, 101
*Independent (The)*, 211
Indian Councils Act of 1892, 175; of 1909, 181
*Indian Express (The)*, 211
Indian Independence Bill, 201
Indian Independence Act (1947), 201
Indian Liberation Federation, 184
Indian Nation Army, 191, 199
Indian National Congress, 173, 174, 175, 178, 180, 181, 184, 185, 186, 187, 189, 190, 191, 192, 195, 198, 202, 203, 206, 207, 210, 220, 222
Indian Peace Keeping Force (IPKF), 214

Indian People's Theatre Association, 228
Indra III, 43
Indo - China, 72, 73
Indo - Pak War, 202
Indonesia, 72
Indore, 123, 138
Indus Valley Civilisation, 3-8, 9
Infallibility Decree, 118
International Monetary Funds (IMF), 222
International Relations, 213-219
Iraq, 78, 214
Iran, 214, 217
Irwin, Lord, 188
Israel, 217
Iyer, Krishna, 229
Iyer, C. P. Ramaswamy, 204-219

Jalalpur, 44, 58, 172
Jah, Asaf Ali, 131
Jahangir, 104, 107, 20, 130
Jaimal, 105, 106
Jainism, 18, 21-24, 98, 117; Angar, 24; Digambaras, 24; Svetambaras, 24; *Tirthankaras,* 21
Jaipal, 44, 45-46
Jaipur *(see also Ambar),* 106, 116, 227
Jaisalmer, 105
Jaitpur, 140
Jaitugi, 58
Jartrapala, 58
Jakarta, 217
Jalal-ud-din, 86
Jalalabad, 45
Jallianwala Bagh, 183, 184
Jammu & Kashmir *(see also Kashmir),* 204, 208, 209, 215, 216, 219, 220
Jamrud, 110
Jamshedpur, 225
Janata Dal, 202-203
Janata Party, 202, 208, 209
Jaoli, 108
Japan, 191, 198, 217
Jatavarman, 59
Jatti, B. D., 201
*Jauhar,* 105
Jaunpur, 61, 86-87, 101
Java, 42, 65

Jayachandra, 50, 52
Jayawardene, 214
Jejakabhukti, 43
Jhansi, 140, 147
Jhaveri sisters, 230
Jija Bai, 108
Jinji, 110
Jinnah, 187, 189, 194
*Jiziya,* 84, 111, 116
Jog, V. G., 227
Joshi, Bhim Sen, 227
Jumla, Mir, 118
Junagadh, 20

Kabir, 97, 98, 99
Kabul, 44, 53, 78, 85, 102, 103, 104, 115, 120
Kadamba, 63
Kafur, Malik Naib, 60, 66, 68, 82, 83
Kagalika, 27
Kakatiyas, 58, 59-60, 67, 82
Kakatipura, 59
Kala Mandir, 228
Kalachari, Gangeyadeva, 51, 58
Kalamukha, 27
Kalidasa, 39, 40
Kalinga, 32, 34, 61, 65, 67, 86
Kalyan, 58
Kamarupa, 50
Kamboja, 50
Kampili, 90
Kanauj, 41, 43, 46, 48, 50, 52, 54, 78, 87
Kanchi, 59, 60, 63, 67
Kandahar, 31, 103, 104, 107
Kangra, 47, 107, 139
Kainishka, 21, 37
Kanpur, 139, 148
Kant, 166
Kanva Dynasty, 37
Kapilavastu, 19, 29
Kapilendra Deva, 93
Kapisi, 78
Kapoor, Prithviraj, 228
Kapurthala, 224
Karikala, 162, 63
Karna, Maharajadhiraja, 51, 52
Karnataka, 208, 209, 210
Kashmir, 36, 41, 43, 71, 78, 104, 120, 123, 190, 203, 211

Kathaioi, 30
Kathiawar, 38, 43
Kathmandu, 139
Kausumbi, 13, 29
Kautilya, 31, 35
Keddah, 65
Kerala, 208, 210
Kesari, 211
Khalifa, 184
Khaljis, 60, 81, 93
Khalji, Ala-ud-din, 66, 81, 82, 83, 84, 88, 95, 101
Khalji, Muhammed bin-Bhaktyar, 54
Khan, Afzal, 108
Khan, Alam, 85
Khan, Alauddin, 227
Khan, Bairam, 103
Khan, Bandu, 227
Khan, Bismillah, 227
Khan, Chhuti, 99
Khan, Dalir, 109
Khan, Hafiz Ali, 227
Khan, Khizri, 85
Khan, Liaquat Ali, 194
Khan, Nawal Alivardi, 131
Khan, Paragal, 99
Khan, Sayyid Abdulla, 122
Khan, Sayyid Hussain, 122
Khan, Seatsta, 130
Khan, Shayesta, 108
Khan, Syed Ahmad, 175
Khan, Yahiya, 215
Khandesh, 86, 104, 110, 112, 115, 120
Khanua, 88
Khasis, 5
Khilafat Movement, 184
Khonds, 143
Khurasan, 95
Khusrau, Amir, 100
Khwaja Jahan, 86
Kinanan, 78
King, Luther, 156
Kira, 42
Kirkee, 139
Kirman, 78
Kirtivarman, 52
Knight, Robert, 211
Kock, 86
Koil, 54

Kolhapur, 58
Kols, 144
Konarak, 61
Kongudesa, 67
Konkan, 59, 108
Kosala, 13, 14, 20, 29, 65
Krishak Party, 207
Krishna Kutty, 230
Krishnamurthy, Yamini, 230
Krithivasa, 99
Kshatriyas, 16, 17, 19, 30, 72, 87
Kudamali, 64
Kukis, 9
Kulasekhara, Marvarman, 67
Kumaradevi, 38
Kumaragupta, 40, 104
Kumbakonam, 73
Kumbh, Roja, 98
Kumbhalgarh, 88
Kumrahar, 32
Kurnool, 59
Kuru, 13, 14
Kurukshetra, 73
Kushanas, 37, 38, 56
Kusumba, 19

Ladakh, 231
Lahore, 114, 115, 120, 161, 187, 228
Lakhanauti, 61
Lakhnor, 61
Lakshmanaraja, 44
Lakshmanasena, Raja, 51, 55, 60
Laldenga, 205
Lalit Kala Akademi, 228
Lalitaditya, 41
Laos, 73
Laxman, Kamala, 230
Lepchas, 10
Li Peng, 217
Lichchavis, 29
Little Theatre Group, 228
Lodi, Bahlol, 85
Lodi, Ibrahim, 85, 88, 90, 102
Lodi, Sikander, 85
London, 158, 187
Longowal, Sant H. S., 209
Lucknow, 147, 175
Lutyens, Edward, 230

Lytton, Lord, 174

Macaulay, 153
Macedonia, 30
Madhya Pradesh, 210, 228
Madra, 42
Madras, 38, 132, 136, 137, 143, 145,
    151, 153, 168, 169, 171, 172, 177,
    227, 228, 229
*Madras Mail*, 211
Madras Native Association, 169
Madurai, 32, 62, 64, 66, 84
Magadha, 20, 29, 30, 31, 51, 67
*Mahabharata*, 40, 99
Mahadeva, 59
Maharashtra, 25, 107, 122, 163, 166,
    182, 205
Mahavira (Vardhamana), 21, 22, 23,
    99
Mahe, 130
Mahendra, 33
Mahendrapala, 43
Mahendravarman, 57
Mahipala, 43, 50, 65; II, 51
Mahmud Sultan, 45-49, 50, 52, 53, 84,
    94
Mahoba, 52
Makran, 34, 78
Mal, Raja Bihari, 105, 116
Malabari, B. M., 161
Malavas, 39
Malaya, 65
Maldive, 64
Malik, Khusru, 53
Malkhed, 57
Mall, Todar, 115, 116
Malloi, 30
Malwa, 29, 38, 39 40, 41 42, 44, 52, 57,
    58, 59, 61, 82, 86, 87, 88, 104, 112,
    15, 122
*Manasamangala*, 99
Manchester Cloth, 176
Manipur, 205, 210
Mansur, Malik Arjvn, 227
*Manusamhita*, 17
Manyakheta, 57
*Marahatta*, 211
Marathas, 107, 111, 112, 123-125, 135-
    136, 137, 137-139, 150

Maraijayottungavarman, 64
Marwar, 106, 107, 110, 111
Masulipatnam, 131
Mathura, 26, 48
Matiya, 13, 42
Mauryas, 29-36, 37, 56, 62, 93, 103; end
    of the empire, 342
Meerut, 85, 147, 172, 173
Megasthenes, 32, 35-36
Meghalaya, 205
Meghavarna, 39
Mehta, Pherozeshah, 180
Mena, Madhava, 229
Menon, V. P., 203
Mewar, 82, 87, 88, 98, 105, 106, 107,
    111, 114
Mihirakula, 40
Mill, James, 165
Minhaj-ud-din, 100
Mir Jafar, 132, 133, 134
Mir Madan, 133
Mir Qasim, 134, 135
Mirabai, 98
Mithila, 51
Mitra, Krishnachandra, 149
Mitra, Naba Gopal, 166
Mizoram, 205, 210
Mohanlal, 133
Mohanta, P. K., 209
Mohenjodaro, 5, 6, 7, 8
Mongols, 81, 82, 95
Monson, Colonel, 138
Montagu, E. S., 182, 195
Moriyas, 30
Morocco, 215
Moti Masjid, 120
Motopalli, 59
Mountbatten, Lord, 193-194, 201, 203,
    204
Muazzam, Prince, 109
Mudgal, 91
Mueller, Max, 165
Mughals, 82, 85, 92, 93, 95, 131, 147,
    150; art, 119-121; fall of the
    empire, 122-125, 225, 228
Mukherji, Harish Chandra, 149
Mukherji, Sailoz, 229
Mukhopadhyaya, Sambu Chandra,
    149

Mularaja, 52
Mullick, Pramatha, 229
Multan, 46, 48, 53, 80, 115, 139, 140, 171
Mumtaz Mahal, 130
Mundas, 5, 9
Murshidabad, 133
Muslim League, 189, 190, 191, 192, 193; 206; direct action of, 192
Muzzafarpur, 172
Mysore, 31, 36, 58, 66, 136-137

Nabodwip, 99
Nadia, 55
Nagas, 9
Nagaland, 205
Nagarkot, 47
Nagpur, 123, 130, 140, 180
Najibullah, 219
Nakulisa, 27
Nalanda, 42
Namdev, 98, 99
Nana Sahib, 141, 148
Nanak, 97, 98, 99
Nandas, 30, 31; Mahapadma, 29
Nandakumar, Maharaja, 132
Naoroji, Dadabhai, 170
Narain Jahan, 229
Narain, Madhav Rao, 138
Narasimha I, 61; II, 61; III, 61
Narasimhavarman, 57, 63, 64
Narendrasena, 59
Nasir-ud-din, 100
National Book Trust, 232
National Centre for Educational Research & Training, 232
National Conference, 172, 173, 174, 208, 209
National Front, 210
National Democratic Alliance, 210
National Fund & Arms Act, 173
*National Herald*, 211
National Planning Committee, 220
Nayak, Haidar, 136
Nedunjeliyan, Adan, 62, 63
Nehru, Jawaharlal, 187, 194, 197, 202, 208, 213, 216, 220
Nehru, Motilal, 185, 186, 211
Nellore, 59, 60, 67

Nepal, 19, 39, 139, 141, 147, 148, 216
*New India*, 211
Nixon, President, 217, 219
Nizam-ul-Mulk, 122
Noakhali, 192
Non-Aligned Movement (NAM), 217, 219
Non-Cooperative Movement, 185, 195, 196
North's Regulating Act (1773), 134
North West Frontier Province, 193
Northern Sarkars, 131

Oman, 217
Orissa, 32, 60, 61, 86, 92-93, 210, 225
Oudh, 115, 134, 148, 150

Padmini, 82
Pai, Laxman, 229
Paithan, 57
Pakistan, 8, 175, 190, 193, 204, 215, 216, 217, 219, 220
Pal, Bipin Chandra, 175
Palas, 41, 51, 58, 65
Pallavas, 57, 63, 67
Palushar, 225
Panchals, 13, 14
Panchsheel, 202
Pandua, 101
Pandyas, 38, 57, 59, 60, 64, 65, 66-68; Jatavarman Sundara, 59, 67; Jatavarman Vira Pandya, 66, 67, 68; Srimara Srivallabha, 67
Panipat, 85, 93, 124
Pant Dhondhu, 141
Parakramababu, 67
Paramahansa Ramakrishna, 158, 159, 160
Paramaras, 44, 52, 58, 59, 87
Paramesvara, Kavindra, 99
Parantaka, Jatila, 66
Parliament of Religions, 158
Paris, 158
Parsvanath, 21, 22
Parthians, 96
Pasupata, 27
Pataliputra (Patna), 32, 33, 35, 38, 40
Patel, Sardar Vallabhbhai, 198, 203
Pathans, 95

Patiala, 224

Patta, 105, 106, 113

Patwardhan, Vinayakrao, 225

Pawar, 218

Peacock Throne, 120

Pen Ganga, 89

Perambur, 224

Permanent Settlement, 142, 175

Persia, 11, 29, 46, 48, 57, 77, 95, 123

Peshwas, 122, 123, 125

Peshawar, 46, 140, 167, 171

*Pioneer*, 211

Pippalavona, 30

Planning Commission, 221; First Plan, 221, 223; Second Plan, 221, 223; Fourth Plan, 223; Eighth Plan, 222

Plato, 166

Pochakanwall, Piloo, 229

Pondicherry, 130, 182, 205

Poland, 217

Polo, Marco, 59, 67

Ponti, Nicolo, 92

Poona, 108, 123, 137, 138

Portuguese, 87, 95, 130, 205

Porus, 30

Praja Socialist Party, 207

Prarthana Sabha, 158

Prasad, Rajendra, 193, 201

Prashar, Sanyal, 229

Pratapgarh, 108

Prathiharas, 41, 42-43, 44, 50, 57, 87

Pratishthana, 57

Pravarasena, 57

Premadasa, R., 214

Press Council of India, 212

Press Trust of India, 212

Pressler Amendment, 220

Prithviraja, 52, 53, 54

Prola I, 59

Provincial Government, 183

Publication Division, 233

Publishing, 232

Puhar, 62

Pulakesi II, 57

Punjab, 4, 5, 8, 11, 29, 30, 31, 35, 37, 39, 40, 44, 45, 48, 53, 85, 86, 103, 113, 124, 138, 139, 141, 157, 163, 167, 177, 182, 190, 193, 209, 210, 211, 219, 220, 228

Purandar, 109

Puri, 60, 61

Purus, 14

Purushapura (Peshawar), 37

Purushottama, 92

Qadam Rasul Masjid, 101

Qasim, Muhammad bin, 79, 80

Quilon, 67

Quit India Movement, 197

*Quran*, 11, 118, 119

Qutub-ud-din Aibak, 54, 55, 81

Qutub Minar, 101

Qutub Mosque, 101

Radhakrishna, Sarvepalli, 201

Raghava, 230

Raghoba, 136

Raghunath, 123,

Rai, Lajpat, 175

Raigadh, 110

Rajagopalachari, C. 201

Rajarajesvara, 64

Rajaram, 111

Rajasimha, 66

*Rajasuya*, 14, 52

Rajgriha (Rajgir), 29

*Rajatarangini*, 71

Rajput States, 50-53. 87-89, 122, 125, 150

Rajputana (Rajasthan), 25, 42, 44, 105, 107, 122, 210

Rama Raja, 91

Ramabai, Pandita, 160

Ramachandra, 59

Ramananda, 97, 98, 99

Ramapala, 51

Ramayana, 40, 99

Ramesvaram, 82

Ranade, M. G., 156, 161

Rangoon, 148, 190

Rani of Jhansi, 147

Ranthambore, 54, 82

Rao, Baji, 122, 123, 141, 148

Rao, Bhaskar, 209

Rao, Madhava, 135

Rao, Narasimha, P. V., 203, 216, 222
Rao, Rama, N. T., 209
Rao, Shanta, 230
Rao, Viswas, 124
Raor, 79
Rashtrakutas, 43, 57; Indra, 43
Rashtiya Samajik Party, 210
Rawal, Bappa, 87, 105
Raya, Krishnadeva, 980, 91
Raya, Sadasiva, 91
Reagan, 219
Reddy, Sanjiva, 201
Renaissance, 151
Reorganisation of States, 205-206
Republican Party of India, 207
Rewari, 114
*Rigveda*, 69, 98, 157
Roe, Sir Thomas, 130
Rohilkhand, 135
Romans, 11, 63, 71, 166
Rowlatt Act, 184
Roy, Rammohan, 144, 155, 156, 157,
    159, 161, 162
Roychoudhry, D. P., 227
Roychoudhry, Hiranmoy, 229
Rudramba, 59, 60
Ruhellas, 124
Russia, 76, 190, 206, 217

SAARC, 216
Sabuktigin, 45, 46
Sagor, 172
Sakas, 38, 39, 56, 96
Sailendra, 64, 65
Saivism, 18, 24, 26-28
Sakambari, 44
Sakyas, 19, 29
Salem, 67
Salim, Prince, 116
Salisbury, Lord, 175
Salivahana, 156
Samachar Bharati, 212
Samajvadi Janata Party, 211
Samarkand, 84, 102
Samar Sinha, 88
Sambalpur, 140
Samhita, 12, 13; Atharvaveda, 12;
    Rigveda, 10, 12, 13, 15, 26;
    Samveda, 12; Yajurveda, 12, 26

Samudragupta, 38-39, 104
Samyukta, 52, 53
Sanga, Rana, 88
Sangeet Natak Akademi, 226, 228
Sanghamitra, 33
Santhals, 5, 9
Sarabhai, Mrinalini, 230
Saraswati, Bala, 230
Saraswati, Dayanand, 157
Sasanka, 41
Sasaram, 113
Satvahanas, 34, 37, 38, 56
Satnami, 119
*Satrudriya*, 25, 26
Satvatas, 25
Satyaputra, 62
Satakarni, Gautamiputra, 56
Satakarni, Yajnasri, 57
Saurashtra, 203
Savarkar, Vinayak Damodar, 149
Sayanacharya, 92
Sayyid, 85
Sehgal, Amarnath, 229
Seleucus, 30, 31, 32, 35
Sen, Keshub Chandra, 156, 157
Senas, 51, 60
Sepoy Mutiny (1857 war), 145; 146,
    150; Nature of the Outbreak, 149-
    150, transference of crown, 148-
    149
Seven Pagodas, 64
Seven Years War, 133
Shah, Ahmed, 87, 89
Shah, Ala-ud-din Husain, 86, 89
Shah, Azam, 86
Shah Bahadur, 87, 122, 147, 148
Shah, G. M., 208
Shah, Hussain, 99
Shah, Islam, 102, 103
Shah Jahan, 104, 107, 120, 121, 130
Shah, Jalandar, 122
Shah, Muhammad Adil, 103, 114,
    122
Shah, Nadir, 49, 123, 125, 139
Shah, Nusrat, 86
Shah, Sher, 99, 102, 112, 113-114, 116
Shahi, Adil, 90
Shahi, Barid, 90
Shahi dynasty, 44

Shahi, Imad, 90
Shahi, Nizam, 90
Shahi, Qutbi, 90
Shahji, 108
Shambaji, 111
Shankar, Ravi, 227
Sharma, Shanker Dayal, 202, 209
Sharqi dynasty, 87
Shastri, Lal Bahadur, 202
Shastri, Shyama, 226
Sharif Nawaz, 216
Shillong, 227
Shimla Agreement, 215, 216, 219
Shivaji, 107-112, 118, 122, 139, 166;
    and Aurangzeb, 108-110;
    character and achievement, 110-
    112
Shivner, 107
Sher-Gill, Amrita, 228
Siddheswari Devi, 227
Sikandara, 120
Sikhs, 99, 107, 122, 139, 141, 150, 167
Sikkim, 140, 208, 209
Sikkim Sangram Parishad, 209
Silaharas, 58, 61
Simon, John, 186; Commission, 187
Sindh, 5, 8, 29, 31, 43, 78, 79, 80, 86, 94,
    104, 139, 190
Singapore, 190, 191
Singh, Ajit, 111
Singh, Balbir, 229
Singh, Banda, 161
Singh, Charan, 202, 210
Singh, Gyani Zail, 201
Singh, Guru Gobind, 139, 166
Singh, Jai, 79, 80, 109, 118
Singh, Jaswant, 105, 110, 111, 118
Singh, Maharaj Dalip, 161
Singh, Maharaja Raja, 111
Singh, Man, 105, 106, 116
Singh, Manmohan, 222, 223
Singh, Pratap, 106, 112
Singh, Rana Amar, 107
Singh, Rana S.
Singh, Ranjit, 139, 140
Singh, Sangram, 105
Singh, Udai, 105, 106
Singh, V. P., 202, 210
Singhana, 58, 59

Sinha, Guru Bipin, 230
Sindhia, Daulat Rao, 137, 138
Sindhia, Mahadji, 123, 137
Siraj-ud-daula, 124, 131, 132, 133
Sirhind, 123
Sisodiyas, 87
Sitara Devi, 230
Skandagupta, 40, 104
Slave dynasty, 81
*Smriti*, 40
Socialist Party of India, 206, 208
Somnath, 48
Sona Majsid, 101
Solar dynasty, 92
South Africa, 217
South Arcot, 110
South Korea, 217
Sravanabelagola, 31
Sravasti, 29
Sri Lanka, 213
*Srikreshnavijayas*, 99
Srinagar, 231, 204
Sriperambadur, 203
Sriramalu, 205
*Statesman (The)*, 176, 211
Subsidiary Alliance, 137, 138
Sudras, 16, 29, 59
Sumatra, 42, 65
Sunga dynasty, 37
Surajmal, 124
Surat, 109, 110, 130, 180, 181
Suri, Sikandar, 103
Swadeshi, 176, 177; Movement 178,
    196
Swaraj, 179, 185
Swarajya Party, 186
Swatantra Party, 207
Syria, 31, 77

*Tabaqat-i-Nasiri*, 100
Tagore, Dwarkanath, 227
Tagore, Debendranath, 156, 168
Tagore, Rabindranath, 183, 226, 227,
    228
Taj Mahal, 120, 130
Takshashila, 25
Talaiyalangam, 62
Talikota, 91
Tamil Nadu, 210, 225

Tanjore, 62, 64, 67, 107, 111, 141
Tansen, 116
Tantia Tope, 148
Tanvir Hafid, 228
Tara Bai, 111
Tarkhadkar, Bhaskar Pandurang, 163
Tashkent, 202
Tejpur, 173
Telengana, 59
Telugu Desam, 208, 209, 210
Thaikaraw, Ahmed Jan, 227
Thakur, Onkarnath, 226
The Bombay Association, 169
The Indian Association, 169, 171, 172, 173
Thyagaraja, 226
Tilak, Bal Gangadhar, 161, 166, 175, 192, 195, 196, 211
*Times of India (The)*, 211
Timur (Tamerlane), 49, 84, 85, 86, 87, 102
Tipu Sultan, 136, 137, 138
Tirhut, 86
Tod, James, 105
Toramana, 40
Travancore, 203
Treaty of Amritsar, 140
Treaty of Arjungaon, 138
Treaty of Bassein, 138
Treaty of Deogaon, 138
Treaty of Friendship, 218
Treaty of Lahore, 140
Treaty of Salbai, 136, 137
Treaty of Surji, 138
Trichinopoly, 60, 66, 67, 107, 111
*Tripitaka*, 11
Tripura, 205, 208, 210
Tritsus, 14
Trivandrum, 64
Tughluq dynasty, 83, 101
Tughluq, Firuz Shah, 61, 84, 86, 87, 89, 100
Tughlaq, Ghiyas-ud-din, 83, 101
Tughlaq, Ilyas Shah, 86
Tughlaq, Muhammad, 60, 66, 83, 84, 89, 100
Tughlaq, Sikandar, 86
Turkey, Turks, 87, 94, 95, 96, 184

Uch, 53
Udagai, 64
Ujjain, 29, 39
Ukcl, Sharada Charan, 228
UK, 217
Ulugh Khan, 60, 61
Umapati, 51
UN, 216; Human Rights Commission, 220
Unification of India, 203-205
United News of India (UNI), 212
*Upanishads*, 12, 13, 22, 23, 25, 28
Upagupta, 33
Uraiyur, 62
USA, 158, 213, 215, 219, 224
USSR (Soviet Union), 207, 213, 215, 217, 218, 224
Utkala, 42
Uttar Pradesh, 19
Uzbekistan, 217

Vaghilas, 59
Vaisali, 21, 29
Vaishnavism, 18, 24, 25, 26, 27
Vaisyas, 17
Vakatakas, 57
*Vanaprastha*, 16
*Vande Mataram*, 176, 177, 179
Vasudeva (Krishna), 25, 26
Vasudeva, 37
Vatsaraja, 29, 43
*Vedanta*, 158, 160
*Vidangas* (Sutras), 13
*Vedas*, 11-13, 16, 18, 24, 156
Vellore, 110
Venkataraman, R., 201, 217
Vernacular Press Act, 171
Victoria Queen, 148
Vidarbha, 13
Videha, 13
Vidisa, 25
Vidyapati, 99
Vidyasagar, Ishwar Chandra, 161
Vietnam, 73
Vijaya Sena, 51
Vijayanagar, 61, 84, 86, 89, 90-92, 101
Vikramaditya (Chalukya), 58, 59
Vikramaditya (Chandragupta II), 39

Vikramjit, 103
Vira Ballal II, 66; III, 66
Vishnuvardhana, 66
Vivekananda, 158, 159, 160

Wahabis, Wahabism, 166, 167
Wandiwash, 133
Warrangal, 59, 61, 82, 84, 89
Wassaf, 67
Watson, 132
Wavell, Lord, 193
Wedderburn, 174
Wellesley, Lord, 137
Wellesley, Sir Arthur, 138

World War I, 182, 184, 198, 211; II, 189, 198, 206, 220

Yadavas, 58, 82
Yadu, 42
Yasodharman, 40, 41
Yasovarman, 41, 43
Yaudheyas, 39
Yavana, 42, 63
*Young India*, 211

Zabulistan, 78
Zia-ul-Haq, 216
Zoroastrianism, 117